£14

108820

F445

PERIODICALS IN TURKISH AND TURKIC LANGUAGES

A UNION LIST OF HOLDINGS IN U.K. LIBRARIES

EDITED BY MUHAMMAD ISA WALEY

MIDDLE EAST LIBRARIES COMMITTEE (U.K.)

OXFORD

1993

Distributed by the Middle East Centre, St Antony's College, Oxford OX2 6JF

ISBN 0-948889-06-3

Printed in Great Britain by BPCC Wheatons Ltd, Exeter

CONTENTS

Editor's Introduction

1. The purpose and scope of this work

This *Union list* covers holdings of periodicals and newspapers published wholly or partly in modern and Ottoman Turkish and in other languages of the Turkic group, regardless of country or date. Libraries covered are those major collections in the U.K. which provided data or partial data, and some others which the editor was able to visit. As for those libraries whose holdings have not been covered here, it is hoped to incorporate their holdings in the bibliographic file from which this *Union list* has been produced, and perhaps to publish them in a future edition.

It is almost inevitable that a bibliographical work involving periodicals, when produced by one individual, will contain numerous errors and be out of date in some respects. The editor will be most grateful to receive emendations, updates and suggestions for improvements; indeed, one must depend upon others for information such as will enable this *List* to continue in a useful and updated form.

This publication is a list of holdings, not a full descriptive catalogue. However, it is intended to continue adding entries and holdings information to the data file after publication. The production of a proper international union catalogue and/or bibliography is much to be desired. The editor ventures to hope that the present work, for all its faults and limitations, will at least help to inspire colleagues more competent than him to embark on a full-scale bibliography.

Meanwhile it is hoped that the *Union list* will be found useful by those interested in Turkish studies, and that it may lead to further cooperation in bibliographical work as well as providing a basis for more effective coverage of current and other periodicals in the languages concerned.

2. Acknowledgements

One can hardly imagine a project of this kind coming to fruition without much help and encouragement from others; this one certainly would not have done so. It is a pleasure to acknowledge the support of those who have contributed to the project.

A number of specialist librarians and scholars supplied data concerning library holdings. Knowing how tiresome a labour this can be, the editor is deeply grateful to Ms. Heather Bleaney, formerly of the Documentation Unit, Centre for Middle Eastern and Islamic Studies, University of Durham and now at the Islamic Bibliography Unit, Cambridge University Library; Mrs. Jill Butterworth, Cambridge University Library; Mr. David Barrett, Mr. Colin Wakefield, and especially the late Mr. Michael Daly, Bodleian Library, Oxford University; Mr. Jim Downey, Institute of Development Studies, University of Sussex; Dr. Derek Hopwood and Ms. Diane Ring, Middle East Centre, St. Antony's College, Oxford; Dr. Paul Starkey, University of Durham; Miss Rosemary Stevens, Library of the School of Oriental and African Studies, University of London; Mr. Stephen de Winter, Slavonic and East European Section, British Library; Mr. George Woodcock, formerly of the Science Reference and Information Service, British Library; and Dr. Christine Woodhead, Centre for Turkish Studies, Durham.

For technical and other assistance the editor is indebted to colleagues at the British Library: Ms. Joan Corney, Ms. Caroline Halcrow, Mr. Arto Kouyoumdjian, Mrs. Diane Neptune, Miss Catherine Pickett, and Dr. Vrej Nersessian. Encouragement from several colleagues made the project feasible: at the British Library, Mr. Barry Bloomfield, Dr. Albertine Gaur, and Mr. Howard Nelson; from MELCOM U.K., Mr. Paul Auchterlonie, Mr. Peter Colvin, and Dr. Derek Hopwood; in Turkey, Mr. Hasan Duman, formerly Director-General for Libraries and Publications. The office-holders and other members of MELCOM U.K. never ceased to offer support throughout the long and difficult gestation of the *Union list*.

During brief visits to the Millî Kütüphane (National Library) at Ankara the editor benefited greatly from the help of Ms. Şahika Ünal and Ms. Altınay Sernikli and the staff of the Periodicals Section.

Very special thanks are due to H.E. Mr. Rahmi Gümrükçüoğlu, former Ambassador of the Republic of Turkey to Great Britain, for a most generous subsidy of £1600 towards the cost of publication.

3. Technical information for users

Libraries included, with abbreviation codes

BL:OIOC	Oriental and India Office Collections, British Library, London.
BL:HSS	Western Language Sections, Humanities and Social Sciences, British Library, London.
BL:DSC	Document Supply Centre, British Library, Boston Spa.
LO:SOAS	School of Oriental and African Studies, University of London.
CA:UL	Cambridge University Library.
DU:UL	Durham University Library.
DU:DC	Documentation Unit, Centre for Middle Eastern and Islamic Studies, University of Durham. Transferred to Durham University Library in Summer 1993.
OX:BOD	Bodleian Library, University of Oxford.
OX:MEC	Middle East Centre, St. Antony's College, Oxford.
SU:IDS	Institute of Development Studies, University of Sussex.
CA:OS	Faculty of Oriental Studies, University of Cambridge.

How the work was compiled

The *Union list* was designed by the editor on the basis of the facilities offered by the British Library's LOCAS bibliographical file system. Much was learned from the approach and layout adopted for the pioneering *Union catalogue of current Chinese serials*. All 1200 records were compiled in standardized form by the editor on the basis of information supplied by colleagues; the entries for British Library holdings are his own. "Bibslips" were then keyboarded into a BL bibliographical file, in a form enabling batch emendation and updating. Largely because of technical difficulties and the complexity of batch processing procedures, the compilation of this *Union List* has involved the writing out of more than three thousand record amendments in all, containing roughly five thousand field amendments. The *Union list* has been printed directly from a printout of the file.

Record structure

The aim has been to comply with international bibliographic standards, in the form of *Anglo-American Cataloguing Rules, Second edition*, so far as practical. Some readers may be interested to know that the full profile of the *Union list* is not included in the printed edition. Also present in the file are full imprint details, and information codes which would enable the file to be searched by various parameters if it were mounted online. Imprint information apart from place(s) of publications is only included where it is not evident from data in other parts of the record.

The data included in most entries as they appear in print are the following: title, subtitle and/or description, issuing body (where appropriate), designation and date of first and last issue, place of publication, and issues held. Many entries have one or more of the following: description note, publication history, language(s) and character(s), frequency, and title cross-reference(s). Cross-references are always made to the Turkish or Turkic title, whether or not this appears as the main title (or first parallel title) in the periodical itself. For periodicals of which the titles have changed, the entry appears under the last or present title.

4. Inclusions and exclusions

Readers are asked to keep in mind the following points regarding the categories of material which are included in the *Union list*. The criterion for inclusion is linguistic, not geographical. Any periodical is omitted, whether from Turkey or the Ottoman Empire or from elsewhere, which does not include Turkish-language content in an original form in every issue. Not included are European-language academic journals in which Turkish texts are only sometimes edited, or quoted. Contemporary titles in the fields of science and technology will not be found here, excepting a few titles which are anomalously held in the humanities collections of the British Library. That exclusion in no way implies any disregard for the importance of Turkish scientific research and writing. Also omitted are many titles which are not evidently periodicals, and some which perhaps fall into the intermediate category of "occasional publications".

In addition, certain elements have been excluded from the notes area, notably (a) editors' and most publishers' names; (b) any data explicitly available in Turkish/Turkic in the main body of the entry, or that can be readily deduced (e.g. scope, subject matter, frequency of publication), unless such data are inaccurate or misleading. The working assumption is that those able to make use of a given periodical will need to know enough of the language in question to understand the data given verbatim in its bibliographical record. As regards the language, unless otherwise stated, any periodical can be assumed to be in modern (if post-1928) or in Ottoman (up to 1928) Turkish. Where that does not apply, or there is an additional language, there will be a note.

It is to be hoped that this work will be built upon in a number of ways. Examples might be its extension to scientific and technical works; the inclusion of the holdings of more libraries in the U.K. and in other countries; and adding valuable data such as descriptions of the contents and particular interests or viewpoints of periodicals, and the names of editors. The present writer can but offer his apologies for being unable to offer fuller bibliographical information in this elementary publication.

5. Filing order

Readers are asked to keep in mind that the LOCAS file management program disregards diacritical points in alphanumerical filing. As a result, unfortunately it has not been possible to accommodate the standard alphabetical order for modern Turkish: each of the pairs c ç, ı i, o ö, s ş, and u, ü will be found filed together indiscriminately, the filing order being determined by the letter(s) following.

6. Romanization systems utilized

Except where otherwise indicated, the romanization systems used are those employed at the British Library. Ottoman, however, has been romanized almost entirely into modern Turkish orthography except that (a) voiced final consonants have been retained in titles and (b) the hyphen has been used in the *izafet* construction. Ottoman titles in Greek (Karamanlitic) or Armenian characters have been romanized according to the British Library systems for those alphabets, Turkish equivalents being added in cross-references. For titles in Russian, Library of Congress romanization is used. Other Turkic elements in Cyrillic characters are romanized according to the British Library system, in which the representation of consonants is based upon modern Turkish rather than Russian orthography; that used by the Bodleian Library is, with one or two exceptions, identical.

7. Holdings in U.K. collections

The circumstances in which this work has been put together precluded any detailed study of the strengths and weaknesses of the collections of Turkish/Turkic periodical publications in this country. The most famous titles are well represented. In broad terms, however, the holdings are in most respects uneven, while a number of well-known and easily obtainable are held by several libraries. All this reflects the relatively low importance generally attached to Turkish studies and library materials until quite recently. There are now heartening signs of improvement, some U.K. libraries having significantly enhanced their collections in the last few years.

Mainstream academic journals and prominent cultural and literary titles are much in evidence. Ottoman titles are well represented, as are Soviet titles from the 1960s on; but acquiring literature from the newly independent Republics may become more difficult. Older Central Asian and Caucasian material is disappointingly scarce; so, despite British connections, are periodicals from Cyprus. Official publications from before the 1960s are in short supply, although there are fairly good holdings of yearbooks. Nobody familiar with the problems faced by chronically understaffed libraries in acquiring, processing and conserving newspapers is likely to be very surprised that holdings of all save a few prominent titles are quite sparse.

Fortunately it is possible to conclude on a more positive note. The trend towards making complete runs of periodicals available in microform or photostat or in book form, with compact discs perhaps to follow before very long, provides grounds for hoping that those interested in periodical publications in Turkish and other Turkic languages will find libraries better supplied in future.

Muhammad Isa Waley
British Library, London

4

Select bibliography

Ahundov, Nazim. *Azĕrbaycanda dövri mĕtbuat (1832-1920): bibliografiya = Periodicheskaĩã pechat' v Azerbaĩdzhane (1832-1920): bibliografiĩã*. Baku, 1965.

Allworth, Edward. *Nationalities of the Soviet East: publications and writing systems*. New York, 1971.

Bloss, Ingeborg, and Schmidt-Dumont, Marianne. *Zeitschriftenverzeichnis Moderner Orient: Stand 1979*. Hamburg, 1980.

Çapanoğlu, Münir Süleyman. *Basın tarihimizde mizah dergileri*. Istanbul, 1970.

Çelik, Fevzi, and Akyüz, Sevgi. *TBMM Kütüphanesi süreli yayınlar kataloğu*. Ankara, 1987.

Donceel-Voûte, P., and Bayrı-Baykan, S. *Catalogue des périodiques concernant l'histoire, l'archéologie, l'histoire de l'art et la philologie dans les bibliothèques d'Istanboul et d'Ankara*. Istanbul, 1980.

Duman, Hasan. *İstanbul kütüphaneleri Arap harfli süreli yayınlar toplu kataloğu, 1828-1928 = Union catalogue of the periodicals in Arabic script in the libraries of Istanbul*. Istanbul, 1986.

--. *Osmanlı yıllıkları (Salnameler ve Nevsaller): bibliyografya ve bazı İstanbul kütüphanelerine göre bir katalog denemesi*. Istanbul, 1982.

Gelişim Yayınları. *Türkiye'de dergiler ansiklopediler (1849-1984)*. Istanbul, 1984.

Gerçek, Selim Nüzhet. *Türk gazeteciliği, yüzüncü yıldönümü vesilesiyle 1831-1931*. Istanbul, 1931.

Günyol, Vedat. *Sanat ve edebiyat dergileri*. Istanbul, 1986.

İçindekileriyle dergiler. Yıl 1, sayı 1 (1-31 Ocak 1993) -. Istanbul.

İskit, Server. *Türkiye'de matbuat idareleri ve politikaları*. Istanbul, 1943.

Kadın Eserleri Kütüphanesi ve Bilgi Merkezi Vakfı. *İstanbul kütüphanelerindeki eski harfli Türkçe kadın dergileri bibliyografyası (1869-1927)*. Istanbul, 1992.

Karagöz, Adem Ruhi. *Bulgaristan Türk basını, 1879-1945*. Istanbul, 1945.

Millî Kütüphane. *Eski harfli Türkçe süreli yayınlar toplu kataloğu (muvakkat basım)*. Ankara, 1963.

--. *Eski harfli Türkçe süreli yayınlar toplu kataloğu*. vol. 1. Ankara, 1987.

--. *Türkiye bibliyografyası*. Ankara, 1933-.

--. *Türkiye makaleler bibliyografyası*. Ankara, 1952-

Mustafayeva, Z. M. *Azĕrbaycan dövri mĕtbuatı, 1920-1970-ci illĕr: bibliografiya*. Baku, 1979.

Okday, İ. H. *Die Türkische Zeitungen und Zeitschrifte die in Bulgarien herausgegenben werden*. Ankara, 1988.

Oral, Fuat Süreyya. *Türk basın tarihi: 1728-1922, 1831-1922, Osmanlı imparatorluğu dönemi*. Ankara, ca. 1968.

--. *Türk basın tarihi: 1919-1965, Cumhuriyet dönemi*. Ankara, ca. 1970.

Özege, M. Seyfettin. *Eski harflerle basılmış Türkçe eserler kataloğu*. 5 vols. Istanbul, 1971.

Tülbentçi, F. Fazıl. *Cumhuriyetten sonra çıkan gazete ve mecmualar, 29 İlk Teşrin 1923 - 31 Ilk Kanun 1940*. Ankara, 1941.

Varlık, M. Bülent. *Türkiye basın-yayın tarihi kaynakçası*. Ankara, 1981.

Addenda and Corrigenda

AFİYET
Numero 1 (29 Teşrinievvel 1329 [11 Nov. 1913]) - Numero 62 (24 Kanunusani 1330 [6 Feb. 1915])
BL:OIOC: 1 (11.11.1913) - 62 (6.2.1915)   [14498.a.101]

MİLLĔTLĔR
Publication suspended, 1967-1973

ÜLTTAR
Publication suspended, 1967-1973

VOLKAN: her gün sabahları neşrolunur, insaniyete hadim dinî, siyasî gazete
Cild 1, sayı 1 (28 Teşrinievvel 1324 [5 Dec. 1908]) - Cild 1, sayı 110 (8 Nisan 1325 [21 Apr. 1909])
Istanbul
Reprinted in book form, Istanbul 1992
LO:SOAS: 1:1 (5.12.1908) - 1:110 (21.4.1909) (reprint)   [Per.10.653118]

ABANT / Bolu Halkevi kültür dergisi
  Cilt 1, sayı 1 (Temmuz-Ağustos 1944) -
  Cilt 3, sayı 13 (Ocak-Şubat 1947)
  Bolu
  Bimonthly

  BL:OIOC: 1:1 (7/8.1944) - 3:13
  (1/2.1947)   [ITA.1989.a.258]

AÇIK SÖZ
  [1] ([date?], 1915) - [?]
  Baku
  Daily newspaper
  Azeri; Arabic characters

  BL:OIOC: 22.8.1917 - 25.8.1917;
  27.8.1917 - 1.9.1917; 7.9.1917 -
  8.9.1917; 10.9.1917 - 13.9.1917;
  18.9.1917 - 22.9.1917; 25.9.1917 -
  28.9.1917; 1.10.1917; 3.10.1917 -
  6.10.1917; 8.10.1917 - 11.101.1917;
  25.10.1917 - 26.10.1917; 29.10.1917 -
  31.10.1917   [OR.MIC.11539 (O.P.243)]

ADABİY MEROS: Üzbek adabiyoti
  tarihindan tadķiķot va materiallar /
  H. S. Sulaymonov nomidagi Ķulyozmalar
  İnstituti
  [1] (1968) -
  Tashkent
  ISSN 0130-3619
  First issue had Russian added title:
  Literaturnoe nasledie; and Uzbek
  subtitle: huccat va tadķiķotlar
  In Uzbek
  Currently quarterly

  BL:OIOC: (a) 1 [1968]; (b) 1 (43) (1988)
  [(a) ITA.1987.a.150; (b)
  ZOR.1989.a.81]
  LO:SOAS: 1; 1987:2 (=40) -
  [Per.10.508862]

ADALET İSTATİSTİKLERİ = Judicial
  statistics / Başbakanlık Devlet
  İstatistik Enstitüsü
  1959/1960 -
  Ankara
  In Turkish and English; previously in
  Turkish only
  Annual; some issues cumulated

  DU:DC: 1960/1967 - 1967/1968; 1978/1980
  -   [25/4/LAW]
  SU:IDS: 1969/1970; 1976; 1978 - 1981;
  1984; 1986 -   [SERIALS/OFFICIAL/TURKEY]

ADANA İL YILLIĞI
  [1] (1967) - [2] (1973)
  Adana, 1968-1973

  BL:OIOC: [1] (1967)   [14498.a.39]
  OX:BOD: [1]   [Turk.d.3324/1]

ADANA VİLÂYETİ SALNAMESİ
  Defa 1 (1287 [1870-1871]) - Defa 12
  (1320 [1902-1903])
  Adana

  OX:BOD: 11 (1900-1901)   [Turk.e.824]

ADIM: edebiyat, san'at gazetesi
  1. sayı ([9 Haziran 1956?]) - [?]
  Lefkoşa
  Bimonthly

  BL:OIOC: 2 (9.8.1956) - 3 (9.10.1956)
  [14498.a.123]

ADIMLAR: aylık fikir ve kültür dergisi
  Yıl 1, sayı 1 (Mayıs 1943) - Yıl 1, sayı
  12 (Nisan 1944)
  Ankara

  BL:OIOC: 1:1 (5.1943) - 1:12 (4.1944)
  [14498.a.121]

ADIYAMAN İL YILLIĞI
  [1] (1967) - [2] (1973)
  Adana, [ca. 1968]-1973

  BL:OIOC: [1] (1967)   [14498.a.54]
  OX:BOD: [1]   [Turk.d.3324/2]

ADLİYE DERGİSİ / Adliye Vekilliği
  tarafından çıkarılır
  Yıl 1, sayı 1 ([date?], 1910) - [?]
  Ankara
  Title of issuing body varies

  LO:SOAS: 35:2 ([2].1944) - 35:8 (8.1944)
  [Per.32.77005]

AFAK: siyasetten başka herşeyden
  bahseder, cüz cüz neşrolunur risale-i
  mevkutedir
  Numero 1 (20 Zilhicce 1299 [2 Nov.
  1882]) - Numero 7 (23 Cemaziyelevvel
  [sic] 1300 [1 Apr. 1883])
  İstanbul
  Cultural and literary journal
  Monthly

  BL:OIOC: 1 [2.11.1882] - 7 [1.4.1883]
  [14498.cc.46]
  LO:SOAS: 1 - 7   [Per.10.137062]
  OX:BOD: 1 - 7   [Turk.d.2382]
  OX:MEC: 1 - 7   [APT Afa]

AFIET
  See: AFİYET

AFİÈTE
  See: AFİYET

AFİYET: munhasıran mesail-i sıhhiye ve
  tıbbiye ile umur-i beytiyeden bahsolarak
  şimdilik haftada bir kere ...
  neşrolunur resimli gazetedir
  Numero 1 (29 Teşrinievvel 1329 [1912])
  - Numero 62 (24 Kanunusani 1330 [1914])
  İstanbul
  Subtitle varies. Some issues have added
  title Afiet or Afiète

  BL:OIOC: 1 (29.10.1912) - 62 (24.1.1914)
  [14498.a.101]
  OX:BOD: 1 - 62   [Per.Turk.c.193]

AFYON İL YILLIĞI
  [1] (1967) - [2] (1973)
  İstanbul, 1968-1973

  OX:BOD: [1] (1967)   [Turk.d.3324/3]

AĞAÇ: sanat, fikir, aksiyon
  1 (14 Mart 1936) - 17 (29 Ağustos 1936)
  İstanbul
  Weekly

  BL:OIOC: (a) 1 (14.3.1936) - 17
  (29.8.1936); (b) 1 - 16 (25.7.1936)
  [(a) ITA.1990.a.441; (b) 14480.d.181]
  OX:BOD: 1 - 17; wanting no. 11
  [Turk.d.728]

AGGELIAPHOROS
  See: ANGELİAFOROS

AĞİDEL: aylık ėdėbi hėm
  ictimagi-politik curnal / Başkortostan
  Yaдıusılar Soyuzı organı
  1 (Mart 1923) -
  Ufa: KPSS-тın Başkortostan Ölkė
  Komitetı neşriėte
  ISSN 0207-1827
  In Bashkir

  BL:OIOC: 1962:1 - 1983:12   [14499.т.12]
  LO:SOAS: 1963:1 - 1964:7
  [Per.10.189711]
  OX:BOD: 1985:5 -   [Per.Turk.d.3385]

AĞRI İL YILLIĞI
[1] (1967) - [2] (1973)
[Ankara?]

BL:OIOC: [1] (1967)   [14498.a.33]
OX:BOD: [1]   [Turk.d.3324/4]

AGRICULTURAL PRODUCTION VALUE OF TURKEY
See: TÜRKİYE TARIMSAL ÜRETİM
DEĞERİ

AGRICULTURAL STRUCTURE AND PRODUCTION
See: TARIMSAL YAPI VE ÜRETİM

AKADEMİ / İstanbul Güzel Sanatlar
Akademisi tarafından yayınlanmaktadır
Sayı 1 (Mart 1964) - Sayı 10 (1981)
Istanbul
Irregular; nominally four-monthly

BL:OIOC: 1 (3.1964) - 8 (4.7.1974)
[14498.a.18]
LO:SOAS: 1 - 7 (1967)
[Per.107.L.133684]
OX:BOD: 1 - 9 [ca. 11 - 977]
[Per.Turk.c.155]

AKİS: haftalık aktüalite mecmuası
Sayı 1 (15 Mayıs 1954) - Yıl 14, sayı 12
[= 706] (31 Aralık 1967)
Ankara: [s.n.], 1954-1967

BL:OIOC: 18:316 (7.9.1960) - 22:379
(2.10.1961); lacking 342, 345, 348, 350,
352, 354, 357, 371-376   [14498.c.23]
LO:SOAS: 1-37; 39-70; 72-74; 81;
301-302; 340; 347-349; 355-359
[Per.10.L.173833]
OX:MEC: 14:226 (6.9.1958) - 14:228;
14:263-21:357 (1.5.1961); lacking
several issues   [APT Aki]

AKŞAM: müstakil siyasi sabah gazetesi
([Date?], 1334 [1918]) -
Istanbul
National daily newspaper

BL:OIOC: 4.4.1960; 28.4.1960; 30.4.1960;
10.10.1960; 26.11.1960; 17.12.1960;
28.4.1961; 22.5.1961   [OR.MIC.12604
(O.P. 552/4)]

ALA-TOO: Kırgız Cazuuçularının ay sayın
çıga turgan adabiy-körköm cana
koomduk-sayasiy curnal
No. 1 ([month?] 1931) -
Bishkek
ISSN 0320-7390
In Kirgiz

BL:OIOC: 1965:1 -; lacking 1979:4
[14499.t.15]
LO:SOAS: 1977:4 -; lacking 1979:1, 4-12
[Per.10.423545]
OX:BOD: 1965:1 -; lacking 1969:2
[Per.Turk.d.1250]

ALBÜM: güzel yazı, güzel resim mecmuası
No.1 (1 Kânunusani 1934) - No. 5 (Nisan
1934)
Istanbul
Nos.1-2 fortnightly, 3-5 monthly

BL:OIOC: 1 (1.1.1934) - 5 (4.1934)
[14448.f.156]

ALEM = Alem: journal humoristique et
satirique paraissant le jeudi
Numero 1 (29 Kanunusani 1324 [10 Feb.
1909]) - Numero 12 (21 Mayıs 1325 [2
June 1909])
Istanbul
Contents in Ottoman or French

BL:OIOC: 1 (10.2.1909) - 12 (2.6.1909)
[14498.a.75]

ALEMDAR: her gün sabahleri neşrolunur
müstakilülefkar Osmanlı gazetesidir
Sene 1, aded 1 [date?] 1314 [1908] - [?]
Istanbul

BL:OIOC: 10:124 (25.4.1919) - 10:186
(27.6.1919); lacking several issues
[OR.MIC.11697 (O.P.246)]

ALİ BABA: haftalık siyasî mizah gazetesi
Yıl 1, sayı 1 (25 Kasım 1947) - Yıl 1,
sayı 4 (16 Aralık 1947)
Istanbul

BL:OIOC: 1:1 (25.11.1947) - 1:4
(16.12.1947)   [OR.FICHE 439]

ÂLİ PEDAGOJİ ENSTİTUTU SALNAMESİ:
Azerbaycan Devleti Türk Âli Pedagoji
Enstitutu üç seneliği ve ilk
mezunları dolayısile [sic] neşr olunur
İlk [1.] sayı (1924) - [?]
Baku
Azeri; in Arabic characters
Annual

BL:OIOC: 1 (1924)   [14499.ss.21]

ALMAN DİL VE EDEBİYATI DERGİSİ =
Studien zur Deutschen Sprache und
Literatur / herausgegeben von der
Abteilung für deutsche Philologie an
der Universität Istanbul
1 (1954) -
Ankara, 1955-
Articles in German or Turkish
Annual from 1954 to 1956; occasional
thereafter

BL:OIOC: **1 (1954 - 6 (1985)   [ITA.1993.a.329]**

AMASYA İL YILLIĞI
[1] (1967) - [2] (1973)
Amasya

BL:OIOC: [1] (1967)   [14498.a.43]
OX:BOD: [1]   [Turk.d.3324/5]

AMCABEY: Cumartesi günleri çıkar siyasî
mizah gazetesi
Cilt 1, sayı 1 (5 Birincikânun 1942) -
Cilt 1, sayı 33 (17 Temmuz 1943)
Istanbul

BL:OIOC: 1:1 (5.12.1942) - 1:33
(17.7.1943)   [ITA.1990.c.13]

AMME İDARESİ DERGİSİ / Türkiye ve
Orta Doğu Amme İdaresi Enstitüsü
tarafından yılda dört defa ...
yayınlanır
Cilt 1, sayı 1 (Haziran 1968) -
Ankara

BL:OIOC: 1:1 (6.1968) - 14:4 (1981)
[14498.bb.17]

ANA SÖZÜ / Azěrbaycan Halg Těhsili
Nazirliyinin aylıg jurnalı
No. 1 (Noyabr 1990) -
Baku
ISSN 0206-4340
In Azeri

BL:OIOC: 1 (11.1990) -   [ZOR.1991.a.70]

ANADOL AHTERİ: fennî ve ahlakî,
musavver, haftada bir defa neşrolunur
risalei mevkutedir
1. sene, 1. cüz (Septembrios 1 1886) -
1. sene, 23. cüz (Martios 24 1887)
[Istanbul]
Title romanized from Greek orthography:
Anatol akhteri
Karamanlitic: Ottoman in Greek
characters

BL:OIOC: 1:1 (1.9.1886) - 1:23
(24.3.1887)   [14498.cc.25]

ANADOLU = Anatolia / Ankara Üniversitesi
Dil ve Tarih-Coğrafya Fakültesi Eski
Önasya-Akdeniz Medeniyetleri Araştırma
Enstitüsü Dergisi
1 (1957) -
Ankara, 1960-
Nos.1-8 are entitled: Anatolia
Articles in Turkish or English
Irregular; nominally annual

BL:OIOC: 18-19   [14498.cc.87]
LO:SOAS: 1 -   [Per.10.116672]
CA:UL: 1 -   [P.617.c.6]
OX:BOD: 5 (1960) -   [Per.Turk.d.2692]

ANADOLU ARAŞTIRMALARI = Jahrbuch für
kleinasiatische Forschung / İstanbul
Üniversitesi Edebiyat Fakültesi,
Hititoloji Protohistorya ve Önasya
Arkeolojisi ve Eskiçağ Tarihi Anabilim
Dalları tarafından yayınlanır
Cilt 1, sayı 1 (1955) -
Istanbul
Nomenclature of publishing body varies
Some articles are in German, some
summaries and a few articles in English
Nominally annual down to 1980; no. 9,
published 1983, has no nominal date

BL:OIOC: 1:1-   [14482.dd.9]
LO:SOAS: 1:1 - 2:2 (1965)
[Per.5.64435]
CA:UL: 1:1 -   [P.516.c.6]
OX:BOD: 1:1 - 2:2   [Or.Per.99*]

ANADOLU MECMUASI: ayda bir neşrolunur
Sene 1, sayı 1 (1 Nisan 1340 [1924]) -
1. sene, sayı 12 (Mart 1341 [1925])
Istanbul
A cultural and literary journal

BL:OIOC: 1:1 (1.4.1924) - 1:9/11
(2.1925)   [14480.d.234]
OX:BOD: 1:1 - 1:12 (3.1925)
[Per.Turk.d.3555]

ANADOLU SANATI ARAŞTIRMALARI / İstanbul
Üniversitesi Mimarlık Fakültesi,
Mimarlık Tarihi ve Rölöve Kürsüsü
1 (1968) - 2 (1970)
Istanbul

BL:OIOC: 1 (1968) - 2 (1970)
[14451.d.14]
LO:SOAS: 1 - 2   [Per.10.277180]
OX:BOD: 1 - 2   [Per.Turk.d.2856]

ANATOL AKHTERI
See: ANADOL AHTERİ

ANATOLIA
See: ANADOLU

ANGELİAFOROS / Amerika Misyonarları
Şirketi tarafından müellif-i gazeta,
E. Bliss
Cilt A, nom. 1 (16 Fevruarios 1872 [29
Feb. 1872]) - [?]
Istanbul: American Missionary Society
Newsletter for Turkish-speaking
Christians
Vol.1 comprises 47 issues
Karamanlitic: Ottoman in Greek
characters
Weekly

BL:OIOC: 1:2 (29.2.1872) - 2:1
(16.1.1873)   [O.P.438]

ANGELİAFOROS ÇOCUKLAR İÇİN
See: ANGELİAFOROS TZOTZOUKLAR İTZOUN

ANGELİAFOROS TZOTZOUKLAR İTZOUN /
Amerika Misionleri Sirketi tarafēntan
Istanbul, [18--?]-[18--?]
Children's supplement to: Angeliaforos

BL:OIOC: 6:3 (1.3.1877)   [O.P.438/2]

ANGELIAPHOROS
See: ANGELİAFOROS

ANIT / Konya ve Mülhakatı Eski Eserleri
Sevenler Derneği tarafından ayda bir
çıkarılır arkeoloji, folklor, tarih
dergisi
Yıl 1, sayı 1 (Şubat 1949) - Yıl 6,
sayı 28 (Nisan 1961)
Konya

BL:OIOC: 1:1 (2.1949) - 2:17 (5.1950)
[14498.a.19]
LO:SOAS: 1:1 - 5:27 (5.1960)
[Per.10.L.63824]
OX:BOD: 1:1 - 6:28 (4.1961)
[Per.Turk.d.731]

ANKARA İL YILLIĞI
[1] (1967) - [2] (1973)
Ankara

BL:OIOC: [1] (1967)   [14498.a.21]
LO:SOAS: [1]   [Per.10.L.266119]
OX:BOD: [1]   [Turk.d.3324/6]

ANKARA SANAYİ ODASI BÜLTENİ
Sayı 1 (24 Şubat 1972 [?]) -
Ankara
Monthly; originally weekly

DU:DC: 3:25 (1.1979) - 3:26 (2.1979);
3:34 (10.1979)   [25/4/INDUSTRY/GENERAL]

ANKARA TİCARET ODASI DERGİSİ
Sayı 1 (Ocak 1976) - [2. dizi], sayı 5
(Eylül 1984)
Ankara
Monthly until Jan. 1979 (issue 13); new
series irregular

DU:DC: 12.1973 - 4.1975; lacking 9.1974,
2.1975 - 3.1975   [25/4/Commerce]

ANKARA ÜNİVERSİTESİ DİL VE
TARİH-COĞRAFYA FAKÜLTESİ DERGİSİ
See: FAKÜLTE DERGİSİ

ANKARA ÜNİVERSİTESİ DİL VE
TARİH-COĞRAFYA FAKÜLTESİ YILLIK
ARAŞTIRMALAR DERGİSİ
1 (1940-1941)
Istanbul, 1944
Only one issue published

LO:SOAS: 1 (1940/1941)   [Per.10.285352]

ANKARA ÜNİVERSİTESİ HUKUK FAKÜLTESİ
DERGİSİ
Cilt 1, sayı 1 ([1943]) -
Ankara
Occasional contributions in English,
French or German
Frequency varies; originally quarterly

BL:OIOC: 1:1 (1943) - 2:1 (1944); 6
(1949) - 28 (1971)   [14458.fff.54]
BL:DSC: 34 (1982/1987) - 41 (1990)
[0905.252000]
OX:BOD: 1:1 -   [Per.Turk.d.3544]

ANKARA ÜNİVERSİTESİ İLÂHİYAT
FAKÜLTESİ DERGİSİ / Ankara
Üniversitesi İlâhiyat Fakültesi
tarafından yılda bir çıkarılır
Yıl 1, sayı 1 (1952) -
Ankara
Original title, vols. 1 (1952) - 13
(1965): İlâhiyat Fakültesi dergisi
Annual, sometimes biennial; quarterly
from 1952 to 1955

BL:OIOC: 1:1 (1952) -   [14498.a.9]
LO:SOAS: 1:1 -   [Per.10.L.93169]
CA:UL: 1:1 -   [P.830.b.19]
OX:BOD: 1:1 -   [Per.Turk.d.314]

ANKARA ÜNİVERSİTESİ SİYASAL
BİLGİLER FAKÜLTESİ DERGİSİ =
Review of the Faculty of Political
Science = Revue de la Faculté des
Sciences Politiques = Zeitschrift der
Staatswissenschaftlichen Fakultät
Cilt 1 (1943) -
Ankara
Early issues have ''Okulu'' for
''Fakültesi''. Initial English title:
Journal of the School of Political
Sciences
Quarterly

LO:SOAS: 1 (1943) -; lacking 4-9
[Per.10.65383]
DU:UL: 10:1 (3.1955) - 28:2 (6.1973)
[Per./PL8]
OX:BOD: 1 -   [Per.Turk.d.407]

ANKARA ÜNİVERSİTESİ SİYASAL
BİLGİLER OKULU DERGİSİ
See: ANKARA ÜNİVERSİTESİ SİYASAL
BİLGİLER FAKÜLTESİ DERGİSİ

ANKARA ÜNİVERSİTESİ YILLIĞI = Annales
de l'Université d'Ankara
1 (1946-1947) -
Ankara: 1947-
Journal containing learned articles
Contents in English, French, or German,
some with Turkish summaries
Some issues cumulated

BL:OIOC: 1 (1946/1947)   [14498.bb.4]
LO:SOAS: 1 - 13 (1974)   [Per.10.51362]
OX:BOD: 1 - 13   [Per.3794.d.597]

ANKARA VİLÂYETİ SALNAME-İ RESMİYESİ
See: ANKARA VİLÂYETİ SALNAMESİ

ANKARA VİLÂYETİ SALNAMESİ
Defa 1 (1288 [1871-1872]) - Defa 15
(1325 [1907-1908])
Ankara
Issues of 1883 and 1891 both numbered
11; 14 numbered 13 on cover
Some issues entitled: Ankara Vilâyeti
salname-i resmiyesi

LO:SOAS: 15 (1907)   [E.Per.280663]
DU:UL: 15   [PL366.A6]
OX:BOD: 11 (1891) - 12 (1893); 15 (1907)
[Per.Turk.d.1037]

ANNALES DE L'UNIVERSITÉ D'ANKARA
See: ANKARA ÜNİVERSİTESİ YILLIĞI

ANNALES MÉDICALES ET BULLETIN DE
STATISTIQUE DE L'HÔPITAL D'ENFANTS
HAMIDIÉ
See: HAMİDİYE ETFÂL HASTAHANE-İ
ÂLİSİ İSTATİSTİK MECMUA-İ
TIBBİYESİ

ANNUAIRE DES EXPORTATIONS ET IMPORTATIONS
DE LA RÉGION D'ÉGÉE
See: EGE BÖLGESİ İHRACAT-İTHALAT
YILLIĞI

ANNUAIRE STATISTIQUE
See: TÜRKİYE İSTATİSTİK YILLIĞI

ANNUAL BULLETIN OF ELECTRICAL STATISTICS
OF TURKEY
See: TÜRKİYE ELEKTRİK
İSTATİSTİKLERİ YILLIĞI

ANNUAL ELECTRIC POWER SURVEY
See: ELEKTRİK ENERJİSİ YILLIK DURUM
BÜLTENİ

ANNUAL MANUFACTURING INDUSTRY STATISTICS
See: YILLIK İMALAT SANAYİ ANKET
İSTATİSTİKLERİ

ANNUAL OF AYASOFYA MUSEUM
See: AYASOFYA MÜZESİ YILLIĞI

ANNUAL OF EXPORTS AND IMPORTS OF THE
AEGEAN REGION
See: EGE BÖLGESİ İHRACAT-İTHALAT
YILLIĞI

ANNUAL OF THE ARCHAEOLOGICAL MUSEUM OF
ISTANBUL
See: İSTANBUL ARKEOLOJİ MÜZELERİ
YILLIĞI

ANNUAL REPORT OF THE TURKISH FOREST
INSTITUTE
See: ORMANCILIK ARAŞTIRMA ENSTİTÜSÜ
YILLIK BÜLTENİ

ANNUAL STATISTICS OF TRADE AND SERVICE
See: YILLIK TİCARET VE HİZMET
İSTATİSTİKLERİ

ANNUAL STATISTICS / SOSYAL SIGORTALAR
KURUMU
See: İSTATİSTİK YILLIĞI / SOSYAL
SIGORTALAR KURUMU

ANT: haftalık dergi
Sayı 1 ([date?], 196-?]) - Sayı 185
(Nisan 1971)
Ankara
Socialist journal
Later issues subtitled: aylık sosyalist
teori ve eylem dergisi
Later issues published monthly

OX:BOD: 158 (6.1.1970) - 185 (4.1971)
[Per.Turk.c.98]

ANTALYA İL YILLIĞI
[1] (1967) - [2] (1973)
Ankara

BL:OIOC: [1] (1967)   [14498.a.46]
OX:BOD: [1]   [Turk.d.3324/7]

ANTHROPOLOGIE
See: ANTROPOLOJİ

ANTİKA: aylık dergi = The Turkish journal
of collectable art
Sayı 1 (Nisan 1985) -
Istanbul: Mısırlı
All contents in Turkish and English
With complete English translations of
all articles

BL:OIOC: 1 (4.1985) -   [14498.cc.91]

ANTROPOLOJİ: fizik antropoloji,
   paleoantropoloji, etnoloji, prehistorya
   / Ankara Üniversitesi Dil ve
   Tarih-Coğrafya Fakültesi Antropoloji
   Bilimleri Araştırma Enstitüsü
   tarafından yayınlanır
   1. cilt, 1. sayı (1963) -
   Ankara
   Subtitle varies. Added t.p. in French:
   Anthropologie
   Biennial; annual from 1963 to 1965

   BL:OIOC: 1 (1963) -   [14498.b.18]
   LO:SOAS: 1 - 9 (1975/1976)
   [Per.10.183055]

ARAŞTIRMA / Dil ve Tarih-Coğrafya
   Fakültesi Felsefe Araştırma
   Enstitüsü dergisi
   1. cilt (1963) -
   Ankara
   Publication suspended between vols. 10
   (1972) and 11 (1979)

   BL:OIOC: 1 (1963) -   [14442.c.5]
   LO:SOAS: 1 -   [Per.10.276440]
   OX:BOD: 1 - 7 (1969)   [Per.Turk.d.1566]

ARAŞTIRMA DERGİSİ
   See: EDEBİYAT FAKÜLTESİ ARAŞTIRMA
   DERGİSİ

ARAY / Kazakstan LKSM Ortalık
   Komitetinin koğamdık-sayasi,
   ėdėbi-körkem cėne bezendirilgen,
   ay sayın kazak cėne orıs tillerinde
   şığatın curnalı
   No. 1 (Aprel 1987) -
   Alma-Ata
   ISSN 0235-1447
   General-interest magazine
   In Kazakh; also published in Russian
   with title: Zaria
   Monthly

   BL:OIOC: 3 (24) (3.1989) -
   [ZOR.1989.a.40]

ARAYIŞ: haftalık dergi
   Sayı 1 (21 Şubat 1981) - Sayı 54 (1
   Mart 1982)
   Ankara
   Political weekly. BL holdings include
   banned issues

   BL:OIOC: 1 (21.2.1981) - 54 (1.3.1982)
   [ITA.1987.a.512]

ARCHIV FÜR GESCHICHTE DER TÜRKISCHEN
MEDIZIN
   See: TÜRK TIB TARİHİ ARKİVİ

ARCHIV FÜR PHILOSOPHIE
   See: FELSEFE ARKİVİ

ARCHIVES DE PHILOSOPHIE
   See: FELSEFE ARKİVİ

ARCHIVES D'HISTOIRE DE LA MÉDICINE TURQUE
   See: TÜRK TIB TARİHİ ARKİVİ

ARCHIVES OF PHILOSOPHY
   See: FELSEFE ARKİVİ

ARKEOLOJİ: sanat tarihi dergisi / Ege
   Üniversitesi Edebiyat Fakültesi
   1 (1982) -
   Izmir
   Annual

   LO:SOAS: 1 (1982) -   [Per.107.475865]
   OX:BOD: 1 -   [Per.Turk.d.3019]

ARKEOLOJİ VE SANAT: üç ayda bir
   yayınlanır; prehistorya arkeoloji,
   eskiçağ tarihi, sanat tarihi,
   etnografya, numismatik dergisi
   Yıl 1, sayı 1 (Nisan-Mayıs 1978) -
   Istanbul: Arkeoloji ve Sanat Yayınları
   Quarterly; bi-monthly for first issue
   only

   BL:OIOC: 1:1 (4-5.1978) -   [14498.a.76]
   OX:BOD: 1:1 -   [Per.Turk.d.3318]

ÂRŞ: üsbuî, siyasî, müstakil Osmanlı
   gazetesidir
   Numero 1 (11 Eylül 1327 [24 Sept.
   1911]) - [?]
   Skopje
   Possibly only one issue published

   BL:OIOC: 1 (24.9.1911)   [ORB.40/68]

ARTVİN İL YILLIĞI
   [1] (1967) - [2] (1973)
   [Ankara?]

   OX:BOD: [1] (1967)   [Turk.d.3324/8]

ASERBAIDSCHAN
   See: AZERBAYCAN

AŞİYAN: edebî, ilmî, siyasî,
   ictimâî, fennî, ahlâkî haftalık
   mecmuadır
   Numero 1 (28 Ağustos 1324 [10 Sep.
   1908]) - Numero 26 (27 Şubat 1325 [12
   Mar. 1909])
   İstanbul
   Contents: mainly plays, poems and
   stories

   BL:OIOC: 1 (10.9.1908) - 26 (12.3.1909)
   [14480.d.190]
   LO:SOAS: 1 - 2   [Per.10.172651]
   CA:UL: 1 - 26   [Q.830.c.23]
   OX:BOD: 1 - 26   [Turk.d.2222]
   OX:MEC: 1 - 26   [APT Asi]

ASKER: ordu ve donanmanın terakkiyatına
   hâdim olmak üzere ayda iki defa
   neşredilir
   Numero 1 (21 Ağustos 1324 [3 Sep.
   1908]) - Cild 2, numero 24 (1 Eylül
   1325 [14 Sep. 1909])
   Istanbul

   BL:OIOC: 1 (3.9.1908) - 2:24 (14.9.1909)
   [ITA.1988.a.64]
   OX:BOD: 1 - 2:24   [Turk.d.1466]

ASKERİ TARİH BELGELERİ DERGİSİ
   See: HARP TARİHİ VESİKALARI DERGİSİ

ASRÎ MÜSLÜMANLIK: dinî, ilmî, ahlakî
   ve felsefî aylık mecmuadır / Kırım
   Müslüman Halk İdare-i Şer'iyesi
   Numero 1 ([5 Nisan], 1925) - [?]
   Simferopol' (Akmescit)
   Crimean Tatar; Arabic characters
   Nominally monthly

   BL:OIOC: 9 (2.1926), 11 (6.1926)
   [ITA.1986.c.17]

O ASTĒR
   See: MİKRASIATİKON ĒMEROLOGİON O
   "ASTĒR"

ATATÜRK ARAŞTIRMA MERKEZİ DERGİSİ
   Cilt 1, sayı 1 (Kasım 1984) -
   Ankara
   Generally published thrice annually

   OX:BOD: 1:1 (11.1984) -
   [Per.Turk.d.3384]

ATATÜRK İLKELERİ VE İNKILÂP TARİHİ
ENSTİTÜSÜ DERGİSİ / Atatürk
Üniversitesi Atatürk İlkeleri ve
İnkılâp Tarihi Enstitüsü
Cilt 1, sayı 1 ([date?], 1988) –
Erzurum

BL:OIOC: 1:3 (19.5.1989)
[ZOR.1989.a.124]

ATATÜRK ÜNİVERSİTESİ İSLÂMİ
İLİMLER FAKÜLTESİ DERGİSİ
1. sayı (Aralık 1975) –
Erzurum, 1976–
Annual?

BL:OIOC: 1 (12.1975)   [14415.d.84]

ATATÜRK ÜNİVERSİTESİ YILLIĞI
Erzurum
Learned science and humanities articles
Publication dates not known
Includes a few articles in English or
German

BL:OIOC: 1960; 1962   [14498.bb.5]
BL:HSS: 1960; 1962   [S.Q.60/40]

ÂTİ
Sayı 1 (1 Ocak 1334 [1918]) – Sayı 2435
(30 Aralık 1340 [1924])
İstanbul: [s.n.], 1334 [1918] – 1340
[1924]
Daily newspaper
Succeeded by: İleri

BL:OIOC: 79 (20.3.1918) – 268
(5.10.1918) ; lacking 96-106, 114-124,
and a few others   [OR. MIC.11701
(O.P.250)]

AVRUPA / Avrupa Topluluğu Komisyonu
Ankara, 1975–
Original title: Avrupa Topluluğu
10 issues annually

DU:DC: 12 (7.1976) – 18 (3.1977); 25
(10.1977) – 33 (7.1978); 35 (10.1978) –
[25/3/INTERNATIONAL RELATIONS]

AVRUPA TOPLULUĞU
See: AVRUPA

AWETABER: umurê tiniyē vē ilmiyē ve
p'olit'igiyēyē tair łazēt'a tēr /
Ameriga Misionerleri Sirk'et'i
t'arafēntan miwēllifi łazēt'a, Č.K.
Krin
Cild 1, no.1 ([date?, 1855) – [?]
Istanbul: American Missionary Society,
1855-1915
Newspaper for Armenians
Subtitle varies
Ottoman in Armenian characters; at least
one issue in Armenian
Weekly; monthly during at least part of
the 1860s

BL:OIOC: [Unnumbered] (7.12.1864); 6:1
(4.1.1865) – 6:13 (6.12.1865; 7:1
(3.1.1866) – 7:13 (19.12.1866); 8:1
(2.1.1867) – 8:13 (4.12.1867); 9:1
(1.1.1868) – 9:14 (30.12.1868); 12:1
(4.1.1871) – 12:19 (10.5.1871); 13:20
(17.5.1872) – 13:52 (27.12.1871); 14:1
(3.1.1872) – 14:52 (25.12.1872); 20:15
(10.4.1877); 22:19 (8.5.1877)
[OR.MIC.12722 (O.P.440/1-3)]

AWETABER ČOČUGLAR İČİN / Ameriga
Misionarlarê Širk'et'i t'arafêntan
miwēllifi kazēt'a E. Plis, Č.G. Krin
Cild 1, no.1 (1 Jan. 1872) – [?]
Istanbul: American Missionary Society,
1872-[1907?]
Illustrated magazine for Armenian
children
Some issues published as: Awetaber
mankanc', or: Awetaber tayoc' bažin
Ottoman in Armenian characters
Monthly

BL:OIOC: 1:1 (1.1.1872) – 1:12
(1.12.1872); 6:2 (1.2.1877), 6:4
(1.4.1877)   [OR.MIC.12721 (O.P.439)]

AWETABER MANKANC'
See: AWETABER ČOČUGLAR İČİN

AWETABER TAYOC' BAŽIN
See: AWETABER ČOČUGLAR İČİN

AY DEDE [1. SERİ]: pazartesi ve perşembe
günleri neşrolunur, bitaraf hoşsohbet
mizah gazetesi
1. cild, sayı 1 (2 Kanunusani 1338
[1922]) – 1. cild, sayı 90 (9
Teşrinisani 1338 [1922])
Istanbul
Subtitle varies

BL:OIOC: 1:1 (2.1.1922) – 1:90
(9.11.1922)   [14498.a.60/4]
LO:SOAS: 1:1 – 1:90   [L.E.Per.552303]
CA:UL: 1:1 – 1:90   [T.830.a.20]
OX:BOD: 1:1 – 1:90; lacking 76, 79, 81
[Turk.b.10]

AYASOFYA MÜZESİ YILLIĞI = Annual of
Ayasofya Museum
No. 1 (1959) –
Istanbul
Most articles in Turkish; others in
English or French
Irregular

BL:OIOC: 1 (1959)   [14498.cc.17]

AYDEDE
See also: AY DEDE

AYDEDE [2. SERİ]
No. 1 (8 Mayıs 1948) – No. 125 (1 Ekim
1949)
Istanbul
Satirical newspaper
Published twice weekly

BL:OIOC: 1 (8.5.1948) – 125 (1.10.1949)
[ORB.30/72]

AYDIN İL YILLIĞI
[1] (1967) – [2] (1973)
Izmir, [ca. 1968]-1973

OX:BOD: [1] (1967)   [Turk.d.3324/9]

AYDIN VİLÂYETİ SALNAMESİ
Defa 1 (1296 [1878-1879]) – Defa 25
(1326 [1908-1909])
Izmir
Some issues entitled: Salname-i
Vilâyet-i Aydın; Aydın Vilâyetine
mahsus salname

LO:SOAS: 2 (1880) – 3 (1881); 18 (1897)
– 19 (1898)   [E.Per.280660]
CA:UL: 13 (1891); 18 – 19
[S.828.01.b.6]
DU:UL: 12 (1890); 25 (1908)   [PL366.A9]
OX:BOD: 6 (1884); 9 (1887); 12 – 13; 25
[Per.Turk.d.1354]

AYDIN VİLÂYETİNE MAHSUS SALNAME
See: AYDIN VİLÂYETİ SALNAMESİ

AYIN TARİHİ: ayın politik ve ekonomik
olayları
Sayı 1 (15 II. Teşrin - 31 I. Kanun
1933) - Sayı 285 (1-31 Ağustos 1957)
Ankara: Basın ve Yayın Genel
Müdürlüğü
Official government view of world events
Nomenclature of issuing body varies

BL:OIOC: 1 (15.11-13.12.1933) - 285
(1-31.8.1957)   [14456.ff.1]

ÂYİNE
See also: AYNA

AYİNE: perşembe günleri intişar eder,
müstakil ül-efkâr millî mizah
gazetesidir
1. sene, numero 1 (18 Ağustos 1337
[1921]) - 2. sene, numero 72 (4
Kanunusani 1339 [1923])
Istanbul

BL:OIOC: 1:1 (18.8.1921) - 2:72
(4.1.1923)   [14498.a.60/3]

AYİNE-İ VATAN
See: İSTANBUL

AYİNE-İ VATAN: perşembe günleri tab'
olunur
Sene 1, vak'a 1 (14 Kanunusani 1867) -
Sene 1, vak'a 10 (9 Şubat 1867)
Istanbul
Cultural review, with some news items
Continued by: Ruzname-i Ayine-i vatan,
then by: İstanbul
Weekly

BL:OIOC: 1:1 (14.1.1867); 1:3 - 1:4
[14498.d.6/1]

AYLIK BÜLTEN
See: ÜÇ AYLIK BÜLTEN

AYLIK DIŞ TİCARET İSTATİSTİKLERİ =
Monthly foreign trade statistics /
Başbakanlık Devlet İstatistik
Enstitüsü
Ankara, [19--?]-
In Turkish and English
Published in quarterly or other
cumulations, 1969-1973

CA:UL: 1.1967 -   [OP.22000.382.01]
DU:DC: 1.1967; 9.1968 - 12.1973
[25/4/TRADE/INTERNATIONAL]
SU:IDS: 1971:1/2
[SERIALS/OFFICIAL/TURKEY]

AYLIK DIŞ TİCARET ÖZETİ = Summary of
monthly foreign trade / Başbakanlık
Devlet İstatistik Enstitüsü
Ankara, [1964?]-
In Turkish and English

DU:DC: 5/6.1971, 10.1971; 12.1983 -
12.1985; 5.1986 - 8.1987
[25/4/TRADE/INTERNATIONAL]

AYLIK FAALİYET RAPORU / Ege Bölgesi
Sanayi Odası
Izmir, [19--?]-
Some cumulated issues

DU:DC: 6/7.1973 - 9/10.1973
[25/4/INDUSTRY/GENERAL]

AYLIK FİYAT İNDEKSLERİ BÜLTENİ
See: TOPTAN EŞYA VE TÜKETİCİ
FİYATLARI AYLIK İNDEKS BÜLTENİ

AYLIK HABERLER BÜLTENİ / Türk
Kütüphaneciler Derneği
Yıl 1, sayı 1 (Ocak 1953) -
Ankara: Türk Kütüphaneciler Derneği,
1953-

DU:UL: 4:47; 5:50 - 5:51; 6:61
(11.1956-1.1958)   [Per./PL18]

AYLIK HAVA VE ZİRAAT VAZİYETİ BÜLTENİ
/ T.C. Tarım Bakanlığı Devlet
Meteoroloji İşleri Umum Müdürlüğü
Sayı 1 (Ocak 1931) - Cilt 43, sayı 12
(Ocak 1984)
Ankara
Tables include English translations

DU:DC: 22:1 (1.1955) - 12.1960
[25/4/AGRICULTURE]

AYLIK İSTATİSTİK BÜLTENİ = Monthly
bulletin of statistics / Başbakanlık
Devlet İstatistik Enstitüsü
Sayı 1 (Eylül 1952) -
Ankara
Issuing body prior to Feb. 1962:
İstatistik Umum Müdürlüğü. Issues
numbered down to 1961, dated thereafter
In Turkish and English

LO:SOAS: 1991:1 (1/2.1991) -
[Per.77.L.317446]
DU:DC: 42-43 (8-9.1957) - 94 (12.1961);
1.1962 - 10.1974; 1.1975 - 3.1977;
8.1977 - 11.1978; 8.1980 - 12.1980;
4.1981 -   [25/1/GENERAL]
SU:IDS: 5-7.1971 -; lacking 3.1972 -
1.1973, 1.1974 - 7.1977, 9.1978 - 6.1979
[SERIALS/OFFICIAL/TURKEY]

AYLIK İSTATİSTİK BÜLTENİ = Monthly
statistical bulletin / T.C. Merkez
Bankası
1990, Ocak-Şubat -
Ankara
Continuation of: İstatistik ve
değerlendirme bülteni
In Turkish and English

LO:SOAS: 1990:1-2 -   [Per.77.L.539397]

AYLIK SİYASİ İLİMLER MECMUASI
See: SİYASİ İLİMLER MECMUASI

AYNA
See: AYİNE

AYNA = Mir'āt = Zerkalo: Türkî ve
Fârisî orta şivede ba'zâ Rusça
herşeyden bâhis musavver haftalik
macalla-i İslâmiyedür
Aded 1 ([date?] 1331 [1913]) - [?]
Samarkand
In Uzbek (Arabic characters) and
Persian; occasionally contains Russian

BL:OIOC: 40 (26.7.1914) - 41 (2.8.1914)
[ITA.1986.a.1625]

AZADÎ-İ ŞARK = Freiheit des Ostens = La
Liberté de l'Orient: siyasî ictimaî
iktisadî nâme-i Azadı-i Şark, mâhî
2 mertebe çâp mîşeved
Şümare 1 (10 May 1921) - Sal 1,
şümare 12 (20 Mars 1922)
Berlin
Contents in Persian, Arabic, Ottoman,
Urdu, German, French, or English
Fortnightly

LO:SOAS: 4 (1.8.1921) - 1:12 (20.3.1922)
[L.E.Per.42491]

AZERBAİDZHANSKIİ MEDIT͡SINSKIİ ZHURNAL
See: AZĚRBAYCAN TİBB MĚCMUĚSİ

AZERBAİDZHANSKIİ NAUCHNYİ FRONT
See: AZĚRBAYCAN ELMİ CĚBHĚSİ

AZERBAYCAN: aylık kültür dergisi /
çıkaran, Azerbaycan Kültür Derneği
Yıl 1, sayı 1 (Nisan 1952) - Yıl 20,
sayı 205 (Mayıs 1971)
Ankara

BL:OIOC: 1:1 - 2:19; 3:26-31, 34-35;
4:37 - 5:53; 5:58-59
OX:BOD: 1:9 (1.12.1952); 2:2-7; 4:10/11;
5:6/7, 8/9; 6:10-15   [Per.Turk.d.3547]

AZĚRBAYCAN / Azěrbaycan Yazıçılar
Birliyinin aylıg ěděbi-bědii curnalı
1 ([date?] 1923) -
Baku
ISSN 0134-3408
In Azeri

BL:OIOC: 1963:1 -; lacking 1975:11;
1977:5; 1982:7,9-12; 1983:1-12; 1984:12
   [14499.t.13]
LO:SOAS: 1964:8 -; lacking 1969:1 -
1971:12   [Per.10.185358]
SU:IDS: []

AZERBAYCAN: Azerbaycan Millî Birliğinin
organıdır
Yıl 1, sayı 1 ([date?], 1951) - [?]
Munich
Added title in German: Aserbaidschan
Mainly monthly

BL:OIOC: 2:4 (8.1952); 2:6/7
(10.12.''1953'' [1952]); 3:8 (1.1953);
3:11 (4.1953)   [14498.cc.12]

AZĚRBAYCAN ARHİVİ / Azěrbaycan SSR
Nazirlěr Soveti yanında Baş Arhiv
İdarěsi
Baku
Publication history not known. Name of
issuing body varies
Articles in Azeri or Russian
Irregular

BL:OIOC: 1973:1 (12); 1975:1-2 (14-15)
   [ZOR.1988.a.171]

AZĚRBAYCAN COĞRAFYA CĚMİYYĚTİNİN
ĚSĚRLĚRİ = Trudy Azerbaidzhanskogo
Geograficheskogo Obshchestva
1. cild ([196-?]) - [?]
Baku
Articles in Azeri or Russian, with a
summary in the other language
Occasional: 2-4 published 1963-1968

LO:SOAS: 3 (1966)   [Per.87.215725]

AZĚRBAYCAN DİLİ VĚ ĚDĚBIYYAT
TĚDRİSİ: Azěrbaycan SSR Maarif
Nazirliyinin organı "Azěrbaycan
měktěbi" jurnalına ělavě
No.1 ([date?] 1954) -
Baku: Azěrbaycan SSR Maarif Nazirliyi
ISSN 0206-4340
In Azeri
Bimonthly

BL:OIOC: 1987:1 -   [ZOR.1987.a.20]

AZĚRBAYCAN DÖVLĚT ELMİ-TĚDGİGAT
PEDAGOKİKA İNSTİTUTUNUN ĚSĚRLĚRİ
1. burahılış ([195-?]) -
Baku: Azěrbaycan SSR Maarif Nazirliyi,
[195-?]-
Added title in Russian: Trudy
Azerbaidzhanskogo Goşudarstvennogo
Nauchno-Issledovatel'skogo Instituta
Pedagogiki
In Azeri
Occasional

BL:OIOC: 5 (1963), 7 (1966), 11 (1976)
   [14499.t.39]

AZĚRBAYCAN ELMİ CĚBHĚSİ =
Azerbaidzhanskii nauchnyi front /
Azěrbaycan Devlět Elmi-Tědkikat
İnstitutu
No.1-2 (1932) - [?]
Baku
Mainly on politics and humanities
subjects
Articles in Azeri (modified roman
characters) or Russian; with a summary
in the other language

LO:SOAS: 1/2 (1932)   [Per.10.29852]

AZĚRBAYCAN ELMLĚR AKADEMİYASININ
HĚBĚRLĚRİ, TARİH, FĚLSĚFĚ VĚ
HÜGUG SERİYASI = Izvestiia Akademii
Nauk Azerbaidzhanskoi SSR, seriia
istorii, filosofii i prava
1966, 1 -
Baku: Elm
ISSN 0321-1606
One of three continuations of:
Azěrbaycan SSR Elmlěr Akademiyasının
hěběrlěri, ictimai elmlěr seriyası
Title down to 1991 has Azěrbaycan SSR
for Azěrbaycan, Azerbaidzhanskoi SSR
for Azerbaidzhana
Articles in Azeri or Russian
Quarterly

BL:OIOC: 1966:1 - 1974:4   [14499.t.9/2]
LO:SOAS: 1966:1 -; lacking 1971:3-4,
1983:1   [Per.10.203424]
OX:BOD: 1966:1 -   [Per.3974.d.1167]

AZĚRBAYCAN HALG TĚSĚRRÜFATI
See: İGTİSADİYYAT VĚ HĚYAT

AZĚRBAYCAN MĚKTĚBİ / Azěrbaycan SSR
Maarif Nazirliyinin aylıg elmi-nězěri
pedagoji jurnalı
1. yıl, sayı 1 [1944] -
Baku
ISSN 0134-3289

BL:OIOC: 1984:5 -   [14499.tt.41]

AZĚRBAYCAN MĚTBUAT SALNAMĚSİ: ayda bir
çıkar = Letopis' pechati Azerbaidzhana
/ Azěrbaycan SSR Dövlět Bibliografiya
organı
No. 1 ([date?] 1926) -
Baku: Azěrbaycan Dövlět Kitab
Palatası
Azeri and Russian

BL:OIOC: 1965:10 - 1973:11 (lacking few
issues); 1974:5, 11; 1975:6-7, 12;
1976:5-6   [14499.tt.9]

AZĚRBAYCAN SSR ELMLĚR AKADEMİYASININ
HĚBĚRLĚRİ, ĚDĚBİYYAT, DİL VĚ
İNCĚSĚNĚT SERİYASI = Izvestiia
Akademii Nauk Azerbaidzhanskoi SSR,
seriia literatury, iazyka i
iskusstvo
1966, 1 -
Baku: Elm
ISSN 0321-1614
One of three continuations of:
Azěrbaycan SSR Elmlěr Akademiyasının
hěběrlěri, ictimai elmlěr seriyası
Articles in Azeri or Russian
Quarterly

BL:OIOC: 1966:1 -; lacking 1975:3
[14499.t.9/1]
LO:SOAS: 1966:1 -; lacking 1967:3-4,
1969:4, 1972:4   [Per.10.203423]
OX:BOD: 1966:1 -; lacking 1969:4, 1972:4
   [Per.3977.d.522]

AZĚRBAYCAN SSR ELMLĚR AKADEMİYASININ
HĚBĚRLĚRİ, İCTİMAİ ELMLĚR
SERİYASI = Izveştiia Akademii Nauk
Azerbaidzhanskoĭ SSR, seriia
obshchestvennykh nauk
1958, 1 - 1965, 12
Baku
Date of issue 1 not known. From 1966
this publication is divided into three
separate titles
Articles in Azeri or Russian
Monthly prior to 1963, then bi-monthly

BL:OIOC: 1960:6; 1961:1 - 1965:6;
lacking 1961:6-7, 1962:10   [14499.t.9]
BL:HSS: 1958:1 - 1965:12; lacking
1959:6, 1960:3   [Ac.1109.d/2 (4)]
LO:SOAS: 1960:1 - 1965:12
[Per.10.143933]
OX:BOD: 1958:1 - 1958:6; 1960:1 - 1965:6
   [Per.3794.d.1154]

AZĚRBAYCAN SSR ELMLĚR AKADEMİYASININ
HĚBĚRLĚRİ, İGTİSADİYYAT
SERİYASI = Izveştiia Akademii Nauk
Azerbaidzhanskoĭ SSR, seriia
ėkonomiki
1966, 1 -
Baku: Elm
ISSN 0321-1630
One of three continuations of:
Azěrbaycan SSR Elmlěr Akademiyasının
hěběrlěri, ictimai elmlěr seriyası
Articles in Azeri or Russian
Quarterly

BL:OIOC: 1966:1 - 1977:3; lacking
1970:1,4; 1972:3-4; 1974:1,3
[14499.t.2/1]
LO:SOAS: 1966:1 -; lacking 1970:4,
1972:3-4   [Per.67.205241]
OX:BOD: 1966:1 -; lacking 1970:4, 1972:3
- 1972:4   [Per.23211.d.1158]

AZĚRBAYCAN SSR ELMLĚR AKADEMİYASININ
HĚBĚRLĚRİ, TARİH, FĚLSĚFĚ VĚ
HÜGUG SERİYASI
   See: AZĚRBAYCAN ELMLĚR AKADEMİYASININ
   HĚBĚRLĚRİ, TARİH, FĚLSĚFĚ VĚ
   HÜGUG SERİYASI

AZĚRBAYCAN TARİHİ MUZEYİNİN
ĚSĚRLĚRİ
   See: AZĚRBAYCAN TARİHİNĚ DAİR
   MATERİALLAR

AZĚRBAYCAN TARİHİNĚ DAİR
   MATERİALLAR / Azěrbaycan Tarihi
   Muzeyinin ěsěrlěri = Materialy po
   istorii Azerbaidzhana / trudy Muzeia
   Istorii Azerbaidzhana
   1. cild [1956] -
   Baku: Azěrbaycan SSR Elmlěr
   Akademiyası Něşriyyatı
   Subtitles given are the main titles in
   issue 1
   Articles in Azeri or Russian
   Irregular; none published between 1973
   and 10 [1988]

   BL:OIOC: 1 [1956] - ; lacking 5 (1962)
   [14499.r.44]
   OX:BOD: 1 -   [24429e.155]

AZĚRBAYCAN TİBB MĚCMUĚSİ =
   Azerbaidzhanskii meditsinskii
   zhurnal / Azěrbaycan Tibb İnistitutu
   [sic] Něşriyyatı
   No. 1-3 (Janvar, Fevral, Mart 1932) -
   [?]
   Baku
   Mainly in Russian, with summaries in
   Azeri in modified roman script
   Nominally monthly

   BL:HSS: 1-3 (1-3.1932)   [P.P.2984.bg]

AZĚRBAYCAN YURT BİLGİSİ
   Yıl 1, sayı 1 (Ocak 1932) - Cilt 4, sayı
   37 (Şubat 1954)
   Istanbul
   Not published between Dec. 1934 and Feb.
   1954. Final issue published by:
   Azerbaycan Kültürünü Tanıtma
   Derneği
   French title: Revue des études
   d'Azerbaidjan
   Articles in Turkish ; literary texts in
   Azeri
   Monthly

   BL:OIOC: (a) 1:1 (1.1932) - 3:35/36
   (11-12.1934); (b) 4:37 (2.1954)   [(a)
   14498.a.2/1; (b) OR. MICROFICHE 303]
   LO:SOAS: 1:1 - 3:34 (10.1934)
   [Per.10.26476]
   OX:BOD: 1:1 - 3:35/36   [Per.Turk.d.626]

AZĚRBAYCANIN MADDİ MĚDĚNİYYĚTİ =
   Material'naia kul'tura Azerbaidzhana
   / Azěrbaycan SSR Elmlěr Akademiyası
   Tarih İnstitutu, arheolokiya vě
   etnografiya sektoru
   1. cild (1949) -
   Baku: Elm
   ISSN 0132-960X
   Articles in Azeri or Russian
   Irregular

   BL:OIOC: 4 (1962) - 9 (1980)
   [14499.d.5]

BAĞ-KUR İSTATİSTİK YILLIĞI =
   Statistical yearbook, Turkey / Bağ-Kur
   Genel Müdürlüğü
   Ankara: Bağ-Kur Genel Müdürlüğü,
   [19--?]-
   In Turkish and English

   DU:DC: 1980/1981 -   [25/4/SOCIAL
   SERVICES]

BAĞÇE: vatan ve milletin te'âlisine,
   Osmanlıların ittihad ve terakkisine
   hâdim siyasî, edebî, ictimaî
   şimdilik haftada bir defa neşrolunur
   musavver risaledir
   Numero 1 (23 Kanunuevvel [1]323 [5 Jan.
   1908]) - 2. sene, 2. cild, numero 52
   ([date?] [1]326 [1910])
   Thessaloniki
   Subtitle varies

   LO:SOAS: 1 (5.1.1908) - 1:2:32
   (7.3.1909)   [L.E.Per.188777]

BAĞDAD SALNAMESİ
   See: BAĞDAD VİLÂYET-İ CELİLESİNE
   MAHSUS SALNAME

BAĞDAD VİLÂYET-İ CELİLESİNE MAHSUS
   SALNAME
   Defa 1 (1292 [1875-1876]) - [Defa 22]
   (1329 [1911])
   Baghdad
   Some issues entitled: Salname-i
   Vilâyet-i Bağdad; Salname; Bağdad
   Salnamesi; Bağdad Vilayetine mahsus
   salname

   LO:SOAS: 16 (1900)   [E.Per.280665]
   CA:UL: 12 (1896)   [S.828.01.b.8]
   DU:UL: 16   [PL366.B2]

BAĞDAD VİLÂYETİNE MAHSUS SALNAME
   See: BAĞDAD VİLÂYET-İ CELİLESİNE
   MAHSUS SALNAME

BAĞDAT VİLÂYET-İ CELİLESİNE MAHSUS
SALNAME
   See: BAĞDAD VİLÂYET-İ CELİLESİNE
   MAHSUS SALNAME

BAHRİYE SALNAMESİ / tertib eden, Bahriye
  Nezareti
  1. defa (1306 [1890-1891] - 24. tab'ı
  (1341/1342 [1925-1926/1926-1927])
  Istanbul, 1306 [1890 or 1891] - 1342
  [1926 or 1927]
  Title of issuing body varies
  Title of issues 1-8: Salname-i bahrî

  BL:OIOC: 2 (1891-1892)   [14496.e.3]
  CA:UL: 18 (1912-1913)   [S.828.01.b.108]

BALIKESİR İL YILLIĞI
  [1] (1967) - [2] (1973)
  Istanbul, 1969-1973

  BL:OIOC: [1] (1967)   [14498.a.65]
  OX:BOD: [1]   [Turk.d.3324/10]

BALKAN TÜRKLERİ'NİN SESİ: aylık tarih,
  kültür, edebiyat ve sanat dergisi /
  Balkan Türkleri Dayanışma ve Kültür
  Derneği
  Yıl 1, sayı 1 (Ocak 1990) -
  Istanbul

  BL:OIOC: 2:3/4 (4.1991) -
  [ZOR.1991.a.114]
  LO:SOAS: 2:[1] (1-5.1990) -; lacking 2:5
  [Per.57.L.619980]

BANKA VE TİCARET HUKUKU DERGİSİ /
  yayınlayan, Banka ve Ticaret Hukuku
  Araştırma Enstitüsü
  Cilt 1, sayı 1 (Ocak 1961) - Cilt 9,
  sayı 4 (Aralık 1978)
  Ankara
  Semi-annual

  LO:SOAS: 1:1 (1.1961) - 9:4 (12.1978)
  [Per.32.252206]

BAŞBAKANLIK ATOM ENERJİSİ KOMİSYONU
  NÜKLEER KİMYA LABORATUVARININ
  RADYOAKTİF YAĞIŞ DEĞERLENDİRMELERİ
  HAKKINDA FAALİYET RAPORU = Turkish
  Atomic Energy Commission activity report
  of the Radioactive Fallout Laboratory
  1 (1961/1964) -
  Ankara, [1965]-
  In English and Turkish; 1965/1966 issue
  published in separate editions
  Nominally annual after issue 1

  DU:DC: 1 (1961/1964) - 6 (1968/1969);
  lacking 4   [25/4/ENERGY]

BAŞÇAVUŞ: mekatib-i askeriye talebesine
  ve sunuf-u muhtelife küçük zabıtân'a
  mahsus musavver haftalık askerî
  risaledir
  Yıl 1, sayı 1 (10 Temmuz 1328 [23 July
  1912]) - Yıl 1, sayı 10 (13 Eylül 1328
  [26 Sep. 1912])
  Istanbul

  OX:BOD: 1:1 (23.7.1912) - 1:10
  (26.9.1912)   [Turk.d.1021]

BAŞDAN: haftalık siyasî magazin
  Yıl 1, sayı 1 (9 Temmuz [1]948) - Yıl 2,
  sayı 4 (24 Temmuz 1950)
  Istanbul
  Publication interrupted between 11 Feb.
  1949 and 30 June 1950
  Title from June 1950: Yeni baştan:
  Türkiyede sosyalist kültürü yayar
  haftalık gazete

  BL:OIOC: 1:1 (9.7.1948) - 2:4
  (24.7.1950)   [OR.FICHE 440]

BASHKURT AYMAGY
  See: BAŞKORT AYMAĞI

BASİRET: menafi'-i vataniye ve havadis-i
  umumiye'ye dair millet gazetesidir
  1 (10 Kanunusani 1285 [22 Jan. 1870]) -
  Sene 14, 19 ([date?] 1324 [1909])
  Istanbul
  Original numbering ends with issue 2448
  Five issues weekly

  BL:OIOC: 2151 (6.7.1877)   [O.P. 3 (22)]
  LO:SOAS: 1 - 102   [L.E.Per.305846]

BAŞKORT AYMAĞI / Başkortostandı Oyranu
  Gilmi Yemğiyeti tarafınan 3 ayga bir
  tabkır sıgarıla turgan bilm koramahı
  No. 1 (Oktabr 1925) - 7 ([date?], 1929)
  Ufa
  Added title in Cyrillic characters:
  Bashkurt aimagy. Subtitle varies
  Bashkir; Arabic characters
  Irregular

  BL:OIOC: (a) 14499.t.25; (b)
  ITA.1986.a.393

BATI DÜNYASI VE TÜRKİYE' NİN
  İTİSADİ DURUMU
  Ankara
  Dates of publication not known
  Annual

  DU:DC: 1962-1964
  [25/4/ECONOMY/GENERAL]
  OX:BOD: 1 [1987]   [Per.Turk.d.3952]

BATI TRAKYA'NIN SESİ / Batı Trakya
  Türkleri Dayanışma Dernekleri yayın
  organı
  Yıl 1, sayı 1 (Kasım-Aralık 1987) -
  Istanbul
  Bi-monthly

  BL:OIOC: 2:10/12 (5-10.1989) -
  [ZOR.1990.a.16]
  LO:SOAS: 4:29 (4.1991) -
  [Per.57.L.619981]

BAYÇEÇEKEY / Kırgızstan LKCS Borborduk
  Komiteti menen V. İ. Lenin atındagı
  pioner uyumunun Respublikalık Sovetinin
  curnalı
  No. 1 ([date?], 1977) -
  Bishkek
  ISSN 0203-9508
  Magazine for young children
  Kirgiz
  Monthly

  BL:OIOC: 6 [162] (6.1990) - 12 [168]
  (12.1990)   [ZOR.1990.a.114]

BAYINDIRLIK DERGİSİ
  See: BAYINDIRLIK İŞLERİ DERGİSİ

BAYINDIRLIK İŞLERİ DERGİSİ /
  Bayındırlık Bakanlığı
  1. yıl, sayı 1 (Haziran 1934) - 44. yıl,
  sayı 16 ([month?] 1972)
  Ankara
  Continued by: Bayındırlık dergisi [2.
  seri]
  Title of later issues: Bayındırlık
  dergisi
  Frequency varies

  DU:DC: 44:3 (8.1966) - 44:5;
  7-15:11.1970
  [25/4/INDUSTRY/CONSTRUCTION]

BAYRAKTAR / Lefkoşa-Kıbrıs Türk Lisesi
  dergisi
  Yıl 1, sayı 1 [1957] - [?]
  Lefkoşa
  Supersedes: Lisemizin dergisi

  BL:OIOC: 1:1 [1957]   [ITA.1987.a.89]
  OX:BOD: 1:1   [Per.Turk.d.293]

BAYRAM: İzmirde Bayram günleri çıkar
siyasî gazete
İzmir
Years of publication not known

BL:OIOC: 20.3.1961   [OR.MIC.12606
(O.P. 552/20)]

BAYRAM GAZETESİ
İstanbul
Years of publication not known
Published on Bayram festivals and
following day(s) each year

BL:OIOC: 9.3.1962, 10.3.1962; 15.5.1962,
17.5.1962   [OR.MIC.12619 (O.P. 552/19)]

BEBE RUHÎ: ayda bir defa çikar Osmanlı
mizah gazetedir
1. sene, numero 1 (1 Şubat 1898) - 1.
sene, numero 5 (1 Teşrinievvel 1898)
İstanbul
Added title: Bébérouhi: journal turc
mensuel

BL:OIOC: 1:1 (1.2.1898) - 1:5
(1.10.1898)   [14498.d.12]

BÉBÉROUHI
See: BEBE RUHÎ

BEBERUHÎ
See: BEBE RUHÎ

BELGELER: Türk tarih belgeleri dergisi /
Türk Tarih Kurumu
Cilt 1, sayı 1-2 (1964) -
Ankara
Currently biennial; 1964-1971,
semi-annual; 1972-1978, suspended; 1979,
annual

BL:OIOC: 1:1-2 (1964) -   [14498.cc.18]
LO:SOAS: 1:1 -   [Per.10.L.180388]
DU:UL: 1:1-2 - 8:12 (1971)   [Per./PL5]
OX:BOD: 1:1 -   [Per.Turk.d.1215]

BELGELERLE TÜRK TARİHİ DERGİSİ [1.
SERİ]
1 (Ekim 1967) - Cilt 14, sayı 82-83-84
(Tem.-Ağustos-Eylül [1974])
İstanbul
Continued by a new series, beginning
March 1985
Monthly

BL:OIOC: 1:1 (10.1967) - 14:82/83/84
(9.1974)   [14498.cc.21]
LO:SOAS: 1:1 - 14:84   [Per.10.L.210971]
CA:UL: 1:1 - 14:84   [P.617.b.11]
OX:BOD: 1:1 - 14:84   [Per.Turk.d.2041]

BELGELERLE TÜRK TARİHİ DERGİSİ [2.
SERİ]: dün, bugün, yarın: aylık dergi
/ Tarihi Araştırmalar ve Dokümantasyon
Merkezleri Kurma ve Geliştirme Vakfı
Sayı 1 (Mart 1985) -
İstanbul

BL:OIOC: 1 (3.1985) -   [14498.cc.21]
OX:BOD: 1 -   [Per.Turk.d.3525]

BELLETEN: üç ayda bir çıkar / Türk
Tarih Kurumu
Cilt 1, sayı 1 (1 İkincikanun 1937) -
Ankara
French added title: Belleten :
périodique trimestrielle / revue
publiée par la Société Turque
d'Histoire
Articles in Turkish, English, French, or
German

BL:OIOC: 1:1 (1.1937) -   [14498.a.3]
LO:SOAS: 1:1 -   [Per.10.33599]
DU:UL: 1:1 -; lacking a few issues
[Per./PL5]
OX:BOD: 1:1:1:1 -   [Per.Turk.d.547]
OX:MEC: 1:1 - 13:50 (4.1949)   [APT
Tur 4]

BEYOĞLU ÂLEMİ: ilmî ve edebî mecmua
Yıl 1, sayı 1 (19 Haziran 1930) - Yıl 1,
sayı 3 (3 Temmuz 1930)
İstanbul
A frivolous magazine for Francophiles
Weekly

BL:OIOC: 1 (19.6.1930) - 3 (3.7.1930)
[14498.a.112]

BEYRUT VİLÂYETİ SALNAMESİ
See: SALNAME-İ VİLÂYET-İ BEYRUT

BIBLIOGRAPHIA
See: BIBLIYOGRAFYA: KITAP HABERLER
BÜLTENI

BIBLIOGRAPHIE DES ARTICLES PARUS DANS LES
PÉRIODIQUES TURCS
See: TÜRKİYE MAKALELER
BİBLİYOGRAFYASI

BIBLIOTEKAR' KIRGIZISTANA
See: KIRGIZSTANDIN KİTEPKANAÇISI

BİBLIYOGRAFİYA: Yurtta çeşitli
konularda yayımlanan kitap ve dergileri
tanıtmak üzere üç ayda bir çıkarılır
/ C.H.P. Halkevleri Bürosu yayımı
Cilt 1, sayı 1 (19 Şubat 1946) - Cilt
1, sayı 3 (19 Ağustos 1946)
[Ankara]: Cumhuriyet Halk Partisi
Halkevleri Bürosu
Quarterly

BL:OIOC: 1:1 (19.2.1946) - 1:2
(19.5.1946)   [14498.cc.5]
OX:BOD: 1:1 - 1:3 (19.8.1946)
[Per.Turk.e.6718]

BİBLİYOGRAFYA: kitap haberleri bülteni
Yıl 1, cilt 1, sayı 1 (Ocak 1972) - Yıl
2, cilt 2, sayı 6 (Kasım 1973)
Ankara: Turhan
Added title: Bibliographia: book news
bulletin
Bi-monthly

BL:OIOC: 1:1 (1.1972) - 2:6 (12.1973)
[14498.cc.29]
LO:SOAS: 1:1 - 2:6   [Per.10.275925]
CA:UL: 1:1 - 2:6   [P.850.c.204]
DU:UL: 1:1   [Per./PL39]
OX:BOD: 1:1 - 2:6   [Per.Turk.d.2245]

BİBLİYOGRAFYA / Türkiyede çıkan kitap,
gazete ve mecmualardan bahsetmek üzere
Maarif Vekâleti Millî Talim ve Terbiye
Heyeti tarafından çıkarılır Neşriyat
Bülltenidir
Cilte [sic] 1, no.1 (1928-Teşrinievvel
1930) - Cilt 3, no.15
(Teşrinievel-Kanunuevel [sic] 1933)
[Ankara], [1930]-[1934]
Generally bimonthly

BL:OIOC: 1:1 (1928-10.1930) - 3:15
(10-12.1933)   [14498.cc.13]

BİLECİK İL YILLIĞI
[1] (1967) - [2] (1973)
[Istanbul?]

BL:OIOC: [1] (1967)   [14498.a.52]
OX:BOD: [1]   [Turk.d.3324/11]

BİLGİ: aylik terbiye, fikir, kültür ve
sanat dergisi
Sayı 1 (Mayıs 1947) - Cilt 25, sayı
291/292 (Ağustos-Eylül 1971)
Istanbul
Previous title: Yeni bilgi

OX:BOD: 1 (5.1947) - 25:291/292
(8/9.1971)   [Per.Turk.d.3358]

BİLİM CĚNE EÑBEK / Ḵazaḵstan LKSM
Ortalıḵ Komitetİnin ayına bir ret
şığatın ğılımı-köpşilik curnalı
No. 1 ([date?] 1960) - 1988 cıl, no. 12
(Dekabr 1988)
Alma-Ata
ISSN 0134-353X
Continued by: Zerde
In Kazakh

BL:OIOC: 1988:1-12   [ZOR.1988.a.37]
LO:SOAS: 1968:9 - 1988:12; lacking
1968:11, 1970:1   [Per.10.L.225649]

BİLİM OÇAĞİ / Türkistan Ma'arif
Komişarliği yanindaği 'Bilim Kingaşi'
ham 'Uzbik Bilim Hay'ati'ning fikir
tarḵatğuçisi olarak çıkaturğan
adabî, tarbiyavî, ictima'î, fannî
curnaldir
Yil 1, san 1 ([date?] 1922) - [?]
Tashkent
Uzbek; Arabic characters
Frequency unknown

BL:OIOC: 2:2/3 (15.5.1923)
[ITA.1986.a.1632]

BİLİM VE SANAT: aylık kültür dergisi
1 (Ocak 1981) -
Ankara

BL:OIOC: 7:1 (1.1987) -   [ZOR.1987.a.7]
OX:BOD: 1 -   [Per.Turk.d.2946]

BİNGÖL İL YILLIĞI
[1] (1967) - [2] (1972)
[Ankara?], [1972]-[197-?]

OX:BOD: [1] (1967)   [Turk.d.3324/12]

[BİRİNCİ] 1 UMUM İTTİFAG TÜRKOLOJİ
KURULTAYINI ÇAĞIRAN TĚŞKİLAT
KOMİSYONUNUÑ BYÜLLETENİ =
Biulleten' Organizaṫsionnoĭ
Komissii po sozyvu 1-go Vsesoĭuznogo
Tiurkologicheskogo S'ezda
No. 1-y (27 Fevralıa 1926) - no.4-y (6
Marta 1926)
Baku
Contents are in Azeri (Arabic
characters) or Russian

BL:OIOC: 1 (27.2.1926) - 4 (6.3.1926)
[14499.t.21]
LO:SOAS: 1 - 4   [Per.10.136637]

BİRLİK: aylık dışpolitika dergisi
1 (Şubat 1977) - 9/10 (Ekim-Kasım 1977)
Ankara
Mainly on the history and current
situation of Turks outside Turkey
Cover title: Dilde, fikirde, işde
Birlik

BL:OIOC: 1 (1.1977) - 9/10 (9-10.1977)
[14498.cc.39]

BİRLİK / Azěrbaycan İstihlâk
Cěmiyyětlěri İttifagının nâşir-i
ěfkârıdır, imdilik ayda bir děfa
něşrolunur
Sayı 1 (15 Kanunuevvel 1921) - [?]
[Baku]
Azeri; Arabic characters

BL:OIOC: 1 (15.12.1921)   [14499.t.28]

BİRLİK / Türkiye Sosyalist İşçi
Partisi merkez organı
Yıl 1, sayı 1 (21 Şubat 1979) - Yıl 1,
sayı 28 (27 Ağustos 1979)
Istanbul
Weekly newspaper

DU:DC: 1 (21.2.1979) - 9 (4.4.1979);
lacking 7   [25/3/POLITICAL PARTIES]

BİRLİK / Kommunistička Partija na
Makedonija
Yıl 1, sayı 1 ([date?], 1944) -
Skopje
Newspaper
Three issues weekly

BL:OIOC: 17:378 (1.1.1960) - 2761/2762
(30.12.1982)   [O.P.847]

BİTLİS İL YILLIĞI
[1] (1967) - [2] (1973)
Ankara

BL:OIOC: [1] (1967)   [14498.a.40]
LO:SOAS: [1]   [Per.10.L.276431]
OX:BOD: [1]   [Turk.d.3324/13]

BİULLETEN' ORGANIZAṪSIONNOĬ KOMISSII
PO SOZYVU 1-GO VSESOĬUZNOGO
TIURKOLOGICHESKOGO S'EZDA
See: 1 UMUM İTTİFAG TÜRKOLOJİ
KURULTAYINI ÇAĞIRAN TĚŞKİLAT
KOMİSYONUNUÑ BÜLLETENİ

BİZDİÑ OTAN: şet eldegi otandastar men
měděni baylanıs casaytın Sovet
''Otan'' ḵoğami Kazaḵ bölimşesiniñ
gazeti
1977, san 1 ([date?], 1977) -
Alma-Ata
Kazakh; Arabic characters
Published twice monthly

OX:BOD: 1977:1 (?.?.1977) -; lacking
some issues   [Per.Turk.b.14]

BİZİM PAŞA: haftalık siyasî mizah halk
gazetesi
Yıl 1, sayı 1 (24 Haziran 1949) - Yıl 1,
sayı 3 (8 Temmuz 1949)
Istanbul

BL:OIOC: 1:1 (24.6.1949) - 1:3
(8.7.1949)   [OR.FICHE 441]

BİZNİÑ VĚTĚN
See: ŞALḴAR

BİZNİÑ YUL: ěděbî, ilmî, ictimaî,
aylık curnal / Tatarstan Cumhuriyěti
Měarif Halk Kamisariyati organı
1nçi yil, san 1 ([date?], 1923) - [?]
Kazan'
Tatar; Arabic characters

BL:OIOC: 3:1 (1.1925); 5:1 (1.1927) -
5:2 (2.1927)   [14499.tt.32]

BOĞAZİÇİ: aylık resimli mecmua
Cilt 1, sayı 1 (1 İlkteşrin [1936]) -
Cilt 3, sayı 18 (Mart 1938)
Istanbul
Original subtitle: aylık Boğaziçi
mecmuası

BL:OIOC: 1:1 (1.10.1936) - 3:18 (3.1938)
[14498.a.17]
OX:BOD: 1:1 - 3:18   [Per.Turk.d.3213]
OX:MEC: 1:1 - 3:18   [APT Boğ]

BOĞAZİÇİ: aylık kültür ve sanat
dergisi
Sayı 1 (Temmuz 1982) -
Istanbul

OX:BOD: 1 (7.1982) -   [Per.Turk.d.3212]

BOĞAZİÇİ ÜNİVERSİTESİ DERGİSİ,
HÜMANİTER BİLİMLER = Boğaziçi
University Journal, Humanities
Vol. 1 (1973) -
İstanbul, 1974-
Articles are in Turkish or English, with
résumés in the other language
Annual

BL:OIOC: 1 (1973) - 8-9 (1980-1981)
[14498.cc.33]
LO:SOAS: 1 - 3   [Per.10.322669]
CA:UL: 1 - 3   [L.911:44.c.4]
DU:UL: 1 -   [Per./PL 1]
OX:BOD: 1 -   [Per.Turk.d.2391a]

BOĞAZİÇİ ÜNİVERSİTESİ DERGİSİ,
SOSYAL BİLİMLER = Boğaziçi
University Journal, Social Sciences
Vol.1 (1973)-
Istanbul
Articles in Turkish or English
Annual

BL:OIOC: 1 (1973)   [14498.cc.34]
CA:UL: 1 - 3 (1975)
DU:UL: 1 -   [Per./PL 1]
OX:BOD: 1 - 3   [Per.Turk.d.2391b]

BOĞAZİÇİ ÜNİVERSİTESİ HALKBİLİM
YILLIĞI / B[oğaziçi] Ü[niversitesi]
F[olklor] K[ulübü]
[1] (1974)
Istanbul

LO:SOAS: [1] (1974)   [Per.10.328240]

BOĞAZİÇİ UNIVERSITY JOURNAL,
HUMANITIES
See: BOĞAZİÇİ ÜNİVERSİTESİ
DERGİSİ, HÜMANİTER BİLİMLER

BOĞAZİÇİ UNIVERSITY JOURNAL, SOCIAL
SCIENCES
See: BOĞAZİÇİ ÜNİVERSİTESİ
DERGİSİ, SOSYAL BİLİMLER

BOLU İL YILLIĞI
[1] (1967) - [2] (1973)
Istanbul, 1968-1973

BL:OIOC: [1] (1967)   [14498.a.22]
OX:BOD: [1]   [Turk.d.3324/14]

BOLU LİVASI SALNAMESİ
[1] (1337/1338 [1921-1922/1922-1923])
Bolu, 1341 [1925 or 1926]
Only one issue published

OX:BOD: [1] (1921-1923)   [Turk.e.1439]

BOŞANMA İSTATİSTİKLERİ = Divorce
statistics / Başbakanlık Devlet
İstatistik Enstitüsü
1932-1958 -
Ankara, 1959-
Turkish and English
Annual

BL:HSS: 1932/1958;
1932,1940,1945,1950-1960 in 1 vol.
[S.Q.170/26]
SU:IDS: 1971 -; lacking 1974 - 1976,
1983   [SERIALS/OFFICIAL/TURKEY]

BOŞBOĞAZ İLE GÜLLÂBİ: haftada iki
defa ... neşrolunur; şathiyât içinde
müdafaa-i hukuk ve vatan ve ve millete
hadim musavver mizah gazetesidir
Sayı 1 (24 Temmuz 1324 [6 Aug. 1908]) -
Sayı 36 (1 Kanunuevvel 1324 [14 Dec.
1908])
Istanbul

BL:OIOC: 1 (6.8.1908) - 36 (14.12.1908)
[ITA.1989.a.6]
OX:BOD: 1 - 36   [Turk.b.13]

BOSNA VİLÂYETİ SALNAMESİ
Defa 1 (1283 [1866-1867]) - Defa 15
(1308 [1890-1891])
Sarajevo
Some issues entitled: Salname-i
Vilâyet-i Bosna

DU:UL: 13 (1878)   [PL366.B7]

BOYUT
See: YENİ BOYUT

BOZKIR: milliyetçi edebiyat ve sanat
mecmuası; onbeş günde bir çıkar
Yıl 1, sayı 1 (5 Haziran 1944) - Yıl 1,
sayı 6 (29 I. Teşrin 1944)
Eskişehir

OX:BOD: 1:1 (5.6.1944) - 1:6
(29.10.1944)   [Per.Turk.c.200]

BOZKURT: günlük müstakil siyasî gazete
Yıl 1, sayı 1 ([date?] [1951 or 1952]) -
[?]
Lefkoşa

BL:OIOC: 16:5814 (2.7.1967); 16:5889
(17.9.1967)   [O.P.925]

BRUSA VİLÂYETİ SALNAMESİ
See: HÜDAVENDİGÂR VİLÂYETİ
SALNAMESİ

BUCAK: aylık dergi; fikir-sanat-aktüalite
Sayı 1 (23 Nisan 1945) - Cilt 2, sayı 1
(4 Haziran 1946)
Zonguldak

OX:BOD: 1 (23.4.1945) - 2:1 (4.6.1946)
[Per.Turk.c.201]

BUDGETS
See: BÜTÇELER: BELEDIYELER, ÖZEL
IDARELER, KÖYLER

BUDGETS AND FINAL ACCOUNTS
See: BÜTÇELER: BELEDIYELER, ÖZEL
IDARELER, KÖYLER

BULAK: Uyğur kilassik ĕdibiyatı vĕ
hĕlk eğiz ĕdibiyatı pĕsillik
jurnılı
1 ([date?], 1980) -
Urumchi: Şincan hĕlk nĕşriyatı
Uygur; Arabic characters
Quarterly; previously irregular

BL:OIOC: 2 (1981) 17 (1985); 26-27
(1989: 1-2)   [ZOR.1989.a.179]
OX:BOD: 2 (1981) -   [Per.Turk.e.5680]

BULLETIN DE L'ASSOCIATION DE
BIBLIOTHÉCAIRES TURCS
    See: TÜRK KÜTÜPHANECİLER DERNEĞİ
    BÜLTENİ

BULLETIN DE STATISTIQUE ANNUELLE DE
L'HÔPITAL D'ENFANTS HAMIDIÉ
    See: HAMİDİYE ETFÂL HASTAHANE-İ
    ÂLİSİ İSTATİSTİK MECMUA-İ
    TIBBİYESİ

BULLETIN MENSUEL
    See: ÜÇ AYLIK BÜLTEN

BULLETIN [MIDDLE EAST TECHNICAL UNIVERSITY
FACULTY OF ARCHITECTURE]
    See: BÜLTEN [ORTA DOĞU TEKNİK
    ÜNİVERSİTESİ MİMARLIK FAKÜLTESİ]

BULLETIN OF ACCOMMODATION STATISTICS
    See: KONAKLAMA İSTATİSTİKLERİ
    BÜLTENİ

BULLETIN OF CONSTRUCTION STATISTICS
    See: İNŞAAT İSTATİSTİKLERİ
    BÜLTENİ

BULLETIN OF TOURISM STATISTICS
    See: TURİZM İSTATİSTİKLERİ

BÜLTEN / ORMAN BAKANLIĞI
    See: ORMAN BAKANLIĞI AYLIK BÜLTENİ

BÜLTEN / ORMAN BAKANLIĞI ORMAN GENEL
BAKANLIĞI
    See: ORMAN BAKANLIĞI AYLIK BÜLTENİ

BÜLTEN [Orta Doğu Teknik Üniversitesi
    Mimarlık Fakültesi] = Bulletin [Middle
    East Technical University Faculty of
    Architecture]
    Cilt 1, sayı 1 (Ekim 1971) - Cilt 2,
    sayı 4 (Eylül 1974)
    Ankara
    Superseded by: Orta Doğu Teknik
    Üniversitesi Mimarlık Fakültesi
    dergisi
    Contributions in Turkish and English
    Frequency uncertain

    DU:DC: 1:1 (10.1971); 2:4 (9.1974)
    [25/4/EDUCATION]

BURDUR İL YILLIĞI / Burdur'u Kalkındırma
    ve Tanıtma Derneği tarafından
    bastırılmıştır
    [1] (1967) - [2] (1973)
    Ankara, 1970-1975

    BL:OIOC: [1] (1967)   [14498.a.50]
    OX:BOD: [1]   [Turk.d.3324/15]

BURSA İL YILLIĞI
    [1] (1967) - [2] (1973)
    Istanbul, 1968-1973

    BL:OIOC: [1] (1967)   [14498.a.49]
    LO:SOAS: [1]   [Per.10.L.266149]
    OX:BOD: [1]   [Turk.d.3324/16]

BURSA VİLÂYETİ SALNAMESİ
    See: HÜDAVENDİGÂR VİLÂYETİ
    SALNAMESİ

BÜTÇELER: belediyeler, özel idareler,
    köyler = Budgets: municipalities,
    special administration, villages /
    Başbakanlık Devlet İstatistik
    Enstitüsü
    [1] (1956-1964) -
    Ankara, [196-?]
    Titles of issues [1] and [2] not known.
    Issue 3: Bütçeler ve kesin hesaplar:
    il özel idareleri ve köyler Budget and
    final accounts: special provincial
    administrations and villages
    In Turkish and English
    Irregular: about every four years

    BL:HSS: [3] (1980-1983)   [S.Q. 170/61]
    SU:IDS: 1984; 1986 -
    [SERIALS/OFFICIAL/TURKEY]

BÜTÇELER VE KESİN HESAPLAR: İL ÖZEL
İDARELERİ VE KÖYLER
    See: BÜTÇELER: BELEDİYELER, ÖZEL
    İDARELER, KÖYLER

BÜYÜK DOĞU: siyasî ve edebî mecmua
    Yıl 1, sayı 1 (2 Kasım 1945) - Yıl 34,
    sayı 5 (5 Haziran 1978)
    İstanbul
    Islamic but nationalist journal
    Published in several series
    Some issues are entitled: Büyükdoğu
    Weekly

    BL:OIOC: 5:1 (14.10.1949) - 7:62
    (29.6.1951); 11:1 (23.4.1954) - 11:10
    (9.7.1954); 12:1 (22.9.1965) - 12:17
    (12.1.1966); 13:1 (19.7.1967) - 13:18
    (15.11.1967); 15:1 (6.1.1971) - 15:17
    (28.4.1971); 34:1 (8.5.1978) - 34:5
    (5.6.1978)   [14498.a.97]
    OX:BOD: 1:1 (2.11.1945) - 3:87
    (2.4.1948) (a); 5:1 - 7:62 (b); 11:1 -
    11:10 (c)   [(a) Per.Turk.c.203; (b)
    Per.Turk.d.3162; (c) Per.Turk.c.202]

BÜYÜK DUYGU: onbeş günde bir çıkar
    Türk risalesidir
    Yıl 1, sayı 1 (2 Mart 1329 [1913]) - Yıl
    1, sayı 26 (18 Kanunusani 1329 [1914])
    Istanbul
    Generally fortnightly

    OX:BOD: 1:1 (2.3.1913) - 1:26
    (18.1.1914)   [Turk.d.1464]

BÜYÜK MECMUA: perşembe günleri çıkar
    edebî ve ilmî haftalık mecmuadır
    Sayı 1 (6 Mart 1919) - Sayı 17 (25
    Aralık 1919)
    Istanbul

    OX:BOD: 1 (6.3.1919) - 10 (19.6.1919)
    [Per.Turk.c.102]

BÜYÜK SALNAME = Grand annuaire illustré
    / Sanayi-i Nefise Sergisi
    2. sene (1341-1342 [1925-1926])
    Istanbul, 1341 [1925]
    Only one issue published: numbered 2
    because it represents the continuation
    of Türk Ticaret Salnamesi, Sene 1
    (1340-1341 [1924-1925])
    Ottoman; also partly in French

    CA:UL: 2 (1925-1926)   [L.830.b.27]

BÜYÜK ŞARK
    1. yıl, no. 1-2 (Nisan-Mayıs 1931) - 5.
    yıl, no. 19 (Mayıs-Nisan 1935)
    Istanbul: [Türk Yükseltme Kurumu]
    A masonic journal
    Quarterly?

    BL:OIOC: 1:1-2 (4-5.1931) - 5:19
    (4-5.1935)   [ITA.1988.a.63]
    OX:BOD: 1:1-2 - 5:19   [Per.Turk.d.3315]

20

BÜYÜKDOĞU
    See: BÜYÜK DOĞU

ÇAĞDAŞ ELEŞTİRİ: edebiyat, sanat,
  sorunlar ve kuramlar dergisi
  1 (Mart 1982) - Yıl 4, 6 (Haziran 1985)
  İstanbul: Gelişim
  Monthly

  OX:BOD: 1 (3.1982) - 4:6 (6.1985)
  [Per.Turk.d.3323]

ÇAĞILTI [2. DÖNEM]: aylık sanat dergisi
  / Zile Kültür Derneği
  Yıl 1, sayı 1 (Mayıs 1973) - Yıl 2, sayı
  12 (Nisan 1974)
  Zile
  Subtitle varies

  OX:BOD: 1:1 (5.1973) - 2:12 (4.1974)
  [Per.Turk.d.3541]

ÇAĞIRIŞ: aylık mecmua = Prizyv:
  ezhemesiachnyi zhurnal: organ
  severo-kavkasskoi natsional'noi
  mysli
  No. 1-2 (Mayıs-Haziran 1938) - [?]
  Warsaw
  Continuation of: Ülkemiz
  In Istanbul Turkish and Russian

  BL:OIOC: 1/2 (5-6.1938)
  [ITA.1986.a.391]

ÇAĞRI: aylık fikir, sanat, folklor
  dergisi
  Yıl 1, sayı 1 ([date?], [1956?]) - [?]
  Ankara

  BL:OIOC: 22:247 (8.1978)
  [ITA.1986.a.1633]

ÇALIŞAN ADAM: aylık siyasî ve meslekî
  dergi / OLEYİS yayın organı
  Yıl 1, sayı 1 (Ekim 1971) - [Yıl 5],
  sayı 29 (Aralık 1975)
  Ankara: Türkiye OLEYİS Sendikası
  Monthly

  DU:DC: 1:7 (10.1971) - 2:20/21 (7.1973)
  [25/3/TRADE UNIONS]

ÇALIŞMA DERGİSİ / Çalışma Bakanlığı
  Cilt 1, sayı 1 (Eylül 1945) - [Yıl 39]
  (Mayıs 1983)
  Ankara
  Previous title: Çalışma Vekâleti
  dergisi
  Initially monthly; later annual or
  irregular

  DU:UL: 5:2 (7-9.1957)   [Per./PL8]

ÇALIŞMA RAPORU VE BİLANÇOSU / İş ve
  İşçi Bulma Kurumu Genel
  Müdürlüğü
  Ankara, [19--?]-
  Previous title: Çalışma raporu

  DU:DC: 1971 - 1973   [25/4/EMPLOYMENT]

ÇALIŞMA RAPORU VE BİLANÇOSU İLE İŞ
  PROGRAMI / Sosyal Sigortalar Kurumu
  1975 - [?]
  Ankara, 1976-[19--?]
  Annual

  SU:IDS: 1975 - 1982
  [SERIALS/OFFICIAL/TURKEY]

ÇALIŞMA VEKÂLETİ DERGİSİ
  See: ÇALIŞMA DERGİSİ

ÇALKAN
  No. 1 (İyun' 1955) -
  Frunze
  A monthly satirical magazine
  In Kirgiz; many contributions in
  Russian, 1955-1967 only

  BL:OIOC: 1.1965 - 11.1987; lacking
  8.1966, 12.1966, 1.1970, 4.1970, 2.1981,
  4.1984, 10.1985   [14499.tt.5]

ÇANAKKALE İL YILLIĞI
  [1] (1967) - [2] (1973)
  [İstanbul?], 1969-[197-?]

  OX:BOD: [1] (1967)   [Turk.d.3324/17]

ÇANKAYA: her ayın onbeşinci günü
  neşrolunur, "halka doğru" fikir ve
  sanat mecmuasıdır
  Numero 1 (1 Mayıs 1928)
  Ankara and İstanbul
  Date on wrapper: 15 Mayıs 1928
  In Arabic characters

  BL:OIOC: 1 (1.5.1928)   [14498.a.110]
  OX:BOD: 1   [Per.Turk.c.210]

ÇANKIRI İL YILLIĞI
  [1] (1967) - [2] (1973)
  Ankara, 1969-[ca. 1973]

  OX:BOD: [1] (1967)   [Turk.d.3324/18]

ÇARDAK: fikir ve sanat dergisi
  Yıl 1, sayı 1 (1 Mayıs 1952) - Yıl 2,
  sayı 12 (Ekim 1954)
  Lefkoşe: Çardak Yayınevi
  Initially (nos. 1-4) monthly; irregular
  thereafter

  LO:SOAS: 1:1 (1.5.1952) - 2:12 (10.1954)
  [Per.10.116824]

LE CAUCASE DU NORD
  See: ŞİMALÎ-KAFKASYA

CEBEL-İ LÜBNAN SALNAMESİ
  See: SALNAME-İ CEBEL-İ LÜBNAN

CEM [1. SERİ]: siyasî edebî musavver
  mizah mecmuası = Djem: revue politique,
  humoristique et satirique illustrée
  Numero 1 (28 Teşrinisani 1326 [10 Nov.
  1910]) - Numero 43 (6 Teşrinievvel 1328
  [19 Oct. 1912])
  İstanbul
  Mainly in Ottoman; numerous
  contributions in French
  Weekly

  BL:OIOC: 1 (10.11.1910) - 43
  (19.10.1912)   [14498.a.91]

CEM [2. TERTİB]
  Nu. 1 (15 Kanunuevvel 1927) - no.49 (2
  Mayıs 1929)
  İstanbul
  Humorous and satirical magazine
  1-34 are partly in Arabic characters,
  35-49 entirely in roman

  BL:OIOC: 1 (15.12.1927) - 49 (2.5.1929)
  [14498.a.90]

CEMAAT: İslami, aylık yayın organı /
  sahibi, İngiltere Türk İslâm
  Derneği
  Yıl 1, sayı 1 (Rabi' ul Ahir 1400, Mart
  1980) - Yıl 1, sayı 8 (Muharrem 1401,
  Kasım 1980)
  London

  BL:OIOC: 1:1 (3.1980) - 1:8 (11.1980);
  lacking 1:3   [14498.a.78]

CEMİYET-İ TEDRİSİYE-İ İSLAMİYE
SALNAMESİ
[1] (1332 [1913])
Istanbul
Only one issue published

BL:OIOC: [1] (1913)   [ITA.1987.a.432;
ORB.30/707]

CEP DERGİSİ: her ayın birinde çıkar,
dünya sanat ve düşünce hareketlerini
izler dergi
1 (1 Kasım 1966) - 3. yıl, sayı 29 (1
Mart 1969)
İstanbul: Varlık

BL:OIOC: 1 (1.11.1966) - 3:29 (1.3.1969)
[14480.c.157]

CERİDE-İ ADLİYE / Adliye Vekâleti
tarafından ayda bir neşrolunur
1. sene, ([date?] 1338 [1922]) - 6.
sene, numero 73-75
(Ağustos-Teşrinievvel 1928)
Ankara
Continuation of: Ceride-i Mahâkim,
Ceride-i Mahâkim-i Adliye

BL:OIOC: 1:22/24 (5-7.1923) - 7:73/75
(8-10.1928)   [14429.d.1]
OX:BOD: 1:22/24 - 6:69/70 (4-5.1928)
[Per.Turk.d.53]

CERİDE-İ HAVADİS
See: RUZNAME-İ CERİDE-İ HAVADIS

ÇEVİRİ: dört aylık düşün ve yayın
dergisi
1 (Eylül 1979)
Ankara: Kültür Bakanlığı
Only one issue published
Translations of western literary and
philosophical texts

OX:BOD: 1 (9.1979)   [Per.Turk.d.2744]

ÇEVREN: toplum, bilim, yazın ve sanat
dergisi; iki ayda bir çıkar
Yıl 1, sayı 1 ([date?] 1974) -
Priština: Tan

OX:BOD: 12:45 (2.1985) -
[Per.Turk.d.3535]

CEZAYİR-İ BAHR-İ SEFİD SALNAMESİ
See: CEZAYİR-İ BAHR-İ SEFİD
VİLÂYETİ SALNAMESİ

CEZAYİR-İ BAHR-İ SEFİD VİLÂYETİ
SALNAMESİ
Defa 1 (1287 [1870-1871]) - Defa 20
(1321 [1903-1904])
Rhodes; Chios
Yearbook of the Dodecanese province
Issues 1-7 published at Kale-i Sultaniye
(Çanakkale), Rhodes; 8 and 10-20 at
Rhodos, Rhodes; 9-11 on Chios (Sakız)
Some issues entitled: Cezayir-i Bahr-i
Sefid salnamesi; Salname-i Vilâyet-i
Cezayir-i Bahr-i Sefid

OX:BOD: 2 (1871); 19 (1901)
[Per.Turk.e.5029]

CHAMBRE DE COMMERCE D'ISTANBUL INDICES DES
PRIX
See: İSTANBUL TİCARET ODASI FİYAT
İNDEKSLERİ

CHEHBAL
See: ŞEHBAL

ÇIĞ: iki ayda bir yayımlanır / Tan'ın
Prizren'de hazırlanıp yayımlanan
yazın/sanat dergisidir
Yıl 1, sayı 1 ([undated] 1990) -
Prizren

BL:OIOC: 2:8 (?.1991)   [ZOR.1991.a.96]

CİHAN: Şimal Ġĕrb Mĕdĕniyit Kuruluş
Cĕmiyiti tĕrĕfidin neşriteldi
[1] tuğum sani (Yanvar 1948) - [?]
Lanzho; Urumchi; Nankin
General-interest magazine
Uygur; in Arabic characters
Bimonthly

BL:OIOC: 1 (1.1948) - 2 (3.1948)
[ITA.1986.a.1986.a.1624/5]

ÇIKRIK
See: İMECE

ÇINARALTI [1. SERİ]: haftalık Türkçü,
fikir ve sanat mecmuası
Sayı 1 (9 Ağustos 1941) - Sayı 130 (18
Mart 1944)
Istanbul

BL:OIOC: 1 (9.8.1941) - 130 (18.3.1944)
[ITA.1987.b.1]

ÇINARALTI [2. SERİ]: dilde, dilekte,
düşüncede birlik
Sayı 1 (17 Mart 1948) - Sayı 11 (9
Haziran 1948)
Istanbul
Weekly

BL:OIOC: 1 (17.3.1948) - 11 (9.6.1948)
[ITA.1988.c.1]
LO:SOAS: 1 - 10   [L.E.Per.305844]

ÇINGIRAKLI TATAR: işbu gazete haftada
iki defa neşrolunur
Sene 1, numero 1 (24 Mart 1289 [6 Apr.
1873]) - Sene 1, numero 89 (6 Temmuz
1289 [19 July 1873])
Istanbul

BL:OIOC: 1:4 (?.4.1873)
[14003.e.3(13)]

ÇOCUK BAHÇESİ: atfalın tehzib-i ahlâk
ve tenvir-i efkârına hadim haftalık
risale
Yıl 1, sayı 1 (13 Kanunusani 1320 [26
Jan. 1905]) - Yıl 1, sayı 43 (1
Kanunuevvel 1321 [14 Dec. 1905])
Thessaloniki

OX:BOD: 1:1 (26.1.1905) - 1:43
(14.12.1905)   [Turk.d.1463]

ÇOCUKLARA KIRAAT: mekâtib-i ibtidâiye
ve sibyaniye şâgirdâni için on beş
günde bir neşr olunur
Numero 1 (1 Safer 1299 [23 Dec. 1881]) -
Numero 18 (15 Zilhicce 1299 [28 Oct.
1882])
[İstanbul]

BL:OIOC: 1 (23.12.1881) - 18
(28.10.1882)   [14475.f.8]

COĞRAFYA ENSTİTÜSÜ DERGİSİ
See: İSTANBUL ÜNİVERSİTESİ
COĞRAFYA ENSTİTÜSÜ DERGİSİ

COĞRAFYA HABERLERİ / Türk Coğrafya
Kurumu tarafından çıkarılır
Yıl 1, sayı 1 (Ocak 1959) - Yıl 2, sayı
4 (Aralık 1961)
Ankara

OX:BOD: 1:1 (1.1959) - 2:4 (12.1961)
[Turk.d.1886]

COLLECTIVE BARGAINING AGREEMENTS
STATISTICS
See: TOPLU SÖZLEŞME İSTATİSTİKLERİ

COMMERCIAL COMPANIES AND FIRMS STATISTICS
See: TİCARET ŞİRKETLERİ VE FİRMA
İSTATİSTİKLERİ

CONJONCTURE
See: KONJONKTÜR

CONSTRUCTION STATISTICS
  See: İNŞAAT İSTATİSTİKLERİ

ÇORUM İL YILLIĞI
  [1] (1967) - [2] (1973)
  Ankara, 1968-1973

  BL:OIOC: [1] (1967) [14498.a.20]
  LO:SOAS: [1] [Per.10.L.279250]
  OX:BOD: [1] [Turk.d.3324/19]

ÇORUMLU / Çorum Halkevi Dil, Edebiyat ve
  Tarih Komitesi çıkarır
  Yıl 1, sayı 1 (15 Nisan 1938) - Sayı 53
  (1 Mart 1945)
  Çorum

  OX:BOD: 1:1 (15.4.1938) - 53 (1.3.1945)
  [Turk.d.724]

CULDIZ: ēdebi-körkem, ķoğamdıķ-sayası
  çurnal / Ķazaķstan cazuşılar
  odağınıņ organı
  1929, 1 -
  Alma-Ata
  In Kazakh
  Monthly

  BL:OIOC: 1977:1 - 1983:12; lacking
  1978:10 [14499.t.37]
  OX:BOD: 1985:5 - [Per.Turk.d.3387]

CULTURAL STATISTICS
  See: KÜLTÜR İSTATİSTİKLERİ

CUMHURİYET
  7 Mayıs 1924 -
  Istanbul
  Daily newspaper
  In Ottoman down to 1928

  BL:OIOC: (microfilm) 1.1.1956 -; (hard
  copy) 1.8.1955 - 31.12.1955; 1.8.1959 -
  30.9.1984; lacking 1957, 1969, 1970, and
  some issues [(microfilm)
  OR.MIC.10827; (hard copy) O.P.552]
  LO:SOAS: Current issues only
  [Newspaper room]
  CA:UL: [?].10.1965 - [?].5.1972; lacking
  some issues [enquire for location]
  DU:UL: 18.7.1942 - 31.12.1961
  (microfilm); 8.12.1961 - (hard copy)
  [not callmarked]
  CA:OS: 2.1.1972 - 21.11.1977; lacking
  some issues; 29.11.1986 - 11.3.1987;
  16.3.1990 - [enquire for shelfmark]

CUMHURİYET: haftalık bağımsız, siyasi
  gazete
  Yıl 1, sayı 1 (16 Ağustos 1960) - [?]
  Lefkoşa

  BL:OIOC: 1:1 (16.8.1960) - 2:89
  (23.4.1962) [14498.a.66]

CUMHURİYET SENATOSU TUTANAK DERGİSİ
  See: T.B.M.M. TUTANAK DERGİSİ

CUMHURİYET YILLIK
  1978 -
  Istanbul
  Review of past year's events in Turkey:
  articles from Cumhuriyet newspaper
  Title up to 1981: Cumhuriyet
  Annual; double issue for 1983 in lieu of
  1982 issue

  BL:OIOC: 1978 - [14489.b.217]
  DU:UL: 1983 [Per./PL1]
  OX:BOD: 1978 - [Per.Turk.d.2748]

CYPRUS MOSLEM LYCÉE MAGAZINE
  See: KIBRIS İSLÂM LİSESİ MECMUASI

DAĞARCIK
  See also: TÜRK KÜLTÜRÜNDE DAĞARCIK

DAĞARCIK: bazı müntehabat-ı asar ile
  fünunun delalet ettiği bir takım
  garaib-i keşfiyat ve hükema-yi
  mütekaddimin ve müteahhirin tarafından
  irad edilen muhakemat-ı müfideyi ve
  bazı teracim-i ahvali havidir /
  müellifi, Ahmed Midhat
  Cüz' numerosu 1 (1288 [1872 or 1873]) -
  cüz' numerosu 10 ([1]289 [1873 or
  1874])
  Istanbul: [Ahmed Midhat]
  Frequency uncertain; issues dated by
  year only

  BL:OIOC: 1-10 [14480.d.236]
  DU:UL: 1-10 [Per./PL10]
  OX:BOD: 1-10 [Per.Turk.d.3214]

DALKAVUK: mizaha ait olmak ve şahsiyât-ı
  muhtevi olmamak üzere gönderilecek
  evrâk âmalmemuniye kabul edilir;
  şimdilik haftada bir defa tasdî' eder
  Numero 1 (30 Ağustos 1324 [12 Sep.
  1908]) - Numero 25 (21 Şubat 1324 [6
  Mar. 1909])
  Istanbul

  OX:BOD: 1 (11.9.1908) - 25 (6.3.1909)
  [Per.Turk.d.3549]

DANIŞMA MECLİSİ TUTANAK DERGİSİ
  See: T.B.M.M. TUTANAK DERGİSİ

DARÜLELHAN MECMUASI / Darülelhan
  hey'et-i tedrisiyesi tarafından iki ayda
  bir neşredilir
  Sene 1, numero 1 (1 Şubat 1340 [1925])
  - Sene 2, numero 7 (1 Şubat [1]926)
  Istanbul
  Journal of Istanbul Conservatoire

  BL:OIOC: 1:1 (1.2.1925) - 2:7 (1.2.1926)
  [ITA.1989.c.5]

DARÜLFÜNUN EDEBİYAT FAKÜLTESİ
  MECMUASI: felsefe, ictimaiyât, tarih,
  coğrafya, edebiyat konularını
  muhtevidir
  Sene 1, sayı 1 (Mart 1332 [1916]) - Cilt
  8, sayı 7 (İkincikanun 1933)
  Istanbul
  Subtitle varies
  Vols. 1-6 (1916-1928) in Arabic
  characters
  Frequency varies

  BL:OIOC: 1:1 (3.1916) - 8:7 (1.1933)
  (a); 1:1 - 3:7 (12.1924) (b) [(a)
  114480.d.3; (b) 14498.b.15]
  LO:SOAS: 1:1-6; 2:1, 3, 5-7; 3:1-2, 5-7;
  4:1-6; 5:1-6; 6:1-4; 7:1-5; 8:1, 3-7
  [Per.10.94862]
  OX:BOD: 1:1 - 8:7 [Turk.d.590]

DARÜLFÜNUN HUKUK FAKÜLTESİ MECMUASI:
  iki ayda bir neşrolunur
  Sene 1, sayı 1 (Mart 1332 [1916]) - Sene
  9, sayı 38 (Teşrinievvel 1928)
  Istanbul
  Continued by: İstanbul Üniversitesi
  Hukuk Fakültesi mecmuası

  OX:BOD: 1:1 (3.1916) - 1:6 (1.1917)
  [Per.Turk.d.3542]

DARÜLFÜNUN İLAHİYAT FAKÜLTESİ
MECMUASI: tarihî, ictimaî, dinî,
felsefî
1. sene, 1. sayı (Teşrinisani 1925) -
6. sene, 25. sayı (1 Şubat 1933)
Istanbul
Issues 1-10 are in Ottoman (Arabic
script)
Irregular

BL:OIOC: 1:1 (10.1925) - 6:25 (1.2.1933)
[14498.a.79]
LO:SOAS: 1:1 - 5:22   [Per.10.136626]
CA:UL: 1:1 - 5:18 (1-3.1931)
[Q.830.c.16]
DU:UL: 1:4 (11.1926)   [Per./PL 10]
OX:BOD: 1:1 - 6:25   [Turk.d.591]

DAVUL: haftalık edebî mizah gazetesi
Numara 1 (14 Teşrinievvel 1324 [27 Oct.
1908] - Numara 24 (14 Mayıs 1325 [27 May
1909])
Istanbul

OX:BOD: 1 (27.10.1908) - 24 (27.5.1909)
[Per.Turk.d.3557]

DEATH STATISTICS (IN PROVINCE AND DISTRICT
CENTERS)
See: ÖLÜM İSTATİSTİKLERİ (İL VE
İLÇE MERKEZLERİNDE)

LA DÉFENCE FINANCIÈRE ET ÉCONOMIQUE
See: MÜDAFAA-İ MALİYE VE
İKTİSADİYE

DEMET: Aylık eğitim ve öğretim dergisi
/ Göller Bölgesi Köy Öğretmenleri
Derneği organıdır
Sayı 1 (Mayıs 1953) - Sayı 70 (Şubat
1959)
Isparta

OX:BOD: 1 (5.1953) - 70 (2.1959)
[Per.Turk.d.3538]

DEMİRYOL: aylık meslekî dergi / TCDD
[i.e. Türkiye Cumhuriyeti Devlet
Demiryolları] Genel Müdürlüğü
Yıl 1, sayı 1 (Mart 1341 [1925]) -
Ankara, [1951?]-

BL:HSS: 39:436/437 (?-?.1962)
[S.Q.162/4]
DU:DC: 56/60 (5-9.1956); 552 (1.1972) -
637 (2.1979); lacking 571-572, 581,
618.626, 635-636   [25/4 / TRANSPORT /
RAILWAYS]

DEMOKRAT EGE: günlük siyasi akşam
gazetesi
Yıl 1, sayı 1 (7 Ekim 1955) - Yıl 3,
sayı 2081 (30 Aralık 1959)
Izmir
Continued from Jan. 1960 by: Ege telgraf

BL:OIOC: 5.5.1960 - 6.5.1960
[OR.MIC.12605 (O.P.552/5)]

DEMOKRAT İZMİR: sabahları çıkar
müstakil siyasi gazete
Yıl 1, sayı 1 ([date?], 1947) - [?]
Izmir

BL:OIOC: 31.5.1960, 1.5.1960, 26.12.1960
[OR.MIC.12614 (O.P. 552/14)]

DENİZLİ İL YILLIĞI
[1] (1967) - [2] (1973)
Ankara

BL:OIOC: [1] (1967)   [14498.a.48]
OX:BOD: [1]   [Turk.d.3324/20]

DERGAH: yarım aylık ilim ve sanat mecmuas
1. sene, 1. cild, numero 1 (15 Nisan
[1]337 [1919]) - 2. sene, 4. cild,
numero 42 (5 Kanunusani [1]339 [1921])
Istanbul

BL:OIOC: 1:1:1 (15.4.1919) - 2:4:42
(5.1.1921)   [14498.a.83]
OX:BOD: 1:1:1 - 2:4:42   [Turk.c.170]
OX:MEC: 1:1:1 - 2:4:42   [APT Der]

DERGİ
See also: İNGİLİZ FİLOLOJİSİ
DERGİSİ

DERGİ / Şovyetler Birliğini Öğrenme
Enstitüsü
1. yıl, 1 (Ocak-Mart 1955) - 16. yıl,
no. 59 ([undated], 1970)
Munich
Issue no.1 published while the
institution was named Sovyet Sosyalist
Cumhuriyetleri Birliği Tarih ve
Kültürünü Tetkik Enstitüsü
Quarterly

BL:OIOC: 1:1 (1-3.1955) - 1:42 ([10-12].
1965)   [14498.cc.60]
OX:BOD: 1-41, 47-48, 51, 56, 58-59
[Per.Turk.d.3210]

DERGİ: İNGİLİZ FİLOLOJİSİ
See: İNGİLİZ FİLOLOJİSİ DERGİSİ

DEVİR: haftalık aktüalite gazetesi
Cilt 1, sayı (28 Ağustos 1954) - Cilt
2, sayı 28 (5 Mart 1955)
Istanbul

LO:SOAS: 1:1 (28.8.1954) - 2:28
(5.3.1955)   [Per.10.L.173834]

DEVLET-İ ALİYE-İ OSMANİYE HARİCİYE
NEZÂRET-İ CELİLESİNİN SALNAMESİ
See: SALNAME-İ NEZÂRET-İ UMUR-I
HARİCİYE

DEVLET YAYINLARI BİBLİYOGRAFYASI
See: T.C. DEVLET YAYINLARI
BİBLİYOGRAFYASI

DEVRİM
Sayı 1 (2 Ekim 1969) - Sayı 78 (20 Nisan
1971)
Ankara
Weekly

OX:BOD: 1 (21.10.1969) - 78 (20.4.1971)
[N.Turk.a.9]

DEVRİMCİ SAVAŞIMDA SANAT EMEĞİ
See: SANAT EMEĞİ

DICHDJILIK ALÉMI
See: DİŞÇİLİK ÂLEMİ

DIE BEFREIUNG
See: KURTULUŞ

DİKEN: her hafta çarşamba günleri
çıkar mesleğinde müstakil, edebî,
siyasî, mizah gazetesidir
Aded 1 (30 Teşrinievvel 1335 [1918]) -
Cilt 3, aded 72 ([date?], 1337 [1920])
Istanbul

OX:BOD: 1 (30.10.1918) - 56 (3.6.1919)
[Turk.c.65]

DİL BİLİMİ İNSTİTUTINIÑ İŞLERİ
See: DİL VE ÉDEBİYAT İNSTİTUTINIÑ
İŞLERİ

DİL VE EDEBİYAT İNSTİTUTININ
İŞLERİ = Trudy Instituta iazyka i
literatury / Türkmenistan SSR Ilımlar
Akademiyası Dil ve edebiyat
instituti
1 (1956) -
Ashkhabad: Türkmenistan SSR Ilımlar
Akademiyasınıñ neşriyatı
Titles from issue 4: Dil Bilimi
İnstitutınıñ işleri = Trudy Instituta
iazykoznaniia
Articles in Turkmen or Russian
Irregular

BL:OIOC: 2 (1957) - 4 (1962)
[14499.p.55]
OX:BOD: 1 (1956) - 3 (1959)
[Per.Turk.d.1227]

DİLBİLİM / İstanbul Üniversitesi
Yabancı Diller Yüksek Okulu Fransızca
Bölümü dergisi = Linguistique / Revue
du Département de Français de l'École
Supérieur des Langues Étrangères de
l'Université d'Istanbul
1 (1976) -
Istanbul: 1977-
French title of 1-5: Revue du
Département de Français, etc.
Articles in Turkish or French
Annual

BL:OIOC: 1 (1976) - 6 (1981)
[14498.cc.43]

DİLDE, FİKİRDE, İŞDE BİRLİK
See: BİRLİK

DİNİMİZDE REFORM KEMALİZM: aylık
siyasal, sosyal, bilimsel, ekonomiksel
güzel yazılar dergisi
1. sene, sayı 1 (Aralık 1957) - Cilt 12,
sayı 67 (Nisan 1967)
Istanbul
Subtitle varies
Monthly until Dec. 1960; therafter
generally bimonthly

OX:MEC: 1:1 (12.1957) - 1:12 (11.1958)
[APT Din]

DIŞ POLİTİKA: üç aylık Türkçe ve
Ingilizce siyasi dergi = Foreign policy
Cilt 1, sayı 1 (Mart 1971) -
Ankara
All articles appear in both Turkish and
English

BL:OIOC: 1 (1971) - 4 (1974); 8:1/2
(1975); 9 (1976) -   [14498.cc.23]
LO:SOAS: 1:1 - 8:4 (12.1980)
[Per.10.259950]
DU:UL: 3 (1973) - ; lacking 3:2-4, 4:1,
4:4, 5:1-3, 7:3-4   [Per./PL351]
SU:IDS: 5:4 (?.1976); 9:1/2 (?.1981)
[SERIALS/NON-OFFICIAL/72]

DIŞ TİCARET AYLIK İSTATİSTİK, ÖZEL
TİCARET, SERİ 1 = Statistique mensuel
du commerce extérieur, commerce
spécial / Başvekâlet İstatistik Umum
Müdürlüğü
Mayıs 1933 - [Nisan 1966?]
Ankara
Dates of publication not known
In Turkish and French
Some issues cumulated

DU:DC: 1.1960/3.1960
[25/4/TRADE/INTERNATIONAL]

DIŞ TİCARET İSTATİSTİKLERİ = Foreign
trade statistics / Başbakanlık Devlet
İstatistik Enstitüsü
(1950) -
Ankara, 1951-
Previous title: Dış ticaret yıllık
istatistik = Foreign trade statistics
In Turkish and English
Nominally annual; some two-year
cumulations

DU:DC: 1961/1962 - 1965/1966; 1967/1968
- 1969; 1976/1977 -
[25/4/TRADE/INTERNATIONAL]
OX:BOD: 1985 -   [Per.23245.d.125]
SU:IDS: 1967 -
[SERIALS/OFFICIAL/TURKEY]

DIŞ TİCARET YILLIK İSTATİSTİK
See: DIŞ TİCARET İSTATİSTİKLERİ

DİŞÇİLİK ÂLEMİ: her ay neşrolunur,
dişçilik fenninin terakkisine hizmet
eder fennî, tıbbî ve meslekî
mecmuadır
Sene 1, numero 1 ([date?], 1340 [1924])
- Sene 4, numero 33 ([date?], 1928)
Istanbul
Added titles: Dichdjilik alémi; Le
monde dentaire
Nominally monthly

BL:OIOC: 2:15 (1.1926) - 2:21 (1.1927)
[14442.dd.2]

DIŞİŞLERİ BAKANLIĞI YILLIĞI
Ankara
Publication history not known

BL:OIOC: 1967   [14495.d.32]

DIVORCE STATISTICS
See: BOŞANMA İSTATİSTİKLERİ

DİYANET
See: DİYANET GAZETESİ

DİYANET GAZETESİ / Diyanet İşleri
Başkanlığınca 15 günde bir yayınlanır
Yıl 1, sayı 1 (22 Kasım 1968/1 Ramazan
1388) - Yıl 7, Cilt 6, sayı 144 (1
Temmuz 1976/3 Recep 1396)
Ankara
Title until (?): Diyanet

BL:OIOC: 1:1 (22.11.1968) - 7:6:144
(1.7.1976)   [ITA.1993.a.344]

DİYANET İŞLERİ BAŞKANLIĞI DERGİSİ:
dini, ahlakî, edebi, meslekî dergi
Cilt 1, sayı 1 (Haziran 1962) -
Ankara
Bimonthly; vols. 1-10 (1962-1971)
monthly

OX:BOD: 1962   [Per.Turk.d.848]

DİYARBAKIR İL YILLIĞI
[1] (1967) - [2] (1973)
Ankara

BL:OIOC: [1] (1967)   [14498.a.26]
OX:BOD: [1]   [Turk.d.3324/21]

DİYARBAKIR VİLÂYETİ SALNAMESİ
Defa 1 (1286 [1869-1870]) - Defa 20
(1321 [1905-1906])
Diyarbakır
Some issues entitled: Salname-i
Vilâyet-i Diyarbakır

CA:UL: 3 (1871); 14 (1894)
[S.828.01.b.29]
OX:BOD: 18 (1901)   [Turk.d.1453]

DİYARBEKİR VİLÂYETİ SALNAMESİ
See: DİYARBAKIR VİLÂYETİ SALNAMESİ

DİYOJEN: haftada iki defa neşrolunur
1. sene, numero 1 (12 Teşrinisani 1286
[25 Nov. 1870]) - 3. sene, numero 183
(29 Kanunuevvel 1288·[11 Jan. 1873])
İstanbul
Pioneering humorous magazine

BL:OIOC: 1:1 (25.11.1870) - 3:183
(11.1.1873)   [ITA.1990.c.6]

DJEM
See: CEM

DOĞU: büyük ülkü gazetesi; ayda bir
çıkar
Sayı 1 (İlkteşrin 1942) - Cild 15, yıl
8, sayı 82/96 (Eylûl-Aralık 1949 -
Ocak-Ekim 1950)
Zonguldak
Final issue numbered 82-106 on back
cover, 82-96 on p. 1

OX:BOD: 1 (10.1942) - 82/96 (9-12.1949 -
1-10.1950)   [Turk.d.3537]

DOĞU DİLLERİ / Ankara Üniversiteşi Dil
ve Tarih-Coğrafya Fakülteşi Doğu
Dilleri ve Edebiyatları Bölümü
dergisi
1. cilt, 1. sayı [1964] -
Ankara

BL:OIOC: 1:1 [1964] -; lacking 3:3-4
[14498.cc.11]
LO:SOAS: 1:1 -; lacking 3:2 - 3:4
[Per.10.186878]

DOĞU TÜRKİSTAN: aylık dergi = Eastern
Turkistan = Turkistān al-Sharqiyah
Yıl 1, sayı 1 ([date?] 1979) - Yıl 4,
sayı 52 [=40] (Nisan-Mayıs 1984)
İstanbul
In Turkish, English and Arabic

OX:BOD: 2:1 (8.1980) - 4:52 (4-5.1984)
[Per.Turk.d.3319]

DOĞU TÜRKİSTAN'IN SESİ: üç aylık
mecmua = Şawt Turkistān al-Sharqiyah
= Voice of Eastern Turkistan
Sayı 1, cilt 1 (Ocak 1984) -
İstanbul

BL:OIOC: 1:1 (1.1984) -   [14499.tt.42]
LO:SOAS: 1:1 -   [Per.10.L.494569]
OX:BOD: 1:1 - 2:7/8 (12.1985)
[Per.Turk.d.3220]

DOKLADY
See: MĚ'RUZĚLĚR

DOKUZ EYLÜL ÜNİVERSİTESİ İLÂHİYAT
FAKÜLTESİ DERGİSİ: yılda bir
neşredilir
1 [1983] -
İzmir

LO:SOAS: 1 [1983] -   [Per.10.563527]

DOLAB: ayda bir neşrolunur Türk mizâh
gazetesidir
1, sene, numero 1 (1 Teşrinisani 1316
[14 Nov. 1900]) - 1. sene, numero 7 (1
Mayıs 1317 [14 May 1901])
Folkestone
Added title in French: Le Dolab: journal
turc mensuel

BL:OIOC: 1:1 (14.11.1900) - 1:7
(14.5.1901)   [14498.d.4]

DOLAB: maarif ve edebiyata müteallık her
guna mebahis ve letaifi şamil ve
teracim-i ahval ile makalât-ı müfide
ve mevadd-ı nafia'ya müştemil
olacaktır
Sayı 1 (1290 [1873]) - Sayı 18 (1291
[1874])
İstanbul
Issues dated by year only

OX:BOD: 1 (1873) - 18 (1874)
[Per.Turk.d.1101]

DOLAP
See: DOLAB

DÖNEMLER İTİBARİYLE İMALAT SANAYİİ,
İSTİHDAM-ÜRETİM-EĞİLİM =
Manufacturing industry (quarterly)
employment-production-expectation /
Başbakanlık Devlet İstatistik
Enstitüsü
Ankara, [197-?]-
In Turkish and English
Nominally quarterly

DU:DC: 1974:2 - 1976:3; 1977:3/1978:3;
1979:1/1980:1
[25/4/INDUSTRY/MANUFACTURING]
SU:IDS: 1976:3/1977:3 -; lacking a few
issues   [SERIALS/OFFICIAL/TURKEY]

DORUK: Türk kültürü ve medeniyeti
dergisi
Yıl 1, sayı 1 (Agustos 1976) - Yıl 1,
sayı 1 [i.e. 2] (1977)
Ankara: Karar

BL:OIOC: 1:1 (8.1976)   [14456.d.456]

DORUK DERGİSİ
See: DORUK

DOST: fikir ve sanat dergisi
Cilt 1, sayı 1 (Ekim 1957) - Cilt 25,
sayı 102 (Nisan 1973)
Ankara
Quarterly

OX:BOD: 22:63 (1.1970) - 25:102 (4.1973)
[Per.Turk.d.1729]

DPT BÜLTENİ: ayda bir çıkar / Devlet
Planlama Teşkilâtı yayın organıdır
Sayı 1 (Mayıs 1970) - [?]
Ankara

BL:HSS: 3 (7.1970) - 5 (9.1970)
[S.Q.145/18]

DSİ BÜLTENİ / Devlet Su İşleri Genel
Müdürlüğünce iki ayda bir
yayınlanır
Ankara: [1959?]-

DU:DC: 158 (4.1972) - 165 (4.1974)
[25/4/ENERGY]

DSİ TEKNİK BÜLTENİ: iki ayda bir
çıkar / Devlet Su İşleri Genel
Müdürlüğü
Sayı 1 ([date?], 1967) -
Ankara
Title prior to Sept. 1972: DSİ teknik
dergisi
Frequency varies

DU:DC: 20 (1.1971) - 29 (1.1974)
[25/4/ENERGY]

DSİ TEKNİK DERGİSİ
See: DSİ TEKNİK BÜLTENİ

DÜNÜN VE BUGÜNÜN DEFTERLERİ: Türkiye
  sorunları dizisi
  1 (Haziran 1987) - 3 (Kasım 1987)
  İstanbul: Alan
  Bi-monthly

  OX:BOD: 1 (6.1987) - 3 (11.1987)
  [Per.Turk.d.3528]

DÜNYA
  Yıl 1, sayı 1 (2 Mart 1952) -
  İstanbul
  Daily newspaper

  BL:OIOC: 27.5.1960, 18.5.1960, 31.5.1960
  [OR.MIC.12608 (O.P.552/8)]

DÜNYA MADEN HABERLERİ / Maden Tetkik ve
  Arama Enstitüsü yayınlarından
  Ankara, [19--?]-[19--?]
  Annual

  BL:HSS: 1969 - 1973   [S.Q.45/12]

DÜŞÜN / Tevfik Fikret Derneğinin
  sosyal ve kültürel fikirlerini yayar
  Sayı 1 (Şubat 1964) - [?]
  İstanbul: Tevfik Fikret Derneği
  Publication history unknown

  LO:SOAS: 1 (2.1964)   [Per.10.167484]

EASTERN TURKISTAN
  See: DOĞU TÜRKİSTAN

EDEBÎ MECMUA
  1. sene, sayı 1 (16 Kanunusani 1919)
  İstanbul
  Only one issue published

  BL:OIOC: 1 (16.1.1919)   [ITA.1989.c.5]

EDEBİYAT: aylık dergi
  Sayı 1 (Şubat 1968) -
  Ankara

  BL:OIOC: 4.1973 - 6.1974; 6.1976 -
  11.1984; lacking a few issues
  [OR.MIC.12117 (O.P.576)]

ĚDĚBİYAT / Ş[imal] Ĝ[ĕrb]
  M[ĕdĕniyit] C[ĕmiyiti] tĕrĕfidin
  neşriteldi
  [1] tuğum sani (Dekabr 1947) - [?]
  Urumchi; Lanzho; Nankin
  Uygur; in Arabic characters
  Monthly?

  BL:OIOC: 1 (12.1947)
  [ITA.1986.a.1624/4]

EDEBİYAT ÂLEMİ: haftalık içtimaî,
  ahlakî, tarihî, edebî gazete
  Sene 1, no. 1 (21 Nisan 1949) - Sene 1,
  cilt 2, no. 34 (8 Aralık 1949)
  İstanbul

  BL:OIOC: 1:1 (21.4.1949) - 1:2:34
  (8.12.1949)   [ORB. 30/271]

EDEBİYAT FAKÜLTESİ ARAŞTIRMA DERGİSİ
  / Atatürk Üniversitesi Edebiyat
  Fakültesi
  Cilt 1, sayı 1 (Ekim 1970) - Cilt 2,
  sayı 12 (Aralık 1980)
  Erzurum
  Continued by: Fen-Edebiyat Fakültesi
  Araştırma dergisi
  Irregular

  BL:OIOC: 1:1 (10.1970) - 2:12 (12.1980)
  [14498.cc.72]
  LO:SOAS: 1:1 -   [Per.10.264558]
  OX:BOD: 1:1 - 2:12   [Per.Turk.d.1889]

EDEBİYAT FAKÜLTESİ DERGİSİ / Fırat
  Üniversitesi Edebiyat Fakültesi
  Cilt 1, sayı 1 (1981) -
  Elazığ
  Annual

  OX:BOD: 1:1 (1981) -   [Per.Turk.d.3380]

EDEBİYAT-I UMUMİYE MECMUASI: haftalık
  siyasî, edebî, ilmî gazetedir
  Cilt 1, sayı 1 (22 Teşrinievvel 1332 [4
  Nov. 1916]) - Cilt 5, sayı 110 (Mart
  1919)
  İstanbul

  OX:BOD: 1:1 (4.11.1916) - 5:110 (3.1919)
  [Turk.e.1130]

EDEBİYAT: SEÇMELER / Türk
  Edebiyatçılar Birliği
  İstanbul
  Anthology of recent Turkish verse
  Publication history not known
  Annual

  BL:OIOC: 1965   [14472.b.32]

ĚDEBİYAT VE SUNGAT / Türkmenistan SSR
  Yazıcılar Soyuzının pravleniesi bilen
  Medeniet Ministrliginin organı
  No. 1 (5 İyuli 1958) -
  Ashkhabad
  In Turkmen
  Twice weekly

  BL:OIOC: 1979:10 (3.2.1979) -; lacking
  very few issues   [O.P.1029]

ĚDĚBİYYAT, DİL VĚ INCĚSĚNĚT
SERİYASI
  See: AZĚRBAYCAN SSR ELMLĚR
  AKADEMİYASI HĚBERLERİ, ĚDĚBİYYAT,
  DİL VE INCĚSĚNĚT SERİYASI

ĚDĚBİYYAT GĚZĚTİ / Azěrbaycan
  Yazıçılar İttifagının vě Azěrbaycan
  Měděniyyět Nazirliyinin organı
  No. 1 (Yanvar 1, 1934) -
  Baku
  Title before 1991: Ěděbiyyat vě
  incěsěnět
  In Azeri
  Weekly

  BL:OIOC: 1977:1 -; lacking several
  issues   [O.P.1006]

ĚDĚBİYYAT VĚ İNCĚSĚNĚT
  See: ĚDĚBİYYAT GĚZĚTİ

EDİRNE İL YILLIĞI
  [1] (1967) - [2] (1973)
  [Edirne], 1968-1973

  BL:OIOC: [1] (1967)   [14498.a.37]
  OX:BOD: [1]   [Turk.d.3324/22]

EDİRNE VİLÂYETİ SALNAMESİ
  Defa 1 (1287 [1870-1871]) - Defa 28
  (1319 [1903-1904])
  Edirne
  Some issues dated by hicrî, others by
  malî calendar
  Title of early issues: Salname-i
  Vilayet-i Edirne

  BL:OIOC: 1 (1870-1871)   [14496.b.3]
  LO:SOAS: 21 (1895)   [E.Per.280671]
  DU:UL: 27 (1902)   [PL.366]
  OX:BOD: 3 (1872-1873); 26 (1900-1901);
  28 (1903-1904)   [Per.Turk.d.1437]

EGE BATI DİLLERİ VE EDEBİYATI DERGİSİ
  / Ege Üniversitesi Edebiyat Fakültesi
  1 (1983) -
  İzmir

  OX:BOD: 1 (1983) -   [Per.Turk.d.3226]

27

EGE BÖLGESİ İHRACAT-İTHALAT YILLIĞI =
Annual of exports and imports of the
Aegean Region = Das Export und Import
Jahrbuch der Aegeischen Region =
Annuaire des exportations et
importations de la Région d'Égée /
İzmir Ticaret Odası
1965 –
Izmir, 1966-
In Turkish, English, German and French

BL:OIOC: 1988   [ZOR.1988.a.231]
BL:HSS: 1974   [S.Q.40/12]
DU:DC: 1969-1970; 1972-1974
[25/4/TRADE/INTERNATIONAL]

EGE COĞRAFYA DERGİSİ / Ege
Üniversitesi Edebiyat Fakültesi
Coğrafya Bölümü
Sayı 1 (Ocak 1983) –
Izmir
Annual

OX:BOD: 1 (1983) –   [Per.Turk.d.3227]

EGE EKSPRES: günlük siyasi sabah
gazetesi
Yıl 1, sayı 1 ([date?] 1952)-
Izmir

BL:OIOC: 3, 29, 31, 5, 1960; 1.6.1961;
6.8.1961; 26.12.1961   [OR.MIC.12603
(O.P.552/3)]

E[GE] Ü[NİVERSİTESİ SOSYAL BİLİMLER
FAKÜLTESİ DERGİSİ
See: SOSYAL BİLİMLER FAKÜLTESİ
DERGİSİ

EGE ÜNİVERSİTESİ TIP FAKÜLTESİ
DERGİSİ = Journal of the Medical
Faculty of Ege University
Cilt 1, sayı 1 ([date?], 1962) –
İzmir
Early issues entitled: Ege Üniversitesi
Tıp Fakültesi mecmuası
In Turkish; with summaries in English
Quarterly

DU:DC: 9:1 (1970) – 11:4 (1972); 12:3
(1973) – 13:4 (1974)   [25/4/HEALTH]

EĞİTİM FAKÜLTESİ DERGİSİ / Ankara
Üniversitesi Eğitim Fakültesi
Yıl 1, sayı 1-4 (1968) –
Ankara: Ankara Üniversitesi Eğitim
Fakültesi, 1968-

BL:HSS: 1:1-4 (1968) – 2:1-4 (1969)
[S.Q.59/16]

EİE BÜLTENİ / Elektrik İşleri Etüt
İdaresi Genel Direktörlüğü yayın
organıdır
Ankara, [196-?]-
Frequency varies: monthly, bi-monthly,
or quarterly; some issues not dated

BL:HSS: 26 (1-5.1970) – 44 (2.1973)
[S.Q.62/7]
DU:DC: 34 (6.1971) – 101/102 [?.1982?];
lacking 47, 56, 61-67   [25/4/ENERGY]

EKONOMİ VE İDARİ BİLİMLER DERGİSİ =
Journal of economics and administrative
studies / Boğaziçi Üniversitesi
İktisadi ve İdari Bilimler Fakültesi
Yıl 1, sayı 1 (Kış 1987) –
Istanbul
Articles in Turkish or English
Quarterly

SU:IDS: 2:1 (winter 1988) – 4:2 (summer
1990)   [SERIALS/NON-OFFICIAL/72]

EKONOMİK DEĞERLENDİRME BÜLTENİ,
YILLIK / T.C. Ticaret Bakanlığı
1 ([1951?] –
Ankara
Also published in English

DU:DC: 25 (1975) [also 1976, 1978-1980
in English]   [25/4/TRADE/INTERNATIONAL]

EKONOMİK RAPOR / [Türkiye İş Bankası]
Ankara, [197-?]-
English title?
Published in Turkish or English
Annual

DU:DC: 1975-1981
[25/4/ECONOMY/GENERAL]

ĚKONOMIKA I ZHIZN'
See: İGTİSADİYYAT VĚ HĚYAT

ĚL-ALTAY: çümdemel-keendik depter /
Tuulu Altaydıñ biçiiçilik
organizatsiyazı beletegen
[19--?], 1-kı çıgargan –
Gorno-Altaisk
ISSN 0235-1218
Periodical anthology of Altai writing
Publication history not known
Subtitle varies
Frequency: two issues in 1987

BL:OIOC: 1987:1 – 1987:2
[ITA.1989.a.435]

EL-HAKİKA
See: EL-HAKİKA

EL-HAKİKA = al-Ḥaqīqah
[Aded 1] (10 Mart 1916) – Aded 120
(Evvel [1] Febrāyir 1921)
London
Illustrated wartime and postwar
propaganda newspaper
In Ottoman, Arabic, Persian, and Urdu

BL:OIOC: [1] (10.3.1916) – 74
(22.1.1919)   [O.P.913]
LO:SOAS: [1] – 120 (1.2.1921); lacking
21 (15.12.1916), 104 (1.6.1920) – 111
(15.10.1920)   [Ex.Per.60489]

ELAZIĞ İL YILLIĞI
[1] (1967) – [2] (1973)
Elazığ, 1970-[197-?]

OX:BOD: [1] (1967)   [Turk.d.3324/23]

ELEKTRİK ENERJİSİ YILLIK DURUM
BÜLTENİ = Annual electric power survey
/ Elektrik İşleri Etüt İdaresi Genel
Direktörlüğü
1957 –
Ankara, 1958-

BL:HSS: 1968   [S.Q.62/6]
DU:DC: 1968   [25/4/ENERGY]

ELM / Azěrbaycan SSR Elmlěr Akademiyası
Rěyasět Hey'ětinin, Partiya,
Birlěşmiş Hěmkarlar İttifagı vě
Komsomol Komitělěrinin organı
No. 1 ([date?], 1984) –
Baku
Four-page newspaper on current and
cultural affairs
Articles in Azeri or Russian
Currently monthly

BL:OIOC: 1 [209] (6.1.1990) –
[O.P.1187]

28

ELM VĚ HĚYAT / Azěrbaycan SSR "Bilik"
Cěmiyyětinin aylıg elmi-kütlěvi
jurnalı
[1961] no.1-
Baku
ISSN 0134-3386
In Azeri
Monthly

　BL:OIOC: 1984:5 -　　[14499.tt.45]

ELMİ GEYDLĚR = Uchenye zapiski / H.
Zěrdabi adına Kirovabad Pedagoji
İnstitutu
1 [195-?] - [?]
Kirovabad
Academic journal of education
Contents in Azeri or Russian
Occasional; dated by year only

　BL:OIOC: 12 (1962) - 13 (1962)
　[14499.t.20]

ĚLYAZMALAR HĚZİNĚSİNDĚ = V
sokrovishchnitše rukopiseǐ: trudy /
Azěrbaycan SSR Elmlěr Akademiyası,
Respublika Ělyazmalar Fondu
Cild 1 (1961) -
Baku: Elm
Journal devoted to studies on Islamic
manuscripts in the Manuscript Library of
Azerbaijan Academy of Sciences
Issues 1 and 2 are entitled: Respublika
Ělyamaları Fondunun ěsěrlěri = Trudy
Respublikanskogo Fonda
Articles in Azeri or Russian
Occasional

　BL:OIOC: 1 (1961) - ; lacking 5
　[14499.t.11]
　LO:SOAS: 1 -　　[Per.10.156799]
　OX:BOD: 1 - ; lacking 5
　[259045.d.Baku 1.1]

EMEK / Türkiye Genel Hizmetler
İşçileri Sendikası yayın organıdır
Cilt 1, sayı 1 (Temmuz 1953) -
Ankara
Fortnightly

　DU:DC: 252 (15.10.1975) - 301
　(1.11.1977); lacking 253, 255-257, 264,
　271-273, 288, 296　　[25/3/TRADE UNIONS]

EMEL: iki aylık fikir-kültür dergisi
Cilt 1, sayı 1 (Kasım 1960) -
Ankara
Journal primarily for Crimean Tatars in
Turkey
Subtitle varies slightly

　BL:OIOC: 1:1 (11.1960) -; lacking 14:82
　(4-5.1974), 14:84 (9-10.1974)
　[14498.c.20]
　OX:BOD: 1:1 -　　[Per.Turk.d.3356]

EMEL: on günde bir neşrolunur, menafi'-i
mülk ve millet'e hâdim Osmanlı
gazetesidir
Sene 1, aded 1 (1-12 Mart 1316 [14-25
Mar. 1899]) - [?]
Cairo

　BL:OIOC: 1:1 (14-25.3.1899) - 1:7
　(24.5.1899-4.6.1899)　　[14498.d.21 (1)]

EMEL: edebî, ilmî, ictimaî, iktısadî
ve siyasî aylık mecmua / Kırım Millî
Kurtuluş Hareketinin organı
Yıl 1, nr. 1 ([date?], 1930) - [?]
Constanza
Added title in Romanian: Emel (Ideal)

　LO:SOAS: 10:141 (8.1939)
　[Per.10.40509]

ENI IRSHAD'
　See: YENİ İRŞAD

ENVÂR-I ZEKÂ: mesail-i siyasiye'den ve
mezhebiye'den maada herşeyden bahseder,
onbeş günde bir kere neşrolunur
risale-i mevkutedir
1. cild, cüz' 1 (1299 [1882]) - 2.
cild, cüz' 34 (1302 [1884 or 1885])
Istanbul
Irregular; nominally fortnightly; issues
dated by year only

　BL:OIOC: 1:1 (1882) - 2:34 (1884-5) (1);
　1:1 - 1:12 (2)　　[14498.c.2 (1);
　14475.bb.18 (2)]
　CA:UL: 1:1 - 1:8　　[Q.830.d.2]
　OX:BOD: 1:1 - 2:34　　[Per.Turk.d.2855]

ERCİYES ÜNIVERSİTESİ İLAHİYAT
FAKÜLTESİ DERGİSİ
Sayı 1 (1983) -
Kayseri, 1984-
Studies on Islam and Islamic culture and
history
Irregular

　BL:OIOC: 1 (1983) -　　[14498.cc.84]

ERDEM / Atatürk Kültür Merkezi dergisi
Cilt 1, sayı 1 (Ocak 1985) -
Ankara
Journal of Turkish studies
Articles in Turkish and / or English
Four-monthly

　BL:OIOC: 1:1 (1.1985) -　　[14498.cc.89]
　BL:DSC: 1:1 -　　[3795.530000]
　LO:SOAS: 1:1 -　　[Per.10.512007]
　CA:UL: 1:1 -　　[enquire in periodicals
　dept.]
　DU:UL: 1:1 -　　[Per./PL 1]
　OX:BOD: 1:1 -　　[Per.Turk.d.3383]

EREĞLI KÖMÜR HAVZASI İSTATİSTİKLERİ
　See: TÜRKİYE TAŞKÖMÜRÜ KURUMU
　GENEL MÜDÜRLÜĞÜ İSTATİSTİK
　YILLIĞI

ERZİNCAN İL YILLIĞI
[1] (1967) - [2] (1973)
Ankara, 1968-1973

　OX:BOD: [1] (1967)　　[Turk.d.3324/24]

ERZURUM İL YILLIĞI
[1] (1967) - [2] (1973)
Istanbul, 1968-1973

　OX:BOD: [1] (1967)　　[Turk.d.3324/25]

ESHIL' ADA
　See: YEŞİL ADA

ESKİŞEHİR İL YILLIĞI
[1] (1967) - [2] (1973)
Ankara; Eskişehir

　BL:OIOC: [1] (1967)　　[14498.a.51]
　OX:BOD: [1]　　[Turk.d.3324/26]

EŞREF: haftalık mizah gazetesidir
Yıl 1, sayı 1 (18 Mart 1325 [31 Mar.
1909]) - Yıl 1, sayı 26 (23 Ağustos
1325 [5 Sep. 1909])
Istanbul
Continued by: Musavver Eşref

　OX:BOD: 1:1 (31.3.1909) - 1:26
　(5.9.1909)　　[Turk.b.12]

E.Ü. SOSYAL BİLİMLER FAKÜLTESİ
DERGİSİ
　See: SOSYAL BİLİMLER FAKÜLTESİ
　DERGİSİ

EVİMİZ / Türkiye Emlâk Kredi Bankası
Sayı 1 (Ekim 1967) -
Ankara
Irregular; initially quarterly

DU:DC: 5 (11.1968) - 15 (3.1973)
[25/4/BANKING]

EVLENME İSTATİSTİKLERİ = Marriage
statistics / Başbakanlık Devlet
İstatistik Enstitüsü
1932/1958 -
Ankara, 1959-
In Turkish and English; early issues
Turkish only
Generally annual; some cumulations

BL:HSS: 1932/1958;
1932,1940,1945,1950-1960 (in 1 vol.)
[S.Q.170/26]
DU:DC: 1932/1958; 1932/1960; 1968 -
1971; 1973 - 1974; 1976 -
[25/4/POPULATION]
SU:IDS: 1980 -
[SERIALS/OFFICIAL/TURKEY]

ĔVRÂK-I NĔFİSĔ
Numara 1 ([Mart?] 1919) - Numara 6 (1
Ağustos 1919)
Baku
Cultural and literary journal
Title on cover: Mĕcmua-i Ĕvrâk-ı
nĕfisĕ
Azeri; Arabic characters
Monthly

BL:OIOC: 1 (3?.1919) - 6 (8.1919)
[14499.tt.20]

EVREN: fikir sanat ve edebiyat dergisi
Cilt 1, sayı 1 (Mayıs 1957) - [?]
Lefkoşa
Monthly

BL:OIOC: 1:1 (5.1957)
[ITA.1986.a.1622]

DAS EXPORT UND IMPORT JAHRBUCH DER
AEGEISCHEN REGION
See: EGE BÖLGESİ İHRACAT-İTHALAT
YILLIĞI

EYLEM [1. SERİ]: aylık düşün ve eylem
dergisi
Sayı 1 (Mart 1964) - Sayı 33 (1 Mayıs
1966)
Istanbul

OX:BOD: 1 (3.1964) - 33 (1.5.1966)
[Per.Turk.d.3216]

EZAN: vaktinde çikar bir nidâ-yi
Hayyalâlfelâh
N. 1 (1 Ramazan [1]314/23 Kanunusani
[1]313/4 Şubat [1]897) - N. 2 (1
Ramazan [1]319 [12 Dec. 1901]
Geneva

BL:OIOC: 1 (4.2.1897)   [ITA.1986.a.394]

FAALİYET RAPORU / Türkiye Elektrik
Kurumu
Ankara
Publication history not known
Annual

SU:IDS: 1980 - 1982
[SERIALS/OFFICIAL/TURKEY]

FAALİYET RAPORU / Türkiye Bilimsel ve
Teknik Araştırma Kurumu
Ankara, [196-?]-
Annual: year from March to February

BL:HSS: 1967; 1969   [S.Q.59/25]

FAALİYET RAPORU / İstanbul Sanayi Odası
Istanbul, [19--?]-
Annual

DU:DC: 1971; 1973
[25/4/INDUSTRY/GENERAL]

FAALİYET RAPORU, MALİ RAPOR / Türkiye
Ticaret Odaları, Sanayi Odaları ve
Ticaret Borsaları Birliği
Ankara
Annual

DU:DC: 1959 - 1961; 1963 - 1970; 1972 -
1973   [25/4/COMMERCE]

FAALİYET RAPORU VE İŞ PROGRAMI / Aydın
Teknik Ziraat Müdürlüğü
Izmir, [19--?]-[19--?]
Annual

DU:DC: 1954 (1955)
[25/4/AGRICULTURE/GENERAL]

FAKÜLTE DERGİSİ / Ankara Üniversitesi
Dil ve Tarih-Coğrafya Fakültesi
dergisi
1 (Sonteşrin-İlkkanun 1942) -
Ankara
Previous title: Ankara Üniversitesi Dil
ve Tarih-Coğrafya Fakültesi dergisi
Frequency varies: 1 (1942) - 6 (1948),
bi-monthly; 7 (1949) - 16 (1959),
quarterly; 18 (1960) - 27 (1969),
semi-annual; 28 onwards, irregular

BL:OIOC: 1 (11-12.1942) -   [14498.c.3]
LO:SOAS: 1 -   [Per.10.L.48181]
OX:BOD: 1 -   [Per.Turk.d.460]

FAN VA TURMUŞ / Üzbekiston SSR Fanlar
Akademiyasining oylik ilmiy-ommabop
curnali
1933, no.1 -
Tashkent
ISSN 0134-4560
In Uzbek

BL:OIOC: 1957:1 (3.1957) - ; lacking
1969:1-12, 1971:6-12 and a few others
[14499.tt.1]

FAROUC ATHÈNES
See: FARUK

FARUK: bilâ tefrik-i cins ü mezheb,
hakimiyet-i milliye-i Osmaniye'ye hadim
bitaraf gazetedir
Numero 1 (25 Teşrinisani 1327 [7 Dec.
1911] - Numero 2 [date?]
Athens
Added title: ''Farouc Athènes''
Frequency unknown

BL:OIOC: 1 (7.12.1911)   [ORB.30/43]

FÂTİH VE İSTANBUL / İstanbul Fethi
Derneği tarafından yayınlayan iki aylık
dergi
1. cild, 1. sayı (29 Mayıs 1953) - 2.
cild, 7-12 sayı (29 Mayıs 1954)
Istanbul
Superseded from 1955 by: İstanbul
Enstitüsü mecmuası
Subtitle varies
Bi-monthly; described in final issue as
annual

BL:OIOC: 1:1 (29.5.1953) - 2:7-12
(29.5.1954)   [14498.a.15]
LO:SOAS: 1:1 - 2:7-12   [Per.10.L.97193]
CA:UL: 1:1 - 2:7-12   [T.830.b.6]
DU:UL: 1:1 - 1:6 (lacking title pages)
[Per./PL14]
OX:BOD: 1:1 - 2:7-12   [Per.Turk.d.409]

FELSEFE ARKİVİ / İstanbul Üniversitesi
  Edebiyat Fakültesi, Felsefe Bölümü
  Cilt 1, no.1 [1945] –
  İstanbul
  Added titles, from 22/23 on: Archives of
  Philosophy; Archives de Philosophie;
  Archiv für Philosophie
  Some articles in French or German
  Irregular

  BL:OIOC: 1:1 [1945] – 21 [1978]
  [14498.cc.47]
  LO:SOAS: 1:1 –   [Per.10.65380]
  OX:BOD: 1:1 – 26 (1987); lacking 25
  (1986)   [Per.Turk.d.2866]

FELSEFE BÖLÜMÜNÜN ESERLERİ =
  Trudy sektora filosofii / Azerbaycan
  SSR Elmler Akademiyası
  Cild 1 [1958] – 4 cild [1963]
  Baku
  Articles in Azeri or Russian
  Occasional

  LO:SOAS: 1 [1958] – 4 [1963]
  [Per.10.268499]

FELSEFE DERGİSİ
  1 (Kasım-Aralık 1977) –
  İstanbul: Kavram
  Quarterly

  BL:OIOC: 1 (11-12.1977) – 11
  (4-5-6.1980)   [14498.cc.41]

FELSEFE VE İCTİMAİYAT MECMUASI: ayda
  bir neşrolunur / Türk Felsefe
  Cemiyetinin resmî organıdır
  Sene 1, sayı 1 (Mayıs [1]927) – 2. yıl,
  sayı 2 (1929/1930)
  İstanbul
  In Ottoman before Year 2, no.1
  (July-Sep. 1929)
  Monthly until no.6, then irregular; not
  published between Oct. 1928 and Sep.
  1929

  OX:MEC: 1:1 (5.1927) – 2:2 (1929/1930)
  [APT Fel 1]

FELSEFE YILLIĞI
  1. sene (1931-1932) – 2 (1934-1935)
  İstanbul, 1932-1935

  BL:OIOC: 1 (1931-1932) – 2 (1934-1935)
  [14498.a.70]

FEN-EDEBİYAT FAKÜLTESİ ARAŞTIRMA
  DERGİSİ / Atatürk Üniversitesi
  Fen-Edebiyat Fakültesi
  Erzurum: Atatürk Üniversitesi, 1985-
  Continuation of: Edebiyat Fakültesi
  Araştırma dergisi
  Occasional

  LO:SOAS: 1:13 (1985) –   [Per.10.264558]

FEVAİD: haftada bir neşrolunur fennî ve
  edebî risale
  1. sene, numero 1 (Şubat? 1308 [1893])
  – 3. sene, numero [?] ([date?] 1311
  [1896])
  Bursa: Kitabhane-i Emrî

  BL:OIOC: 2:2 (17.2.1894) – 2:29, 31, 33,
  30, 46; 3:6-8, 3:20-22 (30.11.1895);
  lacking part of 2:23 pp.1-2
  [14498.cc.93]

FİKİR HAREKETLERİ: ilmî, içtimaî,
  edebî haftalık risale
  Yıl 1, sayı 1 (29 Teşrinievvel 1933) –
  Cild 14, sayı 364 (12 Teşrinievvel
  1940)
  İstanbul

  OX:BOD: 1:1 (29.10.1933) – 14:364
  (12.10.1940)   [Turk.c.70]

FİKİRLER / İzmir Halkevi dergisi
  Sayı 1 ([date?]) – [?]
  İzmir

  BL:OIOC: 296/297 (30.6.1945) (two
  copies)   [ITA.1986.c.18 (7)]

FIRAT ÜNİVERSİTESİ DERGİSİ, SOSYAL
  BİLİMLER
  Cilt 1, sayı 1 (1987) –
  Elazığ
  Semi-annual

  BL:OIOC: 1:1 (1987) –   [ZOR.1988.a.109]

FISHERY STATISTICS
  See: SU ÜRÜNLERİ İSTATİSTİKLERİ

FİYAT İSTATİSTİKLERİ
  See: TOPTAN FİYAT İSTATİSTİKLERİ

FOLKLOR: aylık halkbilimi dergisi / Türk
  Folkloru Kurumu tarafından ayda bir
  çıkarılmaktadır
  Yıl 1, sayı 1 (Mayıs 1969) – Yıl 3, sayı
  31 (10 Mart 1984)
  İstanbul
  Initially monthly; later irregular

  BL:OIOC: 1:1 (5.1969) – 3:31 (10.3.1984)
  [ITA.1988.a.62]
  LO:SOAS: 1:1 – 3:30   [Per.10.259632]
  OX:BOD: 1:1 –   [Per.Turk.d.3314]

FOLKLOR ARAŞTIRMALARI KURUMU YILLIĞI
  [1] (1975)
  Ankara

  BL:OIOC: [1] (1975)   [14439.f.106]

FOLKLOR POSTASI: aylık halk bilgisi
  dergisi
  Cilt 1, sayı 1 [1. Teşrin 1944] – Cilt
  2, no. 19 (Ekim, Kasım, Aralık 1946)
  İstanbul
  Monthly to 2:17 (June 1946); quarterly
  thereafter

  BL:OIOC: 1:1 [10.1944] – 2:19
  (10-12.1946)   [ITA.1989.a.673]

FOLKLOR VE ETNOGRAFYA ARAŞTIRMALARI
  1984 –
  İstanbul
  Includes summaries in English
  Annual?

  BL:OIOC: 1984 –   [14498.cc.83]

FOLKLORA DOĞRU / Boğaziçi Üniversitesi
  Türk Folkloru Kulübü tarafından iki
  ayda bir yayınlanır
  1 (Temmuz-Ağustos [?] 1968) – 47/49
  (1978)
  İstanbul
  Bi-monthly; latterly irregular

  LO:SOAS: 34 (3-4.1974) – 47/49 (1978)
  [Per.10.326713]

FOREIGN POLICY
  See: DIŞ POLİTİKA

FOREIGN TRADE STATISTICS
  See: DIŞ TİCARET İSTATİSTİKLERİ

FORESTRY STATISTICS
  See: ORMANCILIK İSTATİSTİK ALBÜMÜ

FORUM
  See also: YENİ FORUM

FORUM: onbeş günlük tarafsız siyaset
iktisat kültür dergisi
Cilt 1, sayı 1 (1 Nisan 1954) - Cilt 15,
sayı 379 (28 Nisan 1970)
Ankara
No. 36 (15.9.1955) believed to have been
seized before publication ; no. 37
(1.10.1955) bears the number 36

LO:SOAS: 324 (1.10.1967) - 326
(1.11.1967); 331 (15.1.1968) - 343
(15.7.1968)   [L.E.Per.552303]
OX:BOD: 1:1 (1.4.1954) - 379
(28.4.1970); lacking 36 (15.9.1955)
[Per.Turk.c.108]
OX:MEC: 4:106 (15.8.1958) - 15:379
(28.4.1970)   [APT For]

FOTOĞRAF HABERLERİ: her perşembe
çıkar, hadiseleri fotoğrafla bildirir
Numara 1 (1 İkinci Teşrin 1934) -
Numara 9 (27 Birincikânun 1934)
İstanbul

BL:OIOC: 1 (1.11.1934) - 9 (27.12.1934)

FREIHEIT DES OSTENS
See: AZADÎ-İ ŞARK

FUKARA FÜYUZATI: ĕdĕbî, fĕnnî,
siyasî, ictimâî musavvĕr iki
haftalık Türkce mĕcmua-i İslâmiyedir
/ [Azĕrbaycan] Harbi İnkılab
Komitĕsinin nâşir-i efkârıdır
1. sene, numero 1 (1 Sentyabr 1920) - 1.
sene, numero 3 (28 April 1921)
Baku
Azeri; Arabic characters
Irregular; no.2 dated 1 Nov. 1920

BL:OIOC: 1:1 (1.9.1920) - 1:3
(28.4.1921)   [14499.tt.28]

GARAGUM: Türkmen yazıçılarınıñ ayda bir
gezek çikyan ĕdebi-çeper curnalı /
Türkmenistan Yazıçılar Soyuzınıñ
organı
No. 1 ([date?] 1928) -
Ashkhabad
ISSN 0205-9975
Title to end of 1991: Sovet ĕdebiyatı
In Turkmen

BL:OIOC: 1969:1 -; lacking 1974:5,
1976:12, 1977:8, 1982:5, 1984:6
[14499.tt.13]
LO:SOAS: 1967:9 -; lacking 1977:11-12,
1980:6   [Per.10.216221]
OX:BOD: 1985:5 -   [Per.Turk.d.3453]

GARBA DOĞRU: inkılâp kültür mecmuası
Sene 1, cilt 1, no.1 (1 Ağustos 1930) -
Yıl 1, no. 2 (1 Kânunuevvel 1930)
İstanbul

BL:OIOC: 1:1 (1.8.1930) - 1:2
(1.12.1930)   [14498.a.104]

GAS AND WATER STATISTICS
See: HAVAGAZI VE SU İSTATİSTİKLERİ

GAYRET
1. sene, nu. 1 (3 Kanunusani 1301 [16
Jan. 1886]) - 1. sene, nu. 33 (19 Eylül
1302 [2 Oct. 1886])
Istanbul
Weekly newspaper

CA:UL: 1:1 (16.1.1886) - 1:33
(2.10.1886)   [T.830.a.15]

GAZİ EĞİTİM ENSTİTÜSÜ ARAŞTIRMA VE
İNCELEMELERİ BÜLTENİ
No. 1 (Haziran 1961) - [?]
Ankara: Gazi Eğitim Enstitüsü
Öğrenci Derneği
Irregular

LO:SOAS: 1 (6.1961) - 2 (3.1962)
[Per.10.158663]

GAZİANTEP İL YILLIĞI
[1] (1968) - [2] (1973)
Ankara; Gaziantep, 1969-1973

BL:OIOC: [1] (1968)   [14498.a.53]
OX:BOD: [1]   [Turk.d.3324/27]

GELİŞME DERGİSİ
See: ODTÜ. GELİŞME DERGİSİ

GENÇ KALEMLER: onbeşte bir intişar eder
edebî, ilmî mecmua: yeni lisan ve yeni
hayat müdafii
1. cilt, numero 1 ([date?], 1326 [1910])
- 4. cilt, numero 27 ([date?], 1328
[1912]
Thessaloniki
Subtitles vary

BL:OIOC: 1:10 (?.?.1911), 1:13
(31.1.1911) - 1:14 (22.2.1911); 2:1
(?.?.1911) - 4:27 (2.10.1912)
[ITA.1986.c.15]

GENÇLER DÜNYASI: siyasî, ictimaî,
inkılabî, fennî, edebî gençler
mecmua sıdır / Türkiye Komünist
Gençler Birliği Teşkilât Byürosunun
nâşir-i efkârıdır
1. sene, 1 nci sayı (Teşrinisani 1920)
- [?]
Baku
Ottoman
Monthly?

BL:OIOC: 1 (11.1920)   [ITA.1986.c.14]

GENÇLİĞİN SESİ: aylık dergi / T. C.
Kültür Bakanlığı
Sayı 1 (Mayıs 1990) -
Ankara
Serious magazine for Turkish youth

BL:OIOC: 2 (6.1990) -   [ZOR.1990.a.165]
CA:OS: 2 (6.1990) -   [enquire for
location]

GENÇLİK: üç ayda bir çıkar fikrî,
içtimai, kültürel dergi / Kıbrıs
Türk Lisesi Mezunlar Kurumu dergisi
Yıl 1, sayı 1 (Şubat 1951) - Yıl 9,
sayı 1 (Şubat 1959)
Lefkoşa
Generally three issues annually

BL:OIOC: 1:1 (1.1951) - 1:3 (8.1951)
[14498.a.111]

GENEL DİLBİLİM DERGİSİ / Ankara
Dilbilim Çevresi
Cilt 1, sayı 1 ([date?] [1977?]) - [?]
Ankara

BL:OIOC: 1:2 (7.1978)   [ITA.1986.a.564]

GERÇEK: haftalık siyasî gazete
1 (4 Haziran 1975) - 188 (8 Eylül 1980)
Istanbul
Subtitle varies slightly
Weekly; initially fortnightly

DU:DC: 1:5 (10.9.1975)-3:40 (16.5.1978);
lacking 1:1-4, 13-14; 2:16, 21; 3:38
[25/3/POLITICAL PARTIES]

GİRESUN İL YILLIĞI
[1] (1967) - [2] (1973)
Ankara, 1968-1973

BL:OIOC: [1] (1967)   [14498.a.28]
OX:BOD: [1]   [Turk.d.3324/28]

GOBUSTAN: incĕsĕnĕt toplusu /
Azĕrbaycan Sovet Bĕstĕkarlar,
Rĕssamlar, Me'marlar,
Kinematografçılar İttifaglarının vĕ
Teatr Cĕmiyyĕtinin nĕşri
1969, no. 1 - [?]
Baku: Azĕrnĕşr
In Azeri. Some contents in Russian,
English, French, Arabic or Persian
Quarterly

BL:OIOC: 1970:1   [14499.t.41]

GORTSY KAVKAZA
See: KAFKASYA DAĞLILARI

GÖRÜŞ: edebiyat, sanat, tenkit
Cilt 1, sayı 1 (Temmuz 1930) - Cilt 1,
sayı 4 (Şubat 1932)
Ankara

BL:OIOC: 1:1-4   [14480.d.191]

GÖRÜŞ / [Türk Sanayiciler ve İş
Adamları Derneği]
Cilt 1, sayı 1 (Ocak 1973) -
Istanbul
Monthly

DU:DC: 3:10 (10.1975) - 5:9 (9.1977);
lacking 4:6, 4:11, 5:2-6
[25/4/INDUSTRY/GENERAL]

GÖSTERİ: sanat-edebiyat; ayda bir
yayımlanır
Yıl 1, sayı 1 (Aralık 1980) -
Istanbul

OX:BOD: 1:1 (12.1980) -
[Per.Turk.d.3359]

GRAND ANNUAIRE ILLUSTRÉ
See: BÜYÜK SALNAME

GUGUK: cumartesi ve çarşamba günleri
çıkar, doğrudan kıl kadar şaşmaz,
haktan hiçbir vakit ayrılmaz
milliyetperver mizah gazetesidir
1. sene, numero 1 (2 Ağustos 1340
[1924]) - 1. sene, numero 18 (1
Teşrinievvel 1340 [1924])
Istanbul

BL:OIOC: 1:1 (2.8.1924) - 1:18
(1.10.1924)   [14498.a.60/2]

GULİSTON: adabiy-badiy-oynoma / muassisi,
Guliston curanalistlar camoasi; noşir,
Üzbekiston Respublikasi Şark
naşriyot-matbaa kontserni
No. 1 ([date?] 1925) -
Tashkent
ISSN 0134-2207
Uzbek

BL:OIOC: 1967:1 - 1968:12; 1973:11;
1984:4-6,8,10-12; 1985:1 -
[14499.tt.12]
LO:SOAS: 1989:1 (= 467) (1.1989) -
[Per.10.L.588850]
OX:BOD: 1985:1 -   [Per.Turk.c.192]

GÜLŞEN-İ EDEB: risale-i edebiye ve
fenniyedir
Cilt 1, sayı 1 (4 Mart 1315 [17 Mar.
1889]) - Cilt 1, sayı 8 (22 Nisan 1315
[5 May 1889])
Istanbul
Weekly

OX:BOD: 1:8 (5.5.1889)   [Turk.d.2278 33
(3)]

GÜMÜŞHANE İL YILLIĞI
[1] (1967) - [2] (1973)
Ankara, 1968-1973

BL:OIOC: [1] (1967)   [14498.a.45]
OX:BOD: [1]   [Turk.d.3324/29]

ĠUNÇA: maktabgaça yoşdagi bolalar va
boşlangiç sinf ükuvçilari uçun /
Üzbekiston LKSM Markaziy Komiteti va V.
İ. Lenin nomli pioner taşkiloti
Respublika Sovetining curnali
No. 1 (Yanvar' 1967) -
Tashkent
Uzbek
Monthly

BL:OIOC: 1967:1 - 1968:12
[14499.tt.11]

GÜNEŞ: sanat ve edebiyat mecmuası
Sayı 1 (1 Kanunusani 1927) - 1. sene,
sayı 17 (1 Teşrinievvel 1927)
[Istanbul]
Fortnightly

BL:OIOC: 1 (1.1.1927) - 1:17 (1.10.1927)
[14498.a.105]
OX:BOD: 1 - 1:15 (1.9.1927)
[Turk.c.68]

GÜNEŞ: mesail-i siyasiye'den maada
herşeyden bahseder, onbeş günde bir
neşrolunur
Cilt 1, sayı 1 (1301 [1885]) - Cilt 1,
sayı 12 (1301 [1885 or 1886])
Istanbul
Issues dated by year only

OX:BOD: 1:1 (1885) - 1:12 (1885-1886)
[Turk.e.998]

GÜNEY-DOĞU AVRUPA ARAŞTIRMALARI
DERGİSİ / İstanbul Üniversitesi
Edebiyat Fakültesi
1 (1972) -
Istanbul
Some contributions are in western
languages
Annual

BL:OIOC: 1 (1972) -   [14498.cc.79]
LO:SOAS: 1 -   [Per.10.285519]
CA:UL: 1 -   [P.617.c.51]
OX:BOD: 1 -   [Per.Turk.d.3215]

GÜNLÜK YAĞIŞ BÜLTENİ / T. C. Tarım
Bakanlığı Devlet Meteoroloji İşleri
Genel Müdürlüğü
Yıl 1 (1963) - [?]
Ankara
Title of publishing Ministry varies

BL:HSS: 1 (1963) - 10 (1972)
[S.Q.152/2]

GÜNÜMÜZDE KİTAPLAR: aylık kültür
dergisi
Sayı 1 (1 Ocak 1984) - 24 (Aralık 1985)
Istanbul

BL:OIOC: 1 (1.1.1984) - 24 (12.1985)
[ITA.1987.a.313]
OX:BOD: 1 - 24   [Per.Turk.d.3309]

GÜZEL SANATLAR / Maarif Vekilliği
tarafından çıkarılır sanat mecmuası
1 (Ekim 1939) - 6 (Ocak 1949)
Istanbul
Lavishly-produced magazine on the visual
and performing arts
Title of publishing body varies
Title of first issue: Güzelsanatlar
Irregular; initially designated as
four-monthly

BL:OIOC: 1 (10.1939) - 6 (1.1949)
[14498.k.3]
LO:SOAS: 1 - 6   [Per.107.L.56959]

GÜZEL SANATLAR FAKÜLTESİ DERGİSİ /
Ege Üniversitesi Güzel Sanatlar
Fakültesi
Sayı 1 (1980) -
Izmir
Irregular; originally annual

OX:BOD: 1 (1980) -   [Per.Turk.c.190]

GÜZELSANATLAR
See: GÜZEL SANATLAR

HABER BÜLTENİ / ORMAN BAKANLIĞI ORMAN
GENEL BAKANLIĞI
See: ORMAN BAKANLIĞI AYLIK BÜLTENİ

HACETTEPE BULLETIN OF SOCIAL SCIENCES AND
HUMANITIES
See: HACETTEPE ÜNİVERSİTESİ SOSYAL
VE İDARİ BİLİMLER FAKÜLTESİ
BEŞERİ BİLİMLER DERGİSİ

HACETTEPE SOSYAL VE BEŞERİ BİLİMLER
DERGİSİ
See: HACETTEPE ÜNİVERSİTESİ SOSYAL
VE İDARİ BİLİMLER FAKÜLTESİ
BEŞERİ BİLİMLER DERGİSİ

HACETTEPE ÜNİVERSİTESİ BÜLTENİ =
Hacettepe University bulletin
[1] (1969-1970) - [2] (1972)
Ankara
Annual

DU:DC: [1](1969-1970)   [25/4/EDUCATION]

HACETTEPE ÜNİVERSİTESİ EDEBİYAT
FAKÜLTESİ DERGİSİ
Cilt 1, sayı 1 (1983) -
Ankara
Chiefly in Turkish; some contributions
in English, French or German
Biennial

OX:BOD: 1:1 (1983) -   [Per.Turk.d.3545]

HACETTEPE ÜNİVERSİTESİ EĞİTİM
FAKÜLTESİ DERGİSİ
Yıl 1986, sayı 1 -
Ankara
Annual

OX:BOD: 1986:1 -   [Per.Turk.d.3951]

HACETTEPE ÜNİVERSİTESİ SOSYAL VE
İDARİ BİLİMLER FAKÜLTESİ BEŞERİ
BİLİMLER DERGİSİ
Cilt 1, sayı 1 (Mart 1969) -
Ankara
Title of earlier issues: Hacettepe
sosyal ve beşeri bilimler dergisi.
Added English title (earlier issues) :
Hacettepe bulletin of social sciences
and humanities
Articles in Turkish, English, French or
German
Irregular

BL:OIOC: 1980, special issue (B. Cömert
Festschrift)   [14480.d.243]
DU:DC: 2:1 (3.1970) - 8:1 (10.1976)
[25/4/EDUCATION]

HACETTEPE UNIVERSITY BULLETIN
See: HACETTEPE ÜNİVERSİTESİ
BÜLTENİ

HÂDİSELERE TERCÜMAN
See: TERCÜMAN: GÜNLÜK MÜSTAKIL
SIYASI GAZETE

HAFTA: edebiyat ve fünun ve sanayi'e dair
mecmuadır
1. cild, aded 1 (22 Ramazan 1298 [18
Aug. 1881]) - 1. cild, aded 20 (21 Safer
1299 [12 Jan. 1882])
[Istanbul]
Weekly

BL:OIOC: 1:1 (18.8.1881) - 1:20
(12.1.1882)   [14480.d.84]
OX:BOD: 1:1 - 1:20   [Per.Turk.d.3095]

HAFTALIK ENFORMASYON BÜLTENİ / [İhracat
Geliştirme Etüd Merkezi]
Yıl 1, sayı 1 ([date?], 1963) -
Ankara

DU:DC: 20:16 (23.4.1982) - 22:13
(30.3.1984)   [25/4/TRADE/INTERNATIONAL]

HAFTALIK HABER BÜLTENİ / [Eskişehir
Sanayi Odası]
Eskişehir, [1971?] -
Numbering of issues is inconsistent

DU:DC: 1974:1-10, 12-18, 20-34, 37-78;
1975:1-3, 5, 219-235, 237-238, 240-241
[sic]   [25/4/INDUSTRY/GENERAL]

HAFTALIK RESİMLİ İSTANBUL
See: RESİMLİ İSTANBUL

HAKÂİK ÜL-VAKAYİ: umumun menafii için
her nev'-i havadisten bahseder gazetedir
Numero 1 (3 Cemaziyelahir 1287 [3 Sep.
1870] - numero? (23 Zilkade 1289 [6 Feb.
1872])
[İstanbul]
Newspaper. With supplements to each
issue, under the title: İlâve-i
Hakâik
Subtitle of early işsues: menafi-i
şarkiye ve umur-u düveliye'ye dair
Türk gazetesidir
Published five times weekly

BL:OIOC: 1 (3.9.1870) - 98 (7.12.1870);
595 (9.6.1872); lacking 84 (23.11.1870)
[14498.a.61]

HAKİKAT = La Vérité: Cuma ve
Pazarlardan başka her gün yani haftada
beş defa çıkar dahilî ve haricî
bilcümle havadisten bahseder
gayriresmî gazetedir
Numero 1 ([date?] 1293 [1876]) - Numero
305 ([date?] 1294 [1877])
Istanbul
In Ottoman and French
Generally five issues weekly

BL:OIOC: 1:87 (29.3.1877)   [O.P. 3
(11)]

HÂKİMİYET-İ MILLİYE
See: ULUS

HAKKÂRİ İL YILLIĞI
[1] (1967) - [2] (1973)
Ankara, 1972-[197-?]

OX:BOD: [1] (1967)   [Turk.d.3324/30]

HALEB VİLÂYETİ SALNAMESİ
See: SALNAME-İ VİLÂYET-İ HALEB

HALK BİLGİSİ HABERLERİ /
İstanbul-Eminönü Halkevi Dil ve
Edebiyat Şubesi tarafından çıkarılır
aylık folklor mecmuası
Yıl 1, sayı 1 (Teşrinisani 1929) - Yıl
17, sayı 125 (Ocak 1947)
Istanbul, 1930-1942
Early issues published by: H[alk]
B[ilgisi] D[erneği] İstanbul Merkezi

BL:OIOC: 1:1 (1.11.1929) - 11:124
(2.1942)   [14469.g.3]
LO:SOAS: 1:1 - 17:125; lacking 4:48,
5:56, 6:61, 6:65, 8:91, 8:93, 10:109,
10:111 - 10:112, 10:120, ?:123 - ?:124
   [Per.10.389688]
DU:UL: 3:30 (15.11.1933) - 4:41
(15.10.1934)   [Per./PL4]

HALK BİLGİSİ MECMUASI / Halk Bilgisi
Derneği tarafından neşr olunur
1. cild (1928)
Ankara
Only one issue published
In Arabic characters, excepting title
headings of articles

BL:OIOC: 1 (1928)   [14469.g.1;
14498.cc.69; 14498.cc.69*]
OX:BOD: 1   [Turk.d.2487]

HALK EĞİTİMİ BÜLTENİ / Millî
Eğitim Bakanlığı Halk Eğitimi Genel
Müdürlüğü
Cilt 1, sayı 1 (Mart 1966) -
Ankara
Bi-monthly

DU:DC: 4:24 (7.1970)   [25/4/EDUCATION]

HALK KÜLTÜRÜ
1984/1 -
Istanbul
Quarterly

BL:OIOC: 1984:1 -   [14480.d.206]
OX:BOD: 1984:1 -   [Per.Turk.d.3278]

HALKA DOĞRU: haftada bir / "Türk Yurdu"
tarafından çıkarılır
Yıl 1, sayı 1 (11 Nisan 1329 [1913]) -
Yıl 1, sayı 52 (3 Nisan 1330 [1914])
Istanbul

BL:OIOC: 1:1 (11.4.1913) - 1:52
(3.4.1914)   [ITA.1989.a.272]
OX:BOD: 1:1 - 1:52   [Per.Turk.d.3548]

HALKBİLİMİ: yılda dört sayı yayımlanır
/ Halk Sanatları Derneği yayınıdır
86/1 (Temmuz 1986) -
Lefkoşa

BL:OIOC: [19]86:1 (7.1986) - 5:17/18
(1-3.1990)   [ITA.1993.a.342]
OX:BOD: [19]86:1 -   [Per.Turk.c.206]

HALKIN SESİ: hakkın sesi ve halkın
dilidir
Yıl 1, sayı 1 ([date?], 1942) -
Lefkoşa
National newspaper of Turkish Cypriots
Daily

BL:OIOC: 25:7344 (11.8.1966) - 27:8295
(31.12.1968); 30:9070 (1.8.1971) -
31:9518 (31.10.1972); 32:9937 (7.1.1974)
- 33:10084 (30.6.1974); 33:10227
(1.12.1974) - 33:10255 (31.12.1974);
38:12013 (1.12.1979) - 40:15212
(14.10.1981); lacking a few issues
[O.P.913]

HAMİDİYE ETFÂL HASTAHANE-İ ÂLİSİ
İSTATİSTİK MECMUA-İ TIBBİYESİ =
Annales médicales et bulletin de
l'Hôpital d'Enfants Hamidié
1. sene (1316 [1900]) - 8. sene (1323
[1907])
Istanbul
Some issues entitled: Hamidiye Etfâl
Hasatahane-i Âlisi istatistik risalesi
= Bulletin de statistique annuelle de
l'Hôpital d'Enfants Hamidié
Some issues entitled: Hamidiye Etfâl
Hastahane-i Âlisi istatistik risalesi =
Bulletin de statistique annuelle de
l'Hôpital d'Enfants Hamidié
Ottoman and French

BL:OIOC: 2 (1901) - 8 (1907)
[14442.e.2]

HAMİDİYE ETFÂL HASTAHANE-İ ÂLİSİ
İSTATİSTİK RİSALESİ
See: HAMİDİYE ETFÂL HASTAHANE-İ
ÂLİSİ İSTATİSTİK MECMUA-İ
TIBBİYESİ

HAMİYET: âsar-ı edebiye ve mevadd-ı
fenniye'yi hâvidir, onbeş günde bir
neşrolunur
Sene 1, numara 1 (17 Nisan 1302 [30 Apr.
1886]) - Sene 1, numara 17 (15
Kanunuevvel 1302 [28 Dec. 1886])
Istanbul

OX:BOD: 1:1 (30.4.1886) - 1:17
(28.12.1886)   [Per.Turk.c.206]

HAMLE: edebiyatda, sanatda, fikirde,
ilimde
Cild 1, sayı 1 (Ağustos 1940) - Cild 1,
sayı 5 (Birincikânun 1940)
Istanbul
Monthly

OX:BOD: 1:1 (8.1940) - 1:5 (12.1940)
[Per.Turk.d.3546]

HANEHALKI İŞGÜCÜ ANKETİ SONUÇLARI =
Household labour force survey results /
Başbakanlık Devlet İstatistik
Enstitüsü
Ekim 1988 -
Ankara, 1990-
In Turkish and English
Semi-annual

SU:IDS: 10.1988 -
[SERIALS/OFFICIAL/TURKEY]

HANIM KIZLARA MAHSUS
See: HANIMLARA MAHSUS GAZETE'NİN HANIM
KIZLARA MAHSUS KISMI

HANIMLARA MAHSUS GAZETE'NİN HANIM KIZLARA
MAHSUS KISMI
Numero 1 (19 Şubat [1]313 [4 Mar.
1918]) - Numero 52 (25 Şubat 1314 [10
Mar. 1919])
Istanbul
Published in three series: 1-580;
1-[53?]; 1-43
Weekly

OX:BOD: 1 (4.3.1918) - 52 (10.3.1919)
[Per.Turk.d.1847]

AL-ḤAQÎQAH
See: EL-HAKİKA

HARB MECMUASI: onbeş günde bir çıkar
asker ve muharebeden bahseder risale-i
musavvere
Yıl 1, sayı 1 (Teşrinisani 1331 [1915])
- Yıl 3, sayı 27 (Haziran 1334 [1918])
İstanbul
Wartime military propaganda magazine
Irregular, despite subtitle; generally
monthly

BL:OIOC: 1:1 (10.1915) - 3:27 (6.1918)
[14498.a.10]
OX:BOD: 1:1 - 3:27   [Turk.c.171]
OX:MEC: 1:1 - 3:27   [APT Har]

HARB TARİHİ VESİKALARI DERGİSİ
See: HARP TARİHİ VESİKALARI DERGİSİ

HARP MECMUASI
See: HARB MECMUASI

HARP TARİHİ VESİKALARI DERGİSİ: üç
ayda bir çıkarılır / Genelkurmay
Başkanlığı Harp Tarihi Dairesi
Yıl 1, sayı 1 (Eylül 1952) - Yıl 31,
sayı 82 (Ekim 1982)
Ankara
Journal published as a supplement to:
Ordu dergisi
Other titles: issues 68-76: Harb tarihi
vesikaları dergisi; 77-82: Askeri tarih
belgeleri dergisi
Includes many documents in Ottoman

BL:OIOC: 1:1 (9.1952) - 31:82 (10.1982)
[ITA.1988.a.530]
OX:BOD: 1:1 - 10:38   [Per.Turk.d.732]

HATAY İL YILLIĞI
[1] (1967) - [2] (1973)
Istanbul, 1968-1973

BL:OIOC: [1] (1967)   [14498.a.47]
OX:BOD: [1]   [Turk.d.3324/31]

HAVADİS
Yıl 1, sayı 1 ([date?, 1955 or 1956]) -
[?]
İstanbul
Daily newspaper

BL:OIOC: 4:1305 (31.5.1960)
[OR.MIC.12616 (O.P. 552/16)]

HAVAGAZI VE SU İSTATİSTİKLERİ = Gas
and water statistics / Başbakanlık
Devlet İstatistik Enstitüsü
Ankara, [19--?]-
Turkish and English
Annual

SU:IDS: 1984   [SERIALS/OFFICIAL/TURKEY]

HAVÂTIR: vakt-i müsaidde neşrolunur,
fevaid-i Osmaniye' den bâhis gazetedir
Sene 1, numero 1 (5 Ağustos 1314 [18
Aug. 1898]) - Sene 3, numero 15 ([date?]
1316 [1900 or 1901])
Cairo
Irregular

BL:OIOC: 1:11 (30.3.1899) - 1:13
(3.5.1899)   [14498.d.21(2)]

HAVER: onbeş günde bir cüz'
neşrolunur, siyasiyât'den mâ'adâ
herşeyden bahseder
Numero 1 (15 Cemaziyülahire 1301 [12
April 1884]) - Numero 4 (1 Şa'ban 1301
[27 May 1884]
İstanbul

LO:SOAS: 1 (12.4.1884) - 4 (27.5.1884)
[Per.10.188761]

HAYÂL
Numero 1 (27 Mayıs [18]95) - Numero 6
(15 Eylül [18]95)
London
Liberal political and satirical
newspaper
Irregular

BL:OIOC: 1 (27.5.1895) - 6 (15.9.1895)
[14498.d.5]

HAYÂL: onbeş günde bir neşrolunur
Numero 1 (7 Mart 1901) - Numero 5 (25
Mayıs 1901)
Paris
Satirical newspaper

BL:OIOC: 1 (7.3.1901) - 5 (25.5.1901)
[14498.d.17]

HAYÂL [1. SERİ]: işbu gazete haftada
iki defa neşrolunur
1. sene, numero 1 (18 Teşrinievvel 1289
[31 Oct. 1873]) - 2. sene, numero 100 (7
Eylül 1290 [20 Sep. 1874])
Istanbul
Illustrated satirical newspaper
Twice, sometimes thrice, weekly

LO:SOAS: 1:1 (31.10.1873) - 2:100
(20.9.1874)   [L.E.Per.305845]

HAYAT: aylık sanat ve kültür mecmuası
Sayı 1 (İkinci kânun [1939]) - [?]
İstanbul

BL:OIOC: 1 (1.1939) - 5 (6.1939)
[14498.cc.85]

HAYAT: haftalık mecmua
Sayı 1 (6 Nisan 1956) -
İstanbul
Popular general-interest magazine

BL:OIOC: 1 (6.4.1956) - 23:27
(29.6.1978)   [14498.a.10]

HAYAT [1. SERİ]: haftalık ilim, felsefe
ve sanat mecmuası
1. cild, sayı 1 (2 Kanunuevvel 1926) -
Cilt 6, sayı 146 (30 Kanunevvel 1929)
Ankara

BL:OIOC: 1:2 (9.12.1926) - 6:146
(30.12.1928)   [14498.a.14]
LO:SOAS: 1:1 - 6:133 (13.6.1929)
[Per.1O.L.136644]
OX:BOD: 1:1 - 6:146   [Per.Turk.c.63]
OX:MEC: 1:1 (2.12.1926) - 4:104
(22.11.1928)   [APT Hay]

HAYAT TARİH MECMUASI: aylık kültür
mecmuası
Yıl 1, sayı 1 (1 Şubat 1965) - Yıl 18,
sayı 12 (1 Aralık 1982)
İstanbul: Hayat
Title from Year 14, no. 4 (April 1978):
Tarih ve edebiyat mecmuası

LO:SOAS: 1:1 (1.2.1965) - 18:12
(1.12.1982); lacking 12:4 (4.1976), 12:8
(8.1976)   [Per.10.282330]

HAYR ÜL-KELÂM: din ve vatan'a hizmet,
azm-i hâlisanesiyle perşembe günleri
neşr olunur İslâm eseridir
Numero 1 (8 Teşrinisani 1329 (21 Nov.
1913) - 2. sene, numero 38 (24 Temmuz
1330 [6 Aug. 1914])
Istanbul
Subtitle varies

BL:OIOC: 1 (21.11.1913) - 2:38
(6.8.1914)   [ITA.1990.a.684]
CA:UL: 1 (8.11.1913) - 25 (24.4.1914)
[Q.830.b.9]

HAYRÜLKELÂM
See: HAYR ÜL-KELÂM

HAYVANLAR VE HAYVAN ÜRÜNLERİ
İSTATİSTİKLERİ = Livestock and
livestock products statistics /
Başbakanlık Devlet İstatistik
Enstitüsü
1935/1941 -
Ankara

BL:HSS: 1935/1941; 1945/1950
[S.Q.170/7]

HAZER
See: HAZER

HAZER: Azerbaycan edebiyatı dergisi
Yıl 1, sayı 1 (20 Nisan 1979) - Yıl 2,
sayı 17 (20 Ağustos 1980)
Istanbul
Contents in Azeri (roman characters) or
Istanbul Turkish
Monthly

BL:OIOC: 1:1 (20.4.1979) - 2:17
(20.8.1980)   [14499.o.234]
OX:BOD: 1:1 - 2:17   [Per.Turk.d.3362]

HAZİNE-İ FÜNUN: perşembe günleri
neşrolunur edebî ve fennî gazete
1. sene, aded 1 (3 Temmuz 1308 [16 July
1892]) - 4. sene, aded 52 (20 Ağustos
1312 [2 Sep. 1896])
Istanbul: Asır Kütüphanesi
Subtitle varies

LO:SOAS: 1:1 (16.7.1892) - 3:52
(2.9.1896)   [L.E.Per.137064]
CA:UL: 1:1 - 2:52 (21.6.1893)
[Q.830.b.5]

HĚLK MĚÂRİFİ: içtimaî, siyasî,
ělmî, fěnnî vě těrbiyěvî
mǎcmuadır, ayda bir děfa tab' vě
něşrědilěcěktir / Hělk Měârif
Komisarlığı
1. sene, numero 1 (15 Oktyabr 1920) -
[?]
Baku
Azeri; Arabic characters

BL:OIOC: 1:1 (15.10.1920)
[14499.tt.27]

HER AY: siyasa, ilim, sanat
Yıl 1, sayı 1 (20 Mart 1937) - Yıl 1,
sayı 7 (Mart 1938)
Istanbul
Generally monthly

BL:OIOC: 1:1 (20.3.1937) - 1:17 (3.1938)
[14498.cc.48]

HİCAZ VİLÂYETİ SALNAMESİ
Defa 1 (1301 [1883-1884]) - Defa 5 (1309
[1891-1892])
Mecca
Generally biennial

BL:OIOC: 1 (1883-1884)   [14496.c.3]
CA:UL: 4 (1889-1890)   [S.828.01.b.44]
OX:BOD: 1; 4   [Per.Turk.e.1467]

HİKMET: hakikat hadimi, akşamları
intişar eder, özü sözü doğru
Osmanlı gazetesidir
Sene 1, numero 1 (8 Nisan 1326 [21 Apr.
1910]) - Sene 2, numero 77 (9 Haziran
1327 [22 June 1911])
Istanbul
This publication fell foul of the
authorities and later appeared under the
following titles: Millet ile Musahabe,
Münakaşa, Kanad, Coşkun Kalender,
Kalender, Nimet, and (again) Hikmet
Weekly; at one time daily

OX:BOD: 1:1 (21.4.1910) - 2:75
(?.?.1911)   [Per.Turk.c.186]

HİLÂFET: onbeş günde bir defa tab'
olunur
1. sene, aded 1 ([20 Ekim], 1899) - 4.
sene, aded 92 (20 Ağustos 1903)
London
Newspaper on current political events
affecting the Ottoman state
Added title: Khilafat

BL:OIOC: 4:82 (15.12.1902)
[ORB.30/344]

HİLÂL: Meşrutiyetin istikrarına hadım
gazete, her gün neşrolunur
Numero 1 (7 Nisan 1325 [20 Apr. 1909]) -
Numero 3 (14 Nisan 1325 [27 Apr. 1909])
[Istanbul]

BL:OIOC: 1 (20.4.1909) - 3 (27.4.1909)
[14498.a.118]

HİSAR: aylık fikir ve sanat dergisi
Yıl 1, cilt 1, sayı 1 (16 Mart 1950) -
Cilt 20, sayı 199 = 274 (Eylül 1980)
Ankara

OX:BOD: 73 (1.1970) - 180 (=255)
(12.1978)   [Per.Turk.d.1725]

HISTORY OF MEDICINE STUDIES
See: TIP TARİHİ ARAŞTIRMALARI

HOCA NASRATTİN
1. sene, numara 1 (28 Ağustos 1930) -
1. sene, numara 69 (23 Nisan 1931)
İstanbul: [s.n.], 1930-1931
A popular secularist general-interest
magazine
Twice-weekly

BL:OIOC: 1:1 (28.8.1930) - 1:69
(23.4.1931)   [14498.a.98]

HOUKOUK-I-BÉCHÉR
See: HUKUK-İ BEŞER

HOUSEHOLD LABOUR FORCE SURVEY RESULTS
See: HANEHALKI İŞGÜCÜ ANKETI
SONUÇLARI

HÜDAVENDİGÂR VİLÂYETİ SALNAMESİ
Defa 1 (1286 [1869-1870]) - Defa 35
(1927)
Bursa
Title varies: Hüdavendigâr Vilâyeti
salnamesi, Salname, Salname-i
Hüdavendigâr, Bursa Vilâyeti
salnamesi

BL:OIOC: 12 (1885)   [14496.c.4]
LO:SOAS: 12; 28 (1901); 33 (1906) - 34
(1907)   [E.Per.280661]
CA:UL: (a) 33 - 34; (b) 35 (1927)
[S.828.01.b.46; (b) S.828.01.b.19]
DU:UL: 18 (1891); 24 (1897); 33 - 34
OX:BOD: 5 (1874); 8 (1877); 18; 27
(1900); 30 (1903); 33 - 35
[Per.Turk.d.1436]

HUKUK-İ BEŞER: her gün şabahleri
intişar eder müstakilülefkar,
muhtarülichad Osmanlı gazete
Yıl 1, nu. 1 [date? 1334 [1919]) - [?]
Istanbul
French title: Houkouk-i-Béchér: Le
Drit de l'Home [sic]

BL:OIOC: 1:59 (2.4.1919) - 1:67
(10.4.1919); lacking 1:61-62, 66
[OR.MIC.11707 (O.P.257)]

HUKUKİ BİLGİLER MECMUASI = Revue des
sciences juridiques: ayda bir
neşrolunur
Sene 1, numero 1 (Eylül 1926) - [?]
Istanbul, 1926-1942
Articles summarized in French

BL:OIOC: 1:1 (9.1926)   [14458.fff.135]

HULÂSAT ÜL-EFKÂR: tarîk-i terakki'ye
hizmet eder evrâk-i havâdistendir
1. sene, numero 1 (9 Mayıs 1289 [22 May
1873]) - 1. sene, numero 103 (17 Mayıs
1300 [30 May 1874])
Istanbul
Published five times weekly

BL:OIOC: 1:1 (22.5.1873) - 1:103
(30.5.1874)   [14498.a.114]
LO:SOAS: 1:1 - 1:50 (18.8.1873)
[L.E.Per.182843]

L'HUMANITÉ
See: İNSANİYET

HÜR FİKİRLER / Hür Fikirler Yayma
Cemiyetin neşir vasıtasıdır
Cilt 1, sayı 1 (Kasım 1948) - Cilt 1,
sayı 11 (Eylûl 1949)
Istanbul
Monthly

DU:UL: 1:1 (11.1948) - 1:11 (9.1949)
[Per./PL8]

HÜR MARKO PAŞA [1. SERİ]: haftalık
mizah gazetesi
Yıl 1, sayı 1 (7 Ocak 1949) - Yıl 1,
sayı 19 (12 Eylûl 1949)
Istanbul

BL:OIOC: 1:1 (7.1.1949) - 1:19
(12.9.1949)   [OR.FICHE 442]

HÜR MARKO PAŞA [2. SERİ]: haftalık
siyasî mizah gazetesi
Yıl 1, sayı 1 (27 Mart 1950) - [Yıl 1],
sayı 15 (10 Temmuz 1950)
Istanbul

BL:OIOC: 1:1 (27.3.1950) - [1:]15
(10.7.1950)   [OR.FICHE 443]

HURRIET (LA LIBERTÉ)
See: HÜRRİYET

HÜRRİYET: günlük müstakil siyasî
gazete
Sene 1, no.1 (1 Mayıs 1948) -
Istanbul

BL:OIOC: 28.5.1960, 30.5.1960, 1.6.1960,
10.10.1960; 28-29.4.1961, 5.8.1961,
7.8.1961, 12.8.1961, 14-17.9.1961,
10.10.1961, 20.10.1961, 23.11.1961,
8.12.1961   [OR.MIC.12609 (O.P. 552/9)]

HÜRRİYET: haftada bir kere neşredilir,
hâvi olduğu mebâhis millet ve
devlet-i Osmaniye'nin selamet ve
menafi'ine müteallık hüsusât olmakla
memalik-i şarkiye ehalisine mecanen
verilip yalnız posta ücreti alınır /
Yeni Osmanlılar Cemiyeti
Numero 1 (29 Haziran 1325 [12 July
1868]) - Numero 93 (29 Muharrem 1287 [1
May 1870])
London
Added title: Hurriyète (La Liberté)

BL:OIOC: 1 (12.7.1868) - 93 (1.5.1870);
lacking 53 (28.6.1869), 66 (27.9.1869)
[14498.d.1]
OX:BOD: 1 - 50 (7.6.1869)   [Turk.c.101]

HÜRRİYET: onbes günde bir defa Londrada
tab' olunur; bu gazete, teba' a-i
Osmaniye'nin hukuk-i meşrua-i
esasiyesini talıptır ve bütün namuslu
ve hürriyetperest ehalimizin
tercüman-i efkârıdır / müharriri ve
nâşiri, Cevânpir
Numero 1 (25 Receb 1311 [1 February
1894]) - 4. sene, numero 82 (15 Eylûl
1897])
London
Organ of constitutionalist dissent
Added title: Hurriet (La Liberté)
Fortnightly; weekly for issues 12-40

BL:OIOC: 1 (1.2.1894) - 4:82 (15.9.1897)
[14498.d.2]

HÜRRİYET ANSİKLOPEDİK YILLIĞI
See: HÜRRİYET YILLIĞI

HÜRRİYET YILLIĞI
[1] (1973) -
Istanbul: Hürriyet
Yearbook reviewing the past year's
events in Turkey and abroad
Previous title: Hürriyet ansiklopedik
yıllığı

BL:OIOC: [7] (1979) - [9] (1981); [13]
(1985)   [14498.a.77]

HURRIYÈTE (LA LIBERTÉ)
See: HÜRRİYET

İBRET: yevmî gazete
Sayı 1 (1 Haziran 1288 [14 June 1872]) -
Sayı 132 (24 Mart 1289 [6 Apr. 1873])
Istanbul

OX:BOD: (a) 1 (14.6.1872) - 128
(2.4.1874) (hard copy); (b) 126
(31.3.1873) - 132 (6.4.1873) (microfilm)
[Turk.b.11]

İÇ TİCARET İSTATİSTİKLERİ: ticaret
şirketleri, firmalar (ticaret
unvanları) ve tüketim kooperatifleri =
Internal trade statistics: commercial
companies, firms and consumers'
cooperative associations / Başbakanlık
Devlet İstatistik Enstitüsü
Ankara, [19--?]-
In Turkish and English
Annual

DU:DC: 1972; 1975 - 1976; 1980
[25/4/TRADE/INTERNAL]
SU:IDS: 1980 -
[SERIALS/OFFICIAL/TURKEY]

İÇ VARLIK
Cilt 1, sayı 1 (31 Mayıs 1951) - Cilt 6,
fasikül 69 [1957]
Ankara
A religious, ethical and cultural review
for the general public
Monthly

BL:OIOC: 1:1 (31.5.1951) - 6:69 [1957]

İÇEL İL YILLIĞI
[1] (1967) - [2] (1973)
Ankara, 1968-1973

BL:OIOC: [1] (1967)   [14498.a.62]
LO:SOAS: [1]   [Per.10.L.276432]
OX:BOD: [1]   [Turk.d.3324/32]

ICHTIRAK
See: İŞTİRAK

İCRAAT RAPORU VE ÇALIŞMA PROGRAMI
TASARISI / Ankara Teknik Ziraat
Müdürlüğü
Ankara, [19--?]-[19--?]
Annual

DU:DC: 1955 (1956)
[25/4/AGRICULTURE/GENERAL]

İCRAAT RAPORU VE İŞ PROGRAMI TASARISI /
Kayseri Teknik Ziraat Teşkilâtı
Kayseri, [19--?]-[19--?]
Annual

DU:DC: 1956 (1957)
[25/4/AGRICULTURE/GENERAL]

İCTİHAD [1. SERİ] = Idjtihad: libre
examen: ayda bir neşrolunur, serbest,
mecmua-i Osmaniye ve İslamiyedir
1. sene, numero 1 (1 Eylül 1904 [14
Sep. 1904]) - 1. sene, numero 12
(Haziran 1906)
Geneva
Contributions in Ottoman or French

BL:OIOC: 1:1 (14.9.1904) - 1:12
(6.1906); lacking 1:2   [14499.k.2]

İCTİHAD [2. SERİ]: felsefî, ictimaî,
edebî, iktisadî mecmua
1. sene, numero 1 ([date?], 1906) - 24.
sene, numero 265 (30 Teşrinisani 1928)
Cairo; Istanbul
Published first at Cairo, then (from
3:31) at Istanbul
Early issues have added title: Idjtihad:
libre examen. Subtitle varies
Issues 1-11 include contributions in
French
Fortnightly, monthly, or weekly

BL:OIOC: 2:2 (10.1906); 2:4 (9.1907) -
2:5 (1.1908); 3:25 (15.6.1911); 3:31
(15.9.1911); 17:139 (30.11.1921) -
20:169 (1.9.1924)   [14499.k.2]

İCTİMÂİYÂT MECMUASI / Darülfünun
İctimâiyât Darülmesâisi
neşriyatından
Sene 1, sayı 1 (Nisan 1917) - Sene 1,
sayı 6 (Eylül 1333 [1917])
Istanbul
Monthly

BL:OIOC: 1:1 (4.1917) - 1:6 (9.1917)
[ITA.1988.a.884]

İDARE DERGİSİ / İçişleri
Bakanlığınca çıkarılır
Yıl 1, sayı 1 ([date, [1930?]) - [?]
Ankara
Apparently bimonthly

LO:SOAS: 16:174 (5-6.1945) - 16:175
(7-8.1945)   [Per.10.48180]

IDJTIHAD
See: İCTİHAD

İGTİSADİYYAT BÖLMĚSİNİN
ĚSĚRLĚRİ = Trudy Sektora Ėkonomiki
/ Azěrbaycan SSR Ělmlěr Akademiyası
Cild 1 [1949] - 4 [1958]
Baku
Title of no. 4: İgtisadiyyat
İnstitutunun ěsěrlěri
Contents in Azeri or Russian
Occasional

BL:HSS: 1 (1949) - 3 (1956)
[Ac.1109.d.3]
LO:SOAS: 4 [1958]   [Per.67.262131]

İGTİSADİYYAT İNSTİTUTUNUN
ĚSĚRLĚRİ
See: İGTİSADİYYAT BÖLMĚSİNİN
ĚSĚRLĚRİ

İGTİSADİYYAT SERİYASI
See: AZĚRBAYCAN SSR ELMLĚR
AKADEMİYASININ HĚBĚRLĚRİ,
İGTİSADİYYAT SERİYASI

İGTİSADİYYAT VĚ HĚYAT: aylıg igtisadi
jurnal = Ėkonomika i zhizn':
ezhemesiāchnyi ėkonomicheskii
zhurnal / tě'sisçi, Azěrbaycan
Respublikası Nazirlěr Kabineti
1961, no. 1 (Yanvar 1961) -
Baku: Azěrbaycan SSR Dövlět Plan
Komitěsi
ISSN 0207-3021
Titles before 1991: Azěrbaycan halg
těsěrrüfatı = Narodnoe khoziaistvo
Azerbaidzhana
Articles in Azeri or Russian

SU:IDS: 7 (7.1990) -   [ZOR.1991.a.21]

İIBK BÜLTENİ / İş ve İşçi Bulma
Kurumu Genel Müdürlüğü
Sayı 1 ([Aralık 1976]) - sayı
103/104/105 (Haziran-Ağustos 1985)
Ankara
Nominally monthly; generally cumulated
as double or triple issues

DU:DC: 65-67 (4-6.1982) - 103-105
(6-8.1985)   [25/4/EMPLOYMENT]

İKDAM
1. sene, numero 1 (6 Temmuz 1310 [19
July 1894]) - [?] ([date?] 1928)
Istanbul
Daily newspaper

BL:OIOC: 22.8.1917; 14.9.1917 -
25.11.1917; 15.12.1917; 12.2.1918 -
29.6.1918; 13.7.1918 - 17.8.1918;
22.9.1918 - 1.10.1918; lacking 40 issues
[OR.MIC.11700 (O.P.249)]

İKTİSADİ RAPOR / Türkiye Ticaret,
Sanayi, Deniz Ticaret Odaları ve Ticaret
Borsaları Birliği
Ankara, [19--?]-
English edition also currently published
Annual

DU:DC: 1963-1964; 1966-1974; 1977-1981;
1983-   [25/4/ECONOMY/GENERAL]
SU:IDS: 1970; 1973; 1974; 1976
[SERIALS/NON-OFFICIAL/72]

İKTİSAT GAZETESİ
See: TÜRKİYE İKTİSAT GAZETESİ

İLÂHİYAT FAKÜLTESİ DERGİSİ
See also: ANKARA ÜNİVERSİTESİ
İLÂHİYAT FAKÜLTESİ DERGİSİ

İLÂHİYAT FAKÜLTESİ DERGİSİ
See also: SELÇUK ÜNİVERSİTESİ
İLÂHİYAT FAKÜLTESİ DERGİSİ

İLÂHİYAT FAKÜLTESİ DERGİSİ / Dokuz
Eylül Üniversitesi
1 (1984) -
Izmir
Added title in English: Review of the
Faculty of Divinity
Annual

BL:OIOC: 3 (1986) - 4 (1987)
[ZOR.1989.a.111]

İLÂVE-İ HAKÂİK
See: HAKÂİK ÜL-VAKÂYİ

İLERİ: efkâr-ı cezriye'yi neşreder
1 ([date?], 1335 [1919] - [?]
Istanbul
Newspaper
Subtitle varies
Daily

BL:OIOC: 60 (31.3.1919); 84; 150;
152-153; 159-160 (11.7.1919)
[OR.MIC.11704 (O.P.253)]

İLERİ: her ayın dokuzunda çıkar Kıbrıs
Türk çiftçisinin ziraî ekonomik ve
sosyal dergisidir
Sayı 1 (9 Şubat 1945) - [?]
Lefkoşa: Kıbrıs Türk Çiftçiler
Birliği, 1945-[19--?]

BL:OIOC: 1:1 (9.2.1945)   [O.P.219/3
[no.10]]

İLERİ: ayda bir kere çıkar siyasî,
ictimâ'î ilmî ve edebî curnaldır
No. 1 (İyun' 1926) - [?]
Simferopol'
Crimean Tatar; Arabic characters

BL:OIOC: 4 (9.1926) - 8 (12.1926)
[14499.tt.26]

İLERİ MUSİKİ MECMUASI
See: MUSİKİ MECMUASI

İLETİŞİM / Ankara İktisadi ve Ticari
İlimler Akademisi Gazetecilik ve Halkla
İlişkiler Yüksek Okulu yayın organı
1981/1 (Mart 1981) - 1982/4 (1982)
Ankara
Irregular

BL:OIOC: 1981/1 (3.1981) - 1982/4 (1982)
[ITA.1990.a.443]

İLİM VE SANAT
Sayı 1 (Mayıs-Haziran 1985) -
Konya
Journal of Islamic thought and culture
Bi-monthly

BL:OIOC: 1 (5-6.1985) -   [14498.cc.97]
OX:BOD: 1 -   [Per.Turk.d.3524]

İLKE: aylık inceleme yorum belge dergisi
Cilt 1, sayı 1 (Ocak 1974) - Cilt 13,
sayı 73-77 (Ocak-Mayıs 1980)
Istanbul

DU:UL: 5:30 (6.1976) - 7:39 (3.1977)
[Per./PL330]
DU:DC: 4:22/23 (10-11.1975) - 9:52
(4.1978); lacking 5:29 (5.1976)
[25/3/POLITICAL PARTIES]

ILLUSTRATION TURQUE MALUMAT
See: MALUMÂT

İLMİYE SALNAMESİ
[1] (1334 [1915-1916])
Istanbul
Yearbook of the Şeyh ül-İslâm's
office
Only one issue published

BL:OIOC: [1] (1915-1916)   [14495.d.1]
LO:SOAS: [1]   [E.Per.158728]
CA:UL: [1]   [S.828.01.b.130]
DU:UL: [1]   [Per./PL374]

İMALAT SANAYİİ ÜRETİM İNDEKSİ:
dönemler itibariyle (1981=100) =
Manufacturing industry production
indexes / Başbakanlık Devlet
İstatistik Enstitüsü
1982 (I-IV) -
Ankara
In Turkish and English
Quarterly

DU:DC: 4.1983 - 4.1984; 2-4.1985;
2-4.1986   [25/4/INDUSTRY/MANUFACTURING]
SU:IDS: 1982:1/4 - 1983:1-4
[SERIALS/OFFICIAL/TURKEY]

İMDAD ÜL-MİDAD
Cilt 1, aded 1 (1 Safer 1303 [9 Nov.
1885] - Cilt 1, aded 6 (1303 [1886])
Istanbul
Apparently fortnightly; only 1st issue
dated

OX:BOD: 1:1 (9.11.1885)   [Turk.e.2928]

İMECE: aylık fikir ve sanat dergisi
Yıl 1, cilt 1, sayı 1 ([date?] 1961) -
[?]
Ankara
Some issues published under the title:
Çıkrık

OX:BOD: 10:105 (1.1970) - 10:112
(10.1970)   [Per.Turk.d.1727]

İNANÇ [2. DİZİ]: haber, yorum, sanat
dergisi
Sayı 1 (Mart 1984) - Cilt 2, sayı
16-17-18 (Haziran-Temmuz-Ağustos 1985)
Istanbul
Monthly

OX:BOD: 1 (3.1984) - 2:16/17/18
(6-7-8.1985)   [Per.Turk.d.3219]

İNCİLİ ÇAVUŞ: vatan ve milletin
menafiine hâdim, şimdilik pazar ve
çarşamba günleri neşrolunur mizah
gazetesidir
Sayı 1 (10 Ağustos 1324 [23 Aug. 1908])
- Sayı 32 ([date?] 1324 [1909])
Istanbul
Semi-weekly

OX:BOD: 17 (16.11.1908) - 26 (26.1.1909)
[Per.Turk.d.1462 (2)]

L'INDICATEUR CONSTANTINOPOLITAIN
See: TARİF-İ DARÜSSAÂDE

İNGİLİZ FİLOLOJİSİ DERGİSİ:
studies by members of the English
Department, University of Istanbul
1 [1944] - 4 (1953)
İstanbul, 1944-1954
Title of no. 1: Dergi / İngiliz
Edebiyatı Tarihi Zümresi; of no. 2:
Dergi: İngiliz filolojisi
Contributions are in English or Turkish

BL:OIOC: 1 [1944] - 4 (1953)
[14480.d.197]
OX:BOD: 1 - 4   [269.d.161]

İNGİLİZ HUKUK BÜLTENİ / British
Council tarafından hazırlanan bu
bültenden maksat Britanya hukuk
âlemindeki çalışmalar hakkında bir
fikir vermektir
Cilt 1, sayı 1 (1945) - Cilt 1, sayı 2
(Ağustos 1945)
Ankara
Issue 1 dated by year only

BL:OIOC: 1:1 (1945) - 1:2 (8.1945)
[ITA.1986.c.18 (10)]

İNKİLAB VĚ MĚDĚNİYYĚT /
  Azěrbaycan Şura Yazıcıları Tĕşkilat
  Komitĕsinin organı
  1 ([date?] [1925]) - [?]
  Baku
  Azeri; modified roman characters
  Monthly

  BL:OIOC: 109/110 (1-2.1934)
  [ITA.1986.c.18 (9)]

İNQİLAB VĚ MĚDĚNİYYĚT
  See: İNKİLAB VĚ MĚDĚNİYYĚT

İNŞAAT İSTATİSTİKLERİ: inşaat
  ruhsatnameleri ve yapı kullanma izin
  kağıtları = Construction statistics:
  construction permits and occupancy
  permits / Başbakanlık Devlet
  İstatistik Enstitüsü
  Ankara, [19--?]-
  In Turkish and English
  Annual; some cumulated issues

  DU:DC: 1966/1969; 1976/1977; 1981-
  [25/4/INDUSTRY/CONSTRUCTION]
  SU:IDS: 1976 -; lacking 1978, 1980
  [SERIALS/OFFICIAL/TURKEY]

İNŞAAT İSTATİSTİKLERİ BÜLTENİ =
  Bulletin of construction statistics /
  Başbakanlık Devlet İstatistik
  Enstitüsü
  Ankara, [19--?]-
  Dates of publication not known
  In Turkish and English
  Quarterly? Some issues cumulated

  DU:DC: 1-12.1979
  [25/4/INDUSTRY/CONSTRUCTION]

İNSAN BİLİMLERİ DERGİSİ = Journal of
  human sciences / Orta Doğu Teknik
  Üniversitesi / Middle East Technical
  University
  Volume 1, number 1 (1982/1) -
  Ankara
  On humanities subjects, mathematics and
  psychology
  Articles in Turkish or English
  Semi-annual

  BL:OIOC: 1:1 (1982) -   [14480.d.193]
  LO:SOAS: 1:1 -   [Per.10.493804]

İNSAN HAKLARI YILLIĞI / Türkiye ve Orta
  Doğu Amme İdaresi Enstitüsü İnsan
  Hakları Araştırma ve Derleme Merkezi
  Yıl 1 (1979) -
  Ankara

  BL:OIOC: 1 (1979) - 2 (1980)
  [14498.cc.56]

İNSANİYET [1. SERİ]: sosyalizm
  efkârına hâdim insanperver haftalık
  gazetedir
  Numero 1 (5 Ağustos 1326 [18 Aug.
  1910]) - Numero 2 (12 Ağustos 1326 [25
  Aug. 1910])
  Istanbul
  Only two issues. Second series, also
  published in 1326 [1909], comprises
  three issues
  Added title: Journal socialiste
  l'humanité

  BL:OIOC: (reprint) 1 (18.8.1910) - 2
  (25.8.1910)   [ITA.1990.a.425/2]

INTERNAL TRADE STATISTICS
  See: İÇ TİCARET İSTATİSTİKLERİ

İNTİHAB-I EFKÂR
  See: TEVHİD-İ EFKÂR

İNTİHAR İSTATİSTİKLERİ = Suicide
  statistics / Başbakanlık Devlet
  İstatistik Enstitüsü
  Ankara
  Dates of publication not known
  Annual

  DU:DC: 1976 - 1977   [25/4/POPULATION]
  SU:IDS: 1981; 1983 -
  [SERIALS/OFFICIAL/TURKEY]

İNTİKAM: intikamcı Yeni Osmanlıların
  nâşir-i efkârıdır
  1. sene, aded 1 (18 Teşrinisani 1318 [1
  Dec. 1902]) - 2. sene, aded 50 ([date?]
  1319 [1903])
  Genève: [s.n.], 1318 [1902] - 1319
  [1903]
  Published first twice weekly; then
  weekly; then twice monthly

  BL:OIOC: 1:17 (8.2.1901); 1:25
  (18.3.1902); 1:27 (3.4.1902)
  [ITA.1986.c.16]

İRADE-İ MİLLİYE
  See: ULUS

İRŞAD
  See: YENİ İRŞAD

İŞ: aylık felsefe, ahlâk ve içtimaiyat
  mecmuası = Revue turque des sciences
  sociales et économiques = Turkish
  review of economic and social sciences =
  Türkische Monatsschrift für
  Geisteswissenschaft / Türkiye Harsî ve
  İçtimaî Araştırmalar Derneği
  tarafından neşrolunur
  Yıl 1, sayı 1 (İkinci Kânun 1934) -
  Yıl 38, sayı 277/278 (Mart 1973)
  Istanbul; later Ankara
  Later issues entitled: İş ve
  düşünce
  Articles in Turkish, English, French, or
  German
  Sometimes irregular; not published in
  1935

  BL:OIOC: 1:1 (1.1934) - 2:1 (1-3.1936);
  30:248 (12.1964)   [14498.b.4]
  DU:UL: 19:9 (1.9.1953); 21:161
  (1.1.1955) - 22:184 (1.12.1956)
  [Per./PL 8]

İŞ BÜLTENİ / Türkiye İş Bankası
  Yıl 1 (1954) -
  Ankara
  Bimonthly

  DU:UL: 9 (3.1962); 9 (11.1962) - 12
  (6.1965)   [Per./PL8]

İŞ VE DÜŞÜNCE
  See: İŞ

İŞÇİ GÜCÜ: TÜMTİS Sendikasının
  yayın organıdır
  Yıl 1, sayı 1 ([date?]) - Yıl 26, sayı
  462 (1 Eylül 1980)
  Ankara: Türkiye Motorlu Taşıt
  İşçileri Sendikası
  Some issues in year 25 are announced as
  belonging to year 26
  Generally fortnightly?

  DU:DC: 21:318 (15.3.1972) - 26:462
  (1.9.1980); lacking 14 issues
  [25/3/TRADE UNIONS]

İSLÂM: ayda bir mertebe çigaturgan
dinî, ahlakî ilmî ve felsefî meçelle
Yıl 1, san 1 (2 Avgustos 1924nçü yıl)
- [?]
Ufa: Keşşâf Tercümanî
Bashkir; Arabic characters. Also
includes official announcements in
Russian
Bimonthly? Nominally monthly

BL:OIOC: 1:1 (2.8.1924); 1:3
(15.12.1924)   [14499.t.26]

İSLAM DÜNYASI: Cuma günleri çıkar,
ilmî, ahlakî, içtimâ din bilgisi
mecmuası
No. 1 (4 Nisan [1]947) - Cilt 1, no. 28
(26 Eylül [1]947)
Istanbul

BL:OIOC: 1 (4.4.1947) - 1:26 (26.9.1947)
[ITA.1987.a.77]

İSLÂM DÜNYASI
Sene 1, aded 1 (2 Mart 1329 [15 Mar.
1913]) - Sene 2, aded 2 ([date?], 1332
[1916])
Istanbul
Published sporadically; nominally,
fortnightly then weekly

OX:BOD: 1:1 (15.3.1913) - 1:24
(5.3.1914)   [Per.Turk.d.3556]

İSLÂM DÜŞÜNCESİ: üç aylık
İslâmî fikir ve edebiyat mecmuası
Yıl 1, sayı 1 (Mart 1967) - Yıl 2, sayı
8 (Ekim 1969)
Istanbul

BL:OIOC: 1:1 (3.1967) - 2:8 (10.1969)
[14415.d.167]
OX:BOD: 1:1-2:8   [Per.Turk.d.3217]

İSLÂM İLİMLERİ ENSTİTÜSÜ DERGİSİ
[1] [1959] -
Ankara: Ankara Üniversitesi İlâhiyat
Fakültesi, İslâm İlimleri
Enstitüsü
Irregular; no issues between 1959 and
1975

BL:OIOC: [1] (1959) -   [14498.cc.64]
OX:BOD: [1]   [Per.Turk.d.581]

İSLAM MECELLESİ / dinî, millî mecmua
bolup Tamberey İslam mahallesining
imamı Habiburrahman Şakir tarafından
tertib etilüp ayğa bir mertebe neşr
etiledir
1nci san (Ramazan 1369 İyun 1950) - [?]
Tampere (Finland)
Tatar; Arabic characters

BL:OIOC: 2 (7.1950)   [ITA.1986.a.397]

İSLÂM MECMUASI: Müslümanların
faidesine çalışır
Cilt 1, sayı 1 ([Kanunusani] 1330
[1914]) - Cilt 4, sayı 63 (30
Teşrinisani 1334 [1918])
Istanbul
Generally monthly?

OX:BOD: 1:1 (1.1914) - 4:63 (30.10.1918)
[Turk.e.771]

İSLÂM MEDENİYETİ: üç aylık dînî,
ilmî, edebî araştırmalar mecmuası
[Cilt 1, sayı 1] (15 Ağustos 1967) -
Istanbul: İslâm Medeniyeti Vakfı
Published from 1967 to 1969 by Türkiye
İslâm Enstitüleri Talebe Federasyonu,
and from 1979 by İslâm Medeniyeti
Vakfı
1967-1969, generally monthly; 1979
onwards, quarterly

BL:OIOC: [1:1] (8.1967) - 5:4 (10.1982)
[14415.d.143]

İSLÂM TETKİKLERİ DERGİSİ / İstanbul
Üniversitesi Edebiyat Fakültesi
Cild 1, cüz 1-4 (1953) -
İstanbul, 1954-
Title prior to 1984 issue: İslâm
Tetkikleri Enstitüsü dergisi
Irregular

BL:OIOC: 1:1-4 (1953) -   [14498.c.18]
LO:SOAS: 1:1 -   [Per.10.L.100502]
OX:BOD: 1:1 - 7 (1978-1979)
[Per.Or.c.32]

İSLÂM TETKİKLERİ ENSTİTÜSÜ
DERGİSİ
See: İSLÂM TETKİKLERİ DERGİSİ

İŞLETME FAKÜLTESİ DERGİSİ /
Atatürk Üniversitesi İşletme
Fakültesi Araştırma Enstitüsü
Cilt 1, sayı 1 [1974] -
Erzurum
Semi-annual

BL:OIOC: 1:2 [1974] - 2:1 [1976]
[14498.cc.40]
SU:IDS: 9:2 (11.1980)
[SERIALS/NON-OFFICIAL/72]

İŞLETME FAKÜLTESİ DERGİSİ /
İstanbul Üniversitesi İşletme
Fakultesi
Cilt 1, sayı 1 ([date?] 1972) - [?]
Istanbul
Includes articles in English
Nominally bimonthly

SU:IDS: 9:2 (11.1980)
[SERIALS/NON-OFFICIAL/72]

ISPARTA İL YILLIĞI
[1] (1967) - [2] (1973)
Ankara, 1968-1973

BL:OIOC: [1] (1967)   [14498.a.42]
OX:BOD: [1]   [Turk.d.3324/33]

İSTANBUL: aylık dergi
[Yıl 1, no. 1 (Jan. 1944)] - Yıl 5, no.
12 (Oct.-Dec. 1948)
Istanbul
A literary, cultural and political
magazine
Monthly; quarterly during year 5 (1948)

BL:OIOC: 4:1 (1.1947) - 5:12 (12.1948)
[14498.cc.70]
DU:UL: 4:10 (10.1947)   [Per./PL1]

İSTANBUL: kültür dergisi / İstanbul
Halkevleri dergisi
Cilt 1, sayı 1 (1 Birincikânun 1943) -
Cilt 7, sayı 74-75 (31 Aralık 1946)
Istanbul
Twice-monthly

BL:OIOC: 1:1 (1.12.1943) - 7:74/75
(31.12.1946)   [14498.a.94]

İSTANBUL: sanat ve edebiyat dergisi
  Cilt 1, sayı 1 (Kasım 1953) - Cilt 4,
  sayı 4 ([date?], 1957)
  Istanbul
  Monthly. Vols. 1-3 comprise 38 issues

  BL:OIOC: 1:1 (11.1953) - [4]:1 (2.1957)
  [ITA.1989.a.234]
  OX:BOD: 1:1 - 1:14 (12.1954)
  [Turk.d.725]

İSTANBUL
  Istanbul, 1334 [1918]-1335 [1919]
  A daily newspaper

  BL:OIOC: 1:120 (30.3.1919) - 1:217
  (7.7.1919); lacking many issues
  [OR.MIC.11706 (O.P.255)]

İSTANBUL
  Sene 1, defa 1 (24 Eylül 1284 [7 Oct.
  1868]) - Sene 3, defa 23 (15 Mayıs 1285
  [28 May 1869])
  Istanbul
  Political and satirical newspaper
  Originally weekly; later thrice-weekly

  BL:OIOC: 1:1 (7.10.1868) - 2:12
  (7.11.1868); 3:14 (27.4.1869) - 3:23
  (28.5.1869); lacking 1:3, 1:5, 2:13,
  3:16, 3:17   [14498.d.6(2)]

İSTANBUL: bu gazete ... maarif ve
  havadis-i dahiliye ve hülâsa-i
  politika'dan bahsedecektir
  Sene 1, defa 1 (9 Mart 1283 [22 Mar.
  1867]) - Sene 1285, numero 477 (8
  Şevval 1285 [23 Jan. 1869])
  Istanbul
  Previous titles: Ayine-i vatan (nos.
  1-3); Ruzname-i Ayine-i vatan (nos.
  4-79)
  Daily; Ayine-i vatan, weekly; Ruzname-i
  Ayine-i vatan, four or five issues
  weekly

  LO:SOAS: 1:1 (22.3.1867) - 283
  (22.4.1868)   [L.E.Per.29884]

İSTANBUL ARKEOLOJİ MÜZELERİ YILLIĞI =
  Annual of the Archaeological Museum of
  Istanbul / Istanbul Arkeoloji Müzeleri
  yayınlarından
  No. 1 (1934) - 15-16 (1969)
  Istanbul
  Not published between 1937 and 1949.
  Issuing body for no. 1: İstanbul
  Asarıatika Müzesi
  Title of nos. 1-2: İstanbul Müzeleri
  yıllığı
  Articles in Turkish, with translations
  into English, French, or German

  BL:OIOC: 1 (1934) - 15/16 (1969)
  [14498.b.5]
  CA:UL: 3 (1949) - 15/16   [L.617.c.8]
  OX:BOD: 1 - 9 (1960)
  [Or.d.60/11-15-22]

ISTANBUL CHAMBER OF COMMERCE PRICE INDICES
  See: İSTANBUL TİCARET ODASI FİYAT
  İNDEKSLERİ

İSTANBUL ENSTİTÜSÜ DERGİSİ
  See: İSTANBUL ENSTİTÜSÜ MECMUASI

İSTANBUL ENSTİTÜSÜ MECMUASI
  1 (1955) - 5 (1959)
  Istanbul
  Issues 1-3 entitled: İstanbul
  Enstitüsü dergisi
  Annual

  BL:OIOC: 1 (1955) - 5 (1959)
  [14498.a.16]
  LO:SOAS: 1 - 5   [Per.10.L.97193]
  CA:UL: 1 - 5   [Q.830.b.4]
  DU:UL: 1 - 5   [Per./PL14]
  OX:BOD: 1 - 5   [Per.Turk.d.347]

İSTANBUL İL YILLIĞI
  [1] (1967) - [2] (1973)
  Istanbul

  OX:BOD: [1] (1967)   [Turk.d.3324/34]

İSTANBUL MÜZELERİ YILLIĞI
  See: İSTANBUL ARKEOLOJİ MÜZELERİ
  YILLIĞI

İSTANBUL SANAYİ ODASI DERGİSİ
  Yıl 1, sayı 1 ([15 Mart?] 1966) -
  Istanbul
  Monthly

  DU:DC: 6:64 (6.1971) - ; lacking
  11:125-127   [25/4/INDUSTRY]

İSTANBUL TİCARET
  See: İSTANBUL TİCARET ODASI GAZETESİ

İSTANBUL TİCARET ODASI FİYAT
  İNDEKSLERİ = Istanbul Chamber of
  Commerce price indices = Chambre de
  Commerce d'Istanbul indices des prix
  Istanbul, [ca. 1980?]-
  In Turkish, English and French
  Monthly

  DU:DC: 1.1981 -   [25/4/PRICES]

İSTANBUL TİCARET ODASI GAZETESİ /
  İstanbul Ticaret Odası yayın organı
  Yıl 1, sayı 1 (27 Şubat 1958) -
  Istanbul
  Some issues entitled: İstanbul ticaret
  Weekly

  BL:OIOC: 19:957 (3.6.1977) - 19:959
  (17.6.1977); 20:1027 (27.10.1978) -
  20:1036 (19.12.1978); 28:1390 (3.1.1986)
  - ; lacking 20:1035 (22.12.1978),
  29:1403 (4.4.1986), 29:1443 (23.1.1987),
  30:1462 (5.6.1987) - 30:1466 (3.7.1987),
  30:1483 (6.11.1987), 31:1520 (29.7.1988)
  [OR.MIC.12847 (O.P.974)]
  DU:DC: 14:691 (31.12.1971) - 20:1075
  (5.10.1979); 26:1263 (8.7.1983) - ;
  lacking some issues   [25/4/COMMERCE]

İSTANBUL TİCARET ODASI MECMUASI =
  Journal of the Istanbul Chamber of
  Commerce
  Sene 1, sayı 1 (5 Kanunusani 1300 [18
  Jan. 1885]) - 1981, sayı 10-12
  (Ekim-Aralık 1981)
  Istanbul
  Succeeded from 1982 by: ICOC: Journal of
  the Istanbul Chamber of Commerce (in
  English)
  Some issues entitled: İstanbul Ticaret
  ve Sanayi Odası mecmuası, with French
  title: Bulletin de la Chambre de
  Commerce et d'Industrie d'Istanbul
  Mainly in Ottoman, then modern Turkish;
  some issues also in French, or partly in
  English
  Quarterly

  BL:OIOC: 55:10 (10.1939) - 59:8
  (8.1943); lacking 59:1, 59:7   [OR.
  MIC. 11706, reel 3 (O.P. 255)]
  DU:DC: 10/12.1971 - 10/12.1981
  [25/4/COMMERCE]

İSTANBUL TİCARET VE SANAYİ ODASI
MECMUASI
  See: İSTANBUL TİCARET ODASI MECMUASI

İSTANBUL ÜNİVERSİTESİ ATATÜRK
  İLKELERİ VE İNKILAP TARİHİ
  ENSTİTÜSÜ YILLIĞI
  1 (1986) -
  Istanbul

  OX:BOD: 1 (1986) -   [Per.Turk.d.3530]

İSTANBUL ÜNİVERSİTESİ COĞRAFYA
ENSTİTÜSÜ DERGİSİ
Cilt 1 (1951), sayı 1 -
İstanbul
Includes summaries in English or French
Irregular; v. 1 (1951), semi-annual; v.
2 (1952) - 6 (1956), annual

BL:OIOC: 1:1 (1951)-   [14498.aa.4]
DU:UL: 1:1 - 22 (1977)   [Per./PL6]
DU:DC: 1:1 - 1:2; 3:5/6 (1954) - 7:14
(1964)   [25/2/GENERAL]
OX:BOD: 1:1 -   [Per.Turk.d.381]

İSTANBUL ÜNİVERSİTESİ EDEBİYAT
FAKÜLTESİ KÜTÜPHANECİLİK DERGİSİ
See: KÜTÜPHANECİLİK DERGİSİ

İSTANBUL ÜNİVERSİTESİ EDEBİYAT
FAKÜLTESİ TARİH DERGİSİ
Cilt 1, sayı 1-2 (1949-1950) -
İstanbul
Nominally annual

BL:OIOC: 1 (1949/1950) -   [14456.ff.2]
LO:SOAS: 1 -   [Per.10.61958]
CA:UL: 1 -   [P.830.c.29]
DU:UL: 1 - 9; 12 - 31   [Per./PL5]
OX:BOD: 1 -   [Per.Turk.d.401]
OX:MEC: 1 - 17; 22 - 25   [APT Tar 1]

İSTANBUL ÜNİVERSİTESİ EDEBİYAT
FAKÜLTESİ TARİH ENSTİTÜSÜ
DERGİSİ
Sayı 1 (Ekim 1970) -
İstanbul
Annual; two issues sometimes combined

BL:OIOC: 1 (1970)   [14456.k.100]
LO:SOAS: 1 -   [Per.10.262897]
CA:UL: 1 -   [P.617.b.16]
DU:UL: 1 - 9 (1978)   [Per./PL 5]
OX:BOD: 1 -   [Per.Turk.d.2039]

İSTANBUL ÜNİVERSİTESİ EDEBİYAT
FAKÜLTESİ TÜRK DİLİ VE EDEBİYATI
DERGİSİ
Cilt 1 (1946), sayı 1 -
İstanbul
Nominally annual; vols. 1-3 mainly
quarterly

BL:OIOC: 1:1 (1946)-   [14489.bb.1]
LO:SOAS: 1:1 -   [Per.10.55600]
CA:UL: 1:1 -   [L.830.c.54]
DU:UL: 1:1 - 22 (1976)   [Per./PL 2]
OX:BOD: 1:1 -   [Per.Turk.d.206]

İSTANBUL ÜNİVERSİTESİ HUKUK
FAKÜLTESİ MECMUASI: her üç ayda bir
çıkar
Yıl 1, sayı 1 (Şubat 1935) -
İstanbul
Superseded: Darülfünun Hukuk
Fakültesi mecmuası

BL:OIOC: 1:1 (2.1935) - 51:1/4 [1985]
  [14498.a.6]
LO:SOAS: 1:1 -   [Per.10.64841]
CA:UL: 10:1 - 10:2; 11:1 - 13:2
[L.250.c.122]
DU:UL: 19:1 (1953) - 19:4 (1954)
[Per./PL 9]
OX:BOD: 1:1 -   [Per.Turk.d.3543]

İSTANBUL ÜNİVERSİTESİ İKTİSAT
FAKÜLTESİ MECMUASI
Cilt 1, sayı 1 (Ekim 1939) -
İstanbul
Added title: Revue de la Faculté des
Sciences Économiques
Nominally quarterly; generally cumulated
as annual

LO:SOAS: 8:1/4 (10.1946-7.1947) -
[Per.67.97574]
DU:UL: 23:1 (10.1962) - 23:2 (2.1963)
  [Per./PL 8]
OX:BOD: 1:1 (10.1939) - 41
[Per.Turk.d.3231]

İSTANBUL ÜNİVERSİTESİ İLAHİYAT
FAKÜLTESİ MECMUASI
See: DARÜLFÜNUN İLAHİYAT FAKÜLTESİ
MECMUASI

İSTANBUL ÜNİVERSİTESİ İŞLETME
FAKÜLTESİ İŞLETME İKTİSADI
ENSTİTÜSÜ HABER BÜLTENİ
İstanbul, [197-?]-[19--?]
Frequency not known

SU:IDS: 7 (5.1978)
[SERIALS/NON-OFFICIAL/72]

İSTANBUL ÜNİVERSİTESİ ORMAN
FAKÜLTESİ DERGİSİ, SERİ A = Revue
de la Faculté des Sciences Forestières
de l'Université d'Istanbul
Cilt 1, sayı 1 (1951) -
İstanbul
Seri B also published since 1951,
semi-annual
Articles in Turkish or German, with
abstracts in English
Semi-annual

DU:DC: 1:7 (1951)   [25/2/FORESTS]

İSTANBUL VİLÂYET GAZETESİ
Sene 1, numero 1 (28 Kanunuevvel 1338
[10 Jan. 1923]) - Sene 6, numero 1529
(31 Kanunuevvel 1927)
İstanbul
Daily

OX:BOD: 1:1 (10.1.1923) - 6:1529
(31.12.1927)   [Per.Turk.c.88]

İSTATİSTİK CEP YILLIĞI
See: TÜRKİYE İSTATİSTİK CEP
YILLIĞI

İSTATİSTİK VE DEĞERLENDİRME BÜLTENİ
= Monthly statistical and evaluation
bulletin / T.C. Merkez Bankası
[19--?], [date?] - 1989, Aralık
Ankara, [19--?]-1990
Continued by: Aylık istatistik bülteni
In Turkish and English

LO:SOAS: 6:1986 - 12.1989; lacking
1986:7-9, 1988:2   [Per.77.L.539397]

İSTATİSTİK YILLIĞI
See: TÜRKİYE İSTATİSTİK YILLIĞI

İSTATİSTİK YILLIĞI = Annual statistics
/ Sosyal Sigortalar Kurumu
Ankara, [19--?]-
In Turkish and English; formerly in
Turkish only

DU:DC: 1970; 1976 -   [25/4/SOCIAL
SERVICES]
SU:IDS: 1977 - 1981
[SERIALS/OFFICIAL/TURKEY]

İSTATİSTİK YILLIĞI / İş ve İşçi
Bulma Kurumu Genel Müdürlüğü
Ankara, [19--?]-

DU:DC: 1979-1980; 1983-
[25/4/EMPLOYMENT]

İSTİKBÂL: ayda iki defa Londra'da
neşrolunur; hâvi olduğu mebâhis,
vatanımızın selamet ve menfaatına
müteallıktır
Numero 1 ([date?], 1895) - Numero 31 (23
Eylül [18]95)
London
Newspaper of political dissent
Publication history not fully
determined: some issues printed at
Naples and Geneva according to Duman;
27-31 also dated 1312-1313 [lunar A.H.]

BL:OIOC: 27 (2.7.1895) - 31 (23.9.1895)
[14498.d.3]

İŞTİRAK: sosyalizm efkârının
mürevvicidir
Numero 1 (13 Şubat 1325 [26 Feb. 1910])
- Numero 20 (2 Eylül 1326 [15 Sep.
1910])
Istanbul
Added title: Journal socialiste Ichtirak
Weekly, then fortnightly, then irregular

BL:OIOC: (reprint) 1 (26.3.1910) - 20
(15.9.1910)   [ITA.1990.a.425/1]

İSTİŞARE: haftada bir defa neşrolunur
hukuk ve siyasiyat'tan bâhis ilmî,
edebî mecmua
Sayı 1 (4 Eylül 1324 [17 Sep. 1908]) -
Sayı 27 (19 Mart 1325 [1 Apr. 1909])
Istanbul

OX:BOD: 1 (17.9.1908) - 27 (1.4.1909)
[Per.Turk.d.891]

İZMİR İL YILLIĞI
[1] (1967) - [2] (1973)
Izmir, 1969-1973

BL:OIOC: [1] (1967)   [14498.a.55]
OX:BOD: [1]   [Turk.d.3324/35]

İZMİR LİMANI İHRACAT-İTHALAT
İSTATİSTİKLERİ / İzmir Ticaret
Odası
Izmir, [19--?]-
Monthly

DU:DC: 1.1973 - 8.1973
[25/4/TRANSPORT/MARITIME]

İZMİR TİCARET BORSASI İKTİSADİ
RAPORU
(1968) -
Izmir
Former title: İzmir Ticaret Borsası
yıllığı ve iktisadi raporu
Annual

DU:DC: 1968; 1972   [25/4/FINANCE &
INVESTMENT]

İZMİR TİCARET BORSASI YILLIĞI VE
İKTİSADİ RAPORU
See: İZMİR TİCARET BORSASI
İKTİSADİ RAPORU

İZMİR TİCARET BORSASI YÖNETİM KURULU
AYLIK FAALİYET RAPORU
Izmir, [19--?]-

DU:DC: 7.1973; 11.1973   [25/4/FINANCE
& INVESTMENT]

İZMİR TİCARET ODASI AYLIK BÜLTENİ
See: İZMİR TİCARET ODASI DERGİSİ

İZMİR TİCARET ODASI DERGİSİ
Yıl 1, sayı 1 (Ocak 1926) -
Izmir
Previous title: İzmir Ticaret Odası
Aylık Bülteni
Almost entirely in Turkish
Monthly

BL:HSS: 46:6 (6.1973) -   [S.Q.40/6]
DU:DC: 6.1971-   [25/4/COMMERCE]

IZVESTIĬA AKADEMII NAUK AZERBAĬDZHANA,
SERIĬA ISTORII, FILOSOFII I PRAVA
See: AZĚRBAYCAN ELMLĚR AKADEMİYASININ
HĚBĚRLĚRİ, TARİH, FĚLSĚFĚ VĚ
HÜGUG SERİYASI

IZVESTIĬA AKADEMII NAUK
AZERBAĬDZHANSKOĬ SSR
See: AZĚRBAYCAN SSR ELMLĚR
AKADEMİYASI HĚBĚRLĚRİ

IZVESTIĬA AKADEMII NAUK
AZERBAĬDZHANSKOĬ SSR, SERIĬA ISTORII,
FILOSOFII I PRAVA
See: AZĚRBAYCAN ELMLĚR AKADEMİYASININ
HĚBĚRLĚRİ, TARİH, FĚLSĚFĚ VĚ
HÜGUG SERİYASI

IZVESTIĬA AKADEMII NAUK KAZAKHSKOĬ SSR,
SERIĬA FILOLOGII I ISKUSSTVOVEDENIĬA
See: KAZAK SSR ĞILIM AKADEMİYASINIÑ
HABARLARI, FİLOLOGİYA MEN ÖNERTANU
SERİYASI

IZVESTIĬA AKADEMII NAUK KAZAKHSKOĬ SSR,
SERIĬA OBSHCHESTVENNYKH NAUK
See: KAZAKSTAN RESPUBLİKASINIÑ
ĞILIM AKADEMİYASINIÑ HABARLARI,
KOĞAMDIK ĞILIM SERİYASI

IZVESTIĬA AKADEMII NAUK KIRGIZSKOĬ SSR,
OBSHCHESTVENNYE NAUKI
See: KIRGIZ RESPUBLİKASI İLİMDER
AKADEMİYASI KABARLARI, KOOMDUK
İLİMDERİ

IZVESTIĬA AKADEMII NAUK RESPUBLIKI
KAZAKHSTAN, SERIĬA OBSHCHESTVENNYKH NAUK
See: KAZAKSTAN RESPUBLİKASINIÑ
ĞILIM AKADEMİYASINIÑ HABARLARI,
KOĞAMDIK ĞILIM SERİYASI

IZVESTIĬA AKADEMII NAUK RESPUBLIKI
KYRGYZSTAN, OBSHCHESTVENNYE NAUKI
See: KIRGIZ RESPUBLİKASI İLİMDER
AKADEMİYASI KABARLARI, KOOMDUK
İLİMDERİ

IZVESTIĬA AKADEMII NAUK TURKMENISTAN,
GUMANITERNYE NAUKI
See: TÜRKMENİSTAN ILIMLAR
AKADEMİYASININ HABARLARI, GUMANİTAR
ILIMLARI

IZVESTIĬA AKADEMII NAUK TURKMENSKOĬ
SSR, SERIĬA OBSHCHESTVENNYKH NAUK
See: TÜRKMENİSTAN ILIMLAR
AKADEMİYASININ HABARLARI, GUMANİTAR
ILIMLARI

IZVESTIĬA AKADEMII NAUK UZBEKSKOĬ SSR,
SERIĬA OBSHCHESTVENNYKH NAUK
See: ŮZBEKİSTON SSR FANLAR
AKADEMİYASINİNG AHBOROTİ,
İCTİMOİY FANLAR SERİYASİ

JAHRBUCH FÜR KLEINASIATISCHE FORSCHUNG
See: ANADOLU

JOURNAL OF ECONOMICS AND ADMINISTRATIVE
STUDIES
See: EKONOMİ VE İDARİ BİLİMLER
DERGİSİ

JOURNAL OF HUMAN SCIENCES
See: İNSAN BİLİMLERİ DERGİSİ

THE JOURNAL OF OTTOMAN STUDIES
  See: OSMANLI ARAŞTIRMALARI

JOURNAL OF THE ISTANBUL CHAMBER OF
COMMERCE
  See: İSTANBUL TİCARET ODASI MECMUASI

JOURNAL OF THE MEDICAL FACULTY OF EGE
UNIVERSITY
  See: EGE ÜNİVERSİTESİ TIP
FAKÜLTESİ DERGİSİ

JOURNAL OF THE SCHOOL OF POLITICAL
SCIENCES
  See: ANKARA ÜNİVERSİTESİ SİYASAL
BİLGİLER FAKÜLTESİ DERGİSİ

JOURNAL OF TURKISH STUDIES
  See: TÜRKLÜK BİLGİSİ ARAŞTIRMALARI

JOURNAL SOCIALISTE ICHTIRAK
  See: İŞTİRAK

JOURNAL SOCIALISTE L'HUMANITÉ
  See: İNSANİYET

JUDICIAL STATISTICS
  See: ADALET İSTATİSTİKLERİ

KABOTAJ VE ULUSLARARASI DENİZ TAŞIMASI
  İSTATİSTİKLERİ = Statistics of
  coastwise and international sea
  transportation / Başbakanlık Devlet
  İstatistik Enstitüsü
  Ankara, [19--?]-
  In Turkish and English
  Annual; some cumulated issues

  DU:DC: 1975/1980; 1983 -
  [25/4/TRANSPORT/MARITIME]
  SU:IDS: 1986 -
  [SERIALS/OFFICIAL/TURKEY]

KADIN: şimdilik haftada bir defa
  neşrolunur
  Yıl 1, sayı 1 (13 Teşrinievvel 1324 [26
  Oct. 1908]) - Yıl 1, sayı 30 (25 Mayıs
  1325 [7 June 1909])
  Thessaloniki

  OX:BOD: 1:1 (26.10.1908) - 1:30
  (7.6.1909)   [Turk.d.2388]

KADININ SOSYAL HAYATINI ARAŞTIRMA VE
  İNCELEME DERNEĞİ YÖNETİM KURULU
  RAPORU
  Ankara, [197-?]-[197-?]
  Typewritten report
  Annual

  SU:IDS: 1974 - 1977
  [SERIALS/NON-OFFICIAL/72]

KADRO: aylık fikir mecmuası
  1 (II. Kanun 1932) - 35-36
  (İlkkânun-Sonkânun 1934-1935)
  Istanbul

  BL:OIOC: 1 (1.1932) - 36 (1.1935)
  [14498.a.92]
  CA:UL: 1 - 36   [Q.900:9.c.1]
  DU:UL: 1 - 3   [Per./PL 1]
  OX:BOD: 1 - 36; lacking 27, 30, 33,
  [Turk.d.1964]
  OX:MEC: 1 - 36   [APT Kad]

KAFKASYA DAĞLILARI = Gortsy Kavkaza /
  organ Narodnoi Partii Gortsev Kavkaza
  No. 1 ([?] Mart 1931) - [?]
  Warsaw, 1931-[193-?]
  Predecessor of: Ülkemiz = Nash krai
  Added titles: Les montagnards du
  Caucase; The mountaineers of Caucasia
  In Istanbul Turkish and Russian
  Monthly

  BL:OIOC: 49 (3.1934) - 50 (4.1934)
  [ITA.1986.a.388]

KALEM: perşembe günleri neşrolunur
  edebî mizah gazetesi
  1. yıl, sayı 1 (21 Ağustos 1324 [3 Sep.
  1908]) - 2. yıl, sayı 54 (23 Eylül 1325
  [6 Oct. 1909])
  Istanbul

  OX:BOD: 1:1 (3.9.1908) - 2:54
  (6.10.1909)   [Turk.c.121]

KALEM: Perşenbe [sic] günleri çıkar,
  mizah gazetesi
  Sayı 1 (11 Eylül 1930) - Sayı 12 (26
  Teşrinisani 1930)
  Istanbul

  BL:OIOC: 1 (25.9.1930) - 12 (26.11.1930)
  [ITA.1990.c.12]

KAMMUNİST CURNALİ / Ü.K.P.(B.) Markaz
  Koming Orta Asiya Byurasi va Üzbikistan
  Markazi Fırka Komitasi tamanidan ayda
  bir tapkar çıkarılaturgan siyasi,
  iktisadi va ictimai kammunist curnali
  San 1 (Yanvar 1926) - [?]
  Tashkent
  Uzbek; Arabic characters

  BL:OIOC: 7/8 (8.1926) - 7 (=17)
  (7.1927); lacking 6 (=16)   [14499.i.29]

KAMU İKTİSADİ TEŞEBBÜSLERİ VE
  İŞTİRAKLERİ YILLIĞI / T.C. Maliye
  Bakanlığı Hazine Genel Müdürlüğü
  ve Milletlerarası İktisadi İşbirliği
  Teşkilatı Genel Sekreterliği
  (1970) -
  Ankara
  Irregular

  DU:DC: 1976; 1978
  [25/4/ECONOMY/MANAGEMENT & ORGANISATION]

KAMUS UL-ULUM VE 'L-MAARIF
  See: ULUM GAZETESİ

KANUN-U ESASÎ / Osmanlı İttihad ve
  Terakki Cemiyetinin mürevvic-i
  efkârıdır
  Sene 1, numero 1 (21 Kanunuevvel 1896) -
  Sene 2, numero 40 (26 Mayıs 1315 [8 June
  1899])
  Cairo
  Irregular; sometimes weekly

  BL:OIOC: 1:1 (21.12.1869) - 2:25
  (1.9.1898)   [14498.d.10]

KARA-AMİD / Diyarbakırı Tanıtma
  Derneği'nce çıkarılan kültür dergisi
  1. yıl, sayı 1 (Eylül 1956) - Sayı 15
  (Mayıs 1982)
  Diyarbakır
  On history and culture, with emphasis on
  the Amid region
  Irregular; originally intended to appear
  thrice annually
  Subtitle varies

  BL:OIOC: 1:1 (9.1956) - 2-3:2-4
  (1956/1957/1958)   [14498.cc.15]
  OX:BOD: 1:1 - 15 (5.1982)
  [Per.Turk.d.3163]

KARA-GUEUZ
  See: KARAGÖZ

KARA VE DENİZ TAŞITLARI, KABOTAJ VE
   MİLLETLERARASI DENİZ TRAFİĞİ VE
   NAKLİYATI = Vehicles and vessels,
   coastwise and international sea traffic
   and shipping / T. C. Başbakanlık Devlet
   İstatistik Enstitüsü
   Ankara, [196-?]-[197-?]
   Superseded by: Ulaştırma ve trafik
   kazaları istatistikleri; and Kabotaj ve
   uluslararası deniz taşıması
   istatistikleri

   BL:HSS: 1964   [S.Q.170/19]

KARAGÖZ: siyasî, mizahî, musavver halk
   gazetesi
   Sene 1, numero 1 (10 Ağustos 1908) -
   [?]
   Istanbul
   Published at least until 1932
   Subtitle varies. Added title:
   Kara-Gueuz: journal illustré
   Semi-weekly

   LO:SOAS: 6:608 (26.3.1914) - 7:711
   (29.12.1914); 11:1043 (20.3.1919) -
   13:1275 (29.5.1920)   [L.E.Per.305774]

KARAGÖZ SALNAMESİ / naşiri, Karagöz
   gazetesi
   1. sene (1326/1328/1910) - 4. sene
   (1329/1331/1913)
   Istanbul

   CA:UL: 2 (1911)   [L.830.c.84]

KARARLAR MECMUASI: şimdilik üç ayda bir
   neşrolunur / T.C. Şûrayıdevlet
   Sayı 1 (Eylûl 1937) - [?]
   Ankara
   Official review of legislative decisions
   Title of issuing body varies

   BL:OIOC: 1 (9.1937) - 3 (3.1938)
   [14458.fff.116 (1)]

KARAYOLLARI BÜLTENİ / Bayındırlık ve
   İskân Bakanlığı Karayollar Genel
   Müdürlüğü
   Cilt 1, sayı 1 (Kasım 1950) -
   Ankara
   Name of issuing body varies
   Monthly

   DU:DC: 19:241 (4.1970) - 20:250
   (1.1971); lacking 19:242-244, 247
   [25/4/TRANSPORT/ROADS]

KARDAŞ EDEBİYATLAR: üç aylık edebî
   dergi
   Sayı 1 (Mart 1982) - Sayı 16
   (Nisan-Mayıs-Haziran 1987)
   Erzurum

   OX:BOD: 1 (3.1982) - 16 (4-5-6.1987)
   [Per.Turk.d.3381]

KARESİ İDADİ LİSESİNE MAHSUS SALNAME
   1. basılış (1339/1342 [1923])
   Balıkesir
   Only one issue published

   CA:UL: 1 (1923)   [S.828.01.b.53]

KARESİ VİLÂYETİNE MAHSUS SALNAME
   Defa 1 (1305 [1887-1888])
   Balıkesir
   Only one issue published

   OX:BOD: [1] (1887-1888)   [Turk.d.1425]

KARS İL YILLIĞI
   [1] (1967) - [2] (1973)
   Ankara

   BL:OIOC: [1] (1967)   [14498.a.57]
   OX:BOD: [1]   [Turk.d.3324/36]

KARTAL: millî mizah gazetesi
   Yıl 1, no. 1 (1 Temmuz 1929) - Yıl 1,
   no. 10 (1 Ağustos 1929)
   Istanbul
   Twice-weekly

   BL:OIOC: 1:1 (1.7.1929) - 1:10
   (1.8.1929)   [14498.a.108]

KASTAMONİ VİLÂYETİ SALNAMESİ
   See: KASTAMONU VİLÂYETİ SALNAMESİ

KASTAMONU İL YILLIĞI
   [1] (1967) - [2] (1973)
   Ankara, 1968-1973

   BL:OIOC: [1] (1967)   [14498.a.25]
   OX:BOD: [1]   [Turk.d.3324/37]

KASTAMONU VİLÂYETİ SALNAMESİ
   Defa 1 (1286 [1869-1870]) - Defa 21
   (1321 [1903-1904])
   Kastamonu
   Some issues entitled: Salname-i
   Vilâyet-i Kastamonu

   LO:SOAS: 16 (1892)   [E.Per.283629]
   DU:UL: 21 (1903)   [PL367.K2]
   OX:BOD: 3 (1871); 15 (1889) - 16 (1892);
   20 (1899) - 21 (1903)
   [Per.Turk.d.1440]

KAYNAKLAR
   1 (Güz 1983) - Sayı 6 (Kış 1988)
   Ankara: Şekerbank
   Popular academic journal on culture,
   art, and literature
   Irregular

   BL:OIOC: 1 (autumn 1983) - 6 (winter
   1988)   [ITA.1990.a.442]
   OX:BOD: 1 - 6   [Per.Turk.d.3098]

KAYSERİ İL YILLIĞI
   [1] (1968) - [2] (1973)
   Kayseri, 1968-1973

   OX:BOD: [1] (1968)   [Turk.d.3324/38]

KAZAK ĒDEBİETİ / Kazakstan
   Cazuşılar odağı başkarmasınıñ organı
   No. 1 (10 Yanvar 1934) -
   Alma-Ata
   Cultural and literary journal
   Weekly

   BL:OIOC: 1118 (7.7.1972)-; lacking
   16.7.1976, 6.5.1977, 15-29.7.1977,
   24.3.1978, 7.9.1984, 7.12.1984,
   22.3.1985, 26.7.1985   [OR.MIC.12239
   (microfilm), O.P.990 (hard copy)]

KAZAK SSR ĠILIM AKADEMİYASINIÑ
   HABARLARI, FİLOLOGİYA MEN ÖNERTANU
   SERİYASI = Izvestiiā Akademii Nauk
   Kazakhskoi SSR, seriiā filologii i
   iskusstvovedeniiā
   1 ([date? 1957?]) -
   Alma-Ata
   Articles in Russian or Kazakh
   Quarterly

   LO:SOAS: 8/9 (1959) - 22 (1962)
   [Per.10.140197]

KAZAK SSR ĠILIM AKADEMİYASINIÑ
   HABARLARI, KOĞAMDIK ĠILIM SERİYASI
   See: KAZAKSTAN RESPUBLİKASINIÑ
   ĠILIM AKADEMİYASINIÑ HABARLARI,
   KOĞAMDIK ĠILIM SERİYASI

KAZAK SSR ĞILIM AKADEMİYASINIÑ
HABARŞISI = Vestnik Akademii Nauk
Kazakhskoi SSR
No. 1 (Yanvar, 1944) -
Alma-Ata
ISSN 0002-3213
In Russian, with contents lists and very
few articles in Kazakh
Monthly

LO:SOAS: 1964:1 (=226) -; lacking
1964:11, 1965:1-2, 5   [Per.10.206242]
OX:BOD: 1957:1 -   [Per.3974.d.945]

KAZAKSTAN ÉYELDERİ / Kazakstan
Kompartiyası Ortalık Komitetiniñ
ayına birret şığatın éyelderge
arnalğan koğamdık sayasi cène
körkem-èdebi curnalı
[No.1], ([month?], 1925) -
Alma-Ata
In Kazakh
Monthly

BL:OIOC: 1984:4 -   [14499.tt.39]

KAZAKSTAN RESPUBLİKASI ĞILIM
AKADEMİYASINIÑ HABARLARI, KOĞAMDIK
ĞILIM SERİYASI = Izvestiia Akademii
Nauk Respubliki Kazakhstan, seriia
obshchestvennykh nauk
No. 1 (Yanvar' 1962) -
Alma-Ata
No Kazakh series title prior to 1975
Articles in Kazakh or Russian
Bi-monthly

BL:OIOC: 1972:4 - 1976:6; lacking
1974:3, 6, 1975:1   [14499.t.30]
LO:SOAS: 1964:4; 1966:1; 1967:2 -;
lacking 1976:1   [Per.10.203296]

KAZAN: üç aylık dergi / yayınlayan,
Kazan Türkleri Kültür ve Yardımlaşma
Derneği
Yıl 1, sayı 1 (Eylül 1970) -
Istanbul
Nominally quarterly; later semi-annual

BL:OIOC: 1:1 (9.1970) - 9:23 (1980)
[ITA.1988.a.65]
OX:BOD: 1:1 - 9:23   [Per.Turk.d.3363]

KAZAN KALENDARI
1. il (1873) - [?]
Kazan'
Tatar; Arabic characters

BL:OIOC: 3 (1873) - 4 (1874)
[14496.d.1]

KAZAN UTLARI: aylık èdèbi-nèfis hèm
ictimagıy-politik jurnal / Tatarstan
Yazuçılar Soyuzı organı
1922, 1 (May) -
Kazan: KPSSnıñ Tatarstan Ölkè
Komitetının gazeta hèm jurnallar
neşriyatı
ISSN 0206-4189
In Crimean Tatar

BL:OIOC: 1977:1 -   [14499.t.36]
OX:BOD: 1985:8 -   [Per.Turk.d.3386]

KELEBEK: perşembe günleri neşrolunur
edebî, mizah mecmuası
Istanbul

OX:BOD: 1:1 (12.4.1923) - 2:77
(25.9.1924)   [Per.Turk.c.209]

KÈND HÈYATI / Azèrbaycan KP MK-nın
aylığ kütlèvi ictimai-siyasi curnalı
1952, no.1 ([date?], 1952) -
Baku
ISSN 0134-5206
Mainly in Azeri; some items in Russian

BL:OIOC: 1987:1 -   [14499.t.42]

KENTSEL YERLER HANEHALKI İŞGÜCÜ ANKET
SONUÇLARI = Urban places household
labour force survey results /
Başbakanlık Devlet İstatistik
Enstitüsü
1982 -
Ankara, 1984-
In Turkish and English
Irregular

SU:IDS: 1982 - 1984
[SERIALS/OFFICIAL/TURKEY]

KEZEL BAYRAK: yarım aylık jurnal / Junguo
Kommunistik Partiyişi Mèrkiziy
Komitetiniñ başçılığıda nèşr
kilindi
1 san ([date?, 1962?]) - [?]
Beijing
Uygur in Arabic characters (roman from
1975:7 to 1980:18)

LO:SOAS: 1972:3 (=247) - 1981:10;
slightly incomplete   [Per.10.290237]

KEZELTUW / Jonguo Gonçandane Jonyan
Weyüanhaye baskarade
San 1 ([date?, 1962?]) - [?]
Beijing: Ulttar Baspase
Uygur in Arabic characters (roman from
1975:9 to 1980:24)
Monthly; twice-monthly from 1980 on

LO:SOAS: 1972:3 (=247) - 1981:10;
lacking 1974:7-8; 1975:1; 1976:1,10;
1977:1-6,10; 1978:1-6,8
[Per.10.290238]

KHILAFAT
See: HİLÂFET

KIBRIS: şimdilik Pazartesi günleri
neşrolunur, siyasât, edebiyat, ve
fünundan bahistir
Sene 1, aded 1 (10 Ağustos 1308 [23
Aug. 1892]) - [?]
Lefkoşa
Weekly

BL:OIOC: 2:59 (29.10.1893); 4:173
(11.2.1896)   [O.P.3(23)]

KIBRIS İSLÂM LİSESİ MECMUASI = Cyprus
Moslem Lycée magazine
Vol. 1, no. 1 (date? 1939) - [?]
Lefkoşa

BL:OIOC: 2:3 (summer 1940)
[O.P.219/4 (13)]

KIBRIS TÜRK SESİ: haftalık bağımsız
siyasi gazete
Yıl 1, sayı 1 (10 Kasım [1961]) - Yıl 1,
sayı 15 (23 Mart 1962)
London
Not published between 8 Dec. 1961 and 19
Jan. 1962

BL:OIOC: 1:2 (17.11.1961) - 1:15
(23.3.1962)   [OR.MIC.11805 (O.P.737)]

KIBRISTA KOOPERATİFÇİLİK / Kooperatif
Şirketler Mukayyidi tarafından
yayınlanmıştır
No. 1 ([date?], 1947) - [?]
Lefkoşa
Monthly?

BL:OIOC: 8 (3.1948)   [ITA.a.1610]

KİM: haftalık haber dergisi
Cilt 1, sayı 1 (30 Mayıs 1958) - Yıl 9,
sayı 505 (5 Nisan 1968)
Istanbul

LO:SOAS: 1:44 (27.3.1959) - 4:170
(3.10.1961); lacking 2:76, 3:114, 3:141
- 3:146, 4:156, 4:162, 4:168
[Per.10.L.173832]
OX:MEC: 1:16 (12.9.1958) - 1:30; 5:61 -
11:147; 15:112 - 16:209; 21:323 - 25:357
(20.5.1965); lacking some issues
[APT Kim]

KIRGIZ RESPUBLİKASI İLİMDER
AKADEMİYASININ KABARLARI, KOOMDUK
İLİMDERİ = Izvestiíã Akademii Nauk
Respubliki Kyrgyzstan, obshchestvennye
nauki
1966, 1 -
Bishkek
ISSN 0235-0068
Former titles: Kırgız SSR İlimder
Akademiyasının kabarları,
obşçestvennıe nauki = Izvestiíã
Akademii Nauk Kirgizskoĭ SSR,
obshchestvennye nauki
Most contributions in Russian; some in
Kirgiz
Quarterly

BL:OIOC: 1988:1 - [ZOR.1988.a.213]
LO:SOAS: 1969:1 -; lacking 1974:3
[Per.10.226780]

KIRGIZSTAN AYALDARI / Kırgızstan KP
Borborduk Komitetinin koomduk-sayasiy
cana adabiy körköm curnalı
1951, No.1 -
Frunze
In Kirgiz
Monthly

BL:OIOC: 1984:5-   [14499.tt.43]

KIRGIZSTAN SSR İLİMDER AKADEMİYASININ
KABARLARI, OBŞÇESTVENNIE NAUKI
See: KIRGIZ RESPUBLİKASI İLİMDER
AKADEMİYASI KABARLARI, KOOMDUK
İLİMDERİ

KIRGIZSTAN TUUSU / Kırgızstan Kommunisttik
partiyasının Borborduk Komitetinin,
Kırgız SSR Cogorku Sovetinin cana
Ministrler Sovetinin organı
No.1 (7 Noyabr 1924) -
Frunze
Daily newspaper
Title until 24 Feb. 1991: Sovettik
Kırgızstan
In Kirgiz

BL:OIOC: 1.7.1972 - 31.12.1976; 1.2.1979
- 31.12.1980; 1.4.1981 - 31.12.1981;
1.10.1982 - 31.12.1982; 1.1.1988 - ;
lacking a few issues   [OR. MIC. 12012
(O.P. 988)]

KIRGIZSTANDIN KİTEPKANAÇISI:
kitepkanalardın iş tacrıybaları tuuralu
kvartal sayın çıguuçu informatsiyalık
byulleten' = Bibliotekar' Kirgizistana:
ezhekvartal'nyĭ informatsionnyĭ
bíulleten' ob opyme raboty bibliotek /
Kırgız SSRinin N. G. Çernyşevskiy
atındagı Respublikalık Mamlekettik
Kitepkanası
No.1 ([date?], 1963) - [?]
Frunze
Articles in Kirgiz or Russian

LO:SOAS: 1970:3 (=29) - 1976:3 (=53)
[Per.10.206232]

KIRK ANBAR: maarif edebiyat teracim-i
ahval lataifden bahseder onbeş yirmi
günde bir çıkar mecmuadır
Cüz' numerosu 1 (1290 [1873 or 1874]) -
Cüz' numerosu 34 (1293 [1876 or 1877])
Istanbul
Issues dated only by year

BL:OIOC: 1 (1873 or 1874) - 34 (1876 or
1877)   [14498.cc.53]
CA:UL: 1 - 17   [T.830.c.16]
OX:BOD: 21 - 34   [Per.Turk.d.2247]

KIRKLARELİ İL YILLIĞI
[1] (1967) - [2] (1973)
Istanbul, 1968-1973

BL:OIOC: [1] (1967)   [14498.a.32]
OX:BOD: [1]   [Turk.d.3324/39]

KIRŞEHİR İL YILLIĞI
[1] (1967) - [2] (1973)
Ankara

OX:BOD: [1] (1967)   [Turk.d.3324/40]

KİTABLAR ALĚMİNDĚ: ildě dörd děfě
çıhır / Azěrbaycan SSR Nazirlěr
Soveti Dövlět něşriyyat, poligrafiya
vě kitab ticarěti işlěri
komitěsinin, Azěrbaycan SSR
Měděniyyět Nazirliyinin vě
Respublika kitab sevěnlěr
cěmiyyětinin mě' lumat-bibliografik
něşri
1965, 1 - [?]
Baku
In Azeri

BL:OIOC: 1965:1; 1966:1, 1966:3; 1976:4
[14499.t.16]

KİTAP: üçayın kitapları / Kültür ve
Turizm Bakanlığı
Cilt 1, sayı 1 (Eylül 1981) -
Ankara
Nomenclature of issuing body varies
Original subtitle: ayın kitapları
Quarterly; initially monthly

OX:BOD: 1:1 (9.1981) -
[Per.Turk.d.2948]
OX:MEC: 1:1 - 1:6 (2.1982); 7; 10-15
[APT Kit 1]

KİTAP BELLETEN [1. SERİ]: aylık
bibliyografya biografi kültür tarihi
dergisi
Cilt 1, sayı 1 (1 Kasım 1960) - Yıl 2,
sayı 24 (Aralık 1962)
Istanbul: Elif Kitabevi

BL:OIOC: 1:1 (1.11.1960) - 2:24
(12.1962)   [14497.e.17]

KİTAP BELLETEN [2. SERİ]: aylık
bibliyografya biografya dergisi
Yeni seri, sayı 1 (25) (1 Temmuz 1963) -
Nos. 41-43 (Eylül-Ekim-Kasım 1965)
Istanbul: Elif Kitabevi

BL:OIOC: 14497.e.17

KİTAP GAZETEŞİ: ayda bir çıkar /
İstanbul Kütüphanecilik ve
Kitapçılık tarafından çıkarılmaktadır
Yıl 1, sayı 1 (Ekim 1991) -
Istanbul

BL:OIOC: 1:16 (1.1.1993) -
[ZOR.1993.a.128]

KİTLE: haftalık sosyalist gazete
Yıl 1, sayı 1 (27 Mart 1974) - Yıl 5,
sayı 248 (14 Şubat 1979)
Istanbul

DU:DC: 2:72 (15.8.1975) - 5:248
(14.2.1979); lacking 3:104, 106, 113,
115-132, 134-145; 4:188, 210; 5:233
[25/3/POLITICAL PARTIES]

KIYI [1. SERİ]: sanat dergisi
Sayı 1 (Nisan 1981) - Sayı 21
(Haziran-Temmuz 1983)
Trabzon
Monthly

OX:BOD: 1 (4.1981) - 21 (6-7.1983)
[Per.Turk.d.3532]

KIYI [2. SERİ]: kültür ve sanat dergisi
Sayı 1 (Nisan 1986) -
Trabzon
Monthly

OX:BOD: 1 (4.1986) -   [Per.Turk.d.3533]

KIZIL BAYRAK
See: KEZEL BAYRAK

KIZIL GËNCË / Gëncë këza mëavif
[şic, i.e. mëarif] şöbësi vë
mëavif [şic] hëmkarlër ittifakı
tarafındën ''Kızıl kalëm'' Ëdëbiyyat
Cëmiyyëtinin iştirâkiyle aydë bir
nëşr olunan ilmi, ëdëbi, ictimai,
pedagoji mëcmuadır
No. 1 (Mart 1928) - [?]
Ganje (Kirovabad)
Azeri; Arabic characters

BL:OIOC: 1 (3.1928)   [ITA.1986.a.389]

KIZIL KALËM: siyasî, ictimaî, tarihî,
fënnî şëkilli Türkçë mëcmuadır,
aydа bir çıkar / Türkçë ''Kommunist''
gëzetësı nëşriyatından
Sayı 1 (1 Kanunusâni 1924) - [?]
Baku
Azeri; Arabic characters

BL:OIOC: 1 (1.1.1924) - 5 (28.4.1924)
[14499.tt.19]

KIZIL KAZAKSTAN: calpi sayasat, ilm, onar,
çarovaçlık ham adabiyat curnalı /
Kammunist Partiyasınıñ Kazakstan
Aymaktık Kamitesinin atlı [?]
No. 1 ([Yan.?] 1922) - [1929?]
Orenburg; Kızıl Orda; Alma-Ata; Tashkent
Place of publication varies
Kazakh; in Arabic characters
Monthly

BL:OIOC: 1924:7-9 (=31-33)
[14499.ss.24]

KIZIL TUU
See: KEZELTUW

KOCAELİ İL YILLIĞI
[1] (1967) - [2] (1973)
Istanbul, 1970-1973

BL:OIOC: [1] (1967)   [14498.a.64]
OX:BOD: [1]   [Turk.d.3324/41]

KOMMUNİST / Kırgızstan Kommunistik
Partiyasının Borborduk Komitetinin
teoriyalık cana sayasiy curnalı
1926, no. 1 ([date?] 1926) - 1984, no. 6
(İyun' 1984)
Frunze: Kırgızstan KP BKnin basması
Publisher before 1973: Ala-Too basması.
Continued in Russian from July 1984 as:
Kommunist Kirgizstana
In Kirgiz
Monthly

BL:OIOC: 1.1965 - 9.1976; lacking 2.1965
[14499.t.14]
OX:BOD: 1926:1 (?.1926) - 1984:6
(6.1984); lacking several issues from
years 1927 to 1935   [Per.Turk.d.1217]

KONAKLAMA İSTATİSTİKLERİ BÜLTENİ =
Bulletin of accommodation statistics /
Kültür ve Turizm Bakanlığı
1975 -
Ankara
In Turkish and English
Annual

DU:DC: 1981-   [25/4/TOURISM]

KONEVİ: fikir ve sanat dergisi
Sayı 1 (Temmuz 1982) - Sayı 34
(Kasım-Aralık 1986)
Konya
Mainly bimonthly

OX:BOD: 1 (7.1982) - 34 (11-12.1986)
[Per.Turk.d.3364]

KONYA / Halkevi tarafından aydabir
çıkarılır
Yıl 1, no.1 (Eylul 1936) - Yıl 9, sayı
81 (Ağustos 1945)
Konya: Konya Halkevi
Subtitle varies

LO:SOAS: 1:1 (9.1936) - 7:47 (1942)
[Per.10.315043]
OX:BOD: 1:1 - 9:81 (8.1945)
[Per.Turk.d.3540]

KONYA HALKEVİ KÜLTÜR DERGİSİ
Konya
Monthly

BL:OIOC: 1943, special issue (Mevlana)
[14415.d.172]
LO:SOAS: 1943, special issue
[S.VIII.L.50392]

KONYA İL YILLIĞI
[1] (1967) - [2] (1973)
Konya, [ca. 1968]-[ca. 1973]

OX:BOD: [1] (1967)   [Turk.d.3324/42]

KONYA VİLÂYETİ SALNAMESİ
Defa 1 (1285 [1868-1869]) - [Defa 30]
(1330 [1914-1915])
Konya
Many issues entitled: Salname-i
Vilâyet-i Konya

OX:BOD: 29 (1906)   [Turk.e.1507]

KOSOVA VİLÂYETİ SALNAMESİ
See: SALNAME-İ VİLÂYET-İ KOSOVA

KÖZ / Atatürk Üniversitesi
Mediko-Sosyal Hizmetler Daire
Başkanlığı'nın folklor-haber dergisi
Sayı 1 (Ağustos 1979) - Sayı 6 (Kasım
1980)
Erzurum, 1980-1981
Quarterly

OX:BOD: 1 (8.1979) - 6 (11.1980)
[Per.Turk.d.3382]

KUBBEALTI AKADEMİ MECMÛASI: üc ayda bir
çıkar, akademik mecmûadır
Yıl 1, sayı 1 (1 Ocak 1972)-
İstanbul: Kubbealtı Cemiyeti

BL:OIOC: 1:1 (1.1972) - 14:4 (10.1985)
[ITA.1987.a.50]
DU:UL: 1:1 -   [Per./PL4]
OX:BOD: 1 -   [Per.Turk.d.3100]

KÜÇÜK İSTATİSTİK YILLIĞI
See: TÜRKİYE İSTATİSTİK CEP
YILLIĞI

KÜÇÜK MECMUA: haftada bir çıkar ilmî,
edebî, siyasî, iktisadî mecmuadır
Yıl 1, sayı 1 (5 Haziran 1338 [1922]) -
Yıl 1, sayı 33 (5 Mart 1339 [1923])
Diyarbakır

BL:OIOC: 1:1 (5.6.1922) - 1:33
(5.3.1923) (microfiche)
[OR.MICROFICHE 91]
LO:SOAS: 1:1 - 1:33   [Per.10.188768]
OX:BOD: 1:1 - 1:33 (microfiche)   [Or.
Microfiches 59]

KÜLLÜK: fikir ve sanat mecmuası
Yıl 1, sayı 1 (Eylûl [1940])
[İstanbul]
Only one issue published

BL:OIOC: 1:1 (9.1940)   [14498.a.99]

KÜLTÜR BAKANLIĞI DERGİSİ
Sayı 1 ([date?], [1936?]) - [?]
Ankara
Frequency unknown

LO:SOAS: 20 (1.1.1937)   [Per.10.34960]

KÜLTÜR DÜNYASI / UNESCO Türkiye Millî
Komisyonu tarafından her ayın onbeşinde
çıkarılır dergi
Sayı 1 (15 Ocak 1954) - Sayı 28-29
(Eylül-Ekim 1956)
Ankara

BL:OIOC: 1 (15.1.1954) - 28/29
(9-10.1956)   [14456.k.94]
DU:UL: 2 - 4; 7; 19 - 23; 28/29
[Per./PL1]
OX:BOD: 1 - 28/29   [Per.Turk.d.3159]

KÜLTÜR HAFTASI
1 (15 İkici [sic] Kânun 1936) - 21 (3
Haziran 1936)
İstanbul
Weekly

BL:OIOC: 1 (15.1.1936) - 21 (3.6.1936)
[14498.a.100]
LO:SOAS: 1 - 21   [Per.10.L.285571]

KÜLTÜR İSTATİSTİKLERİ = Cultural
statistics = Başbakanlık Devlet
İstatistik Enstitüsü
Ankara, [19--?]-
In Turkish and English
Published in cumulations of several
years

OX:BOD: 1981/1983 -   [Per.247162.d.38]
SU:IDS: 1981/1983 -
[SERIALS/OFFICIAL/TURKEY]

KÜLTÜR VE SANAT
See: SANAT

KURTULUŞ: aylık mecmua / Azerbaycan
Millî Kurtuluş Hareketinin organı
1. yıl, sayı 1 (II-nci Teşrin 1934) -
Yıl 6, sayı 56/57 (Haziran-Temmuz 1939)
Berlin: Millî Azerbaycan Neşriyatı
Added titles in German and French: Die
Befreiung, La Délivrance
In ''Istanbul Turkish''

BL:OIOC: 1:1 (11.1934) - 6:55 (5.1939)
[14499.n.25]
LO:SOAS: 1:1; 2:7-8; 3:15-16; 4:32-38;
5:41-50; 6:51-57   [Per.57.35431]
OX:BOD: 1:1 (11.1934) - 6:56/57
(6-7.1939)   [Turk.d.801]

KURTULUŞ: Avrupa'da Türkiyeli
işçilerin gazetesi
1 ([date?], 1972) -
Berlin (West): Avrupa Türkiyeli
Toplumcular Federasyonu
Fortnightly

DU:DC: 104 (7.6.1974); 115; 117-118
(23.11.1974)   [25/3/POLITICAL PARTIES]

KURUN
See: VAKİT

KÜTAHYA İL YILLIĞI
[1] (1967) - [2] (1973)
Izmir

BL:OIOC: [1] (1967)   [14498.a.30]
OX:BOD: [1]   [Turk.d.3324/43]

KÜTÜPHANECİLİK DERGİSİ: belge bilgi
kütüphane araştırmaları / İstanbul
Üniversitesi Edebiyat Fakültesi
Sayı 1 [1987] -
İstanbul
Occasional

OX:BOD: 1 [1987] -   [Per.Turk.d.3952]

LA DÉLIVRANCE
See: KURTULUŞ

LALA PAŞA: haftalık siyasî mizah ve
tenkid gazetesi
Yıl 1, sayı 1 (25 Mayıs [1]947)
İstanbul
Only one issue published. Continued by:
Merhum Paşa

BL:OIOC: 1:1 (25.5.1947)   [OR.FICHE
444]

LÂLE / Türkpetrol Vakfı'nın yayın
organıdır
Yıl 1, sayı 1 (Temmuz 1982) -
İstanbul
Illustrated studies on Turkish art,
antiquities and culture
Irregular; generally annual

BL:OIOC: 1 (7.1982) -   [14498.a.119]

LE DOLAB
See: DOLAB

LENİN BAYRAĞI / Uzbekistan Kommunist
Partiyası Merkeziy Komiteti, UzSSR
Yuk'arı Soveti ve Ministrler Sovetiniñ
organı
No.1 (1 Mayıs 1957) -
Tashkent
In Tatar
Published thrice weekly

BL:OIOC: 1.2.1979 -; lacking some issues
[O.P.1027]

LETOPIS' PECHATI AZERBAĬDZHANA
See: AZĔRBAYCAN MĔTBUAT SALNAMĔSİ

LİBERAL OTOMAN = Le Libéral ottoman:
  organe des revendications du peuple
  ottoman, bi-mensuel
  1re année, no.1 (15 janvier 1901) - 1re
  année, no.5 (16 mars 1901)
  Paris
  Contents in Ottoman or French

  BL:OIOC: 1:1 (15.1.1901) - 1:5
  (16.3.1901)   [14999.k.3]

LE LIBÉRAL OTTOMAN
  See: LİBERAL OTOMAN

LA LIBERTÉ DE L'ORIENT
  See: AZADÎ-İ ŞARK

LIMBA ROMÂNĂ
  See: ROMEN DİLİ

LINGUISTIQUE
  See: DİLBİLİM

LİTERA / published yearly by the English
  Department of the University of Istanbul
  Volume 1 (1954) - Volume 8 (1965)
  Istanbul
  Not published between 1960 and 1965
  Mainly in English; some articles in
  Turkish

  BL:HSS: 1 (1954) - 8 (1965)
  [Ac.2657.aa]

LITERATURNOE NASLEDIE
  See: ADABİY MEROS

LIVESTOCK AND LIVESTOCK PRODUCTS
STATISTICS
  See: HAYVANLAR VE HAYVAN ÜRÜNLERİ
  İSTATİSTİKLERİ

LONDRA TÜRK SESİ
  See: TÜRK SESİ

MAADİN İSTATİSTİKİ / Orman ve Maadin
  ve Ziraat Nezareti İstatistik İdaresi
  1. sene (1323 [1907-1908]) - [3-5. sene]
  (1325, 1326, 1327 [1909-1912])
  Istanbul, 1325 [1909-1910] - 1330
  [1914-1915]
  Annual; some cumulated issues

  BL:OIOC: 1 (1907-8)   [ITA.1988.a.273]

MAARİF: perşembe günleri neşrolunur
  fenni ve edebî musavver gazete
  1. sene, numero 1 (19 Ağustos 1307 [1
  Sep. 1891]) - 5. sene, numero 35 (29
  Ağustos 1312 [11 Sep. 1896])
  Istanbul: Kasbar
  Years 1-4 comprise 204 issues; new
  numbering for Year 5

  OX:BOD: 1:1 (1.9.1891) - 2:85 (?.?.1892)
    [Turk.d.952]
  OX:MEC: 1:1 - 3:134 (?.2.1893)   [APT
  Mar]

MAARİF VA MADANİYAT: ayda bir
  çıkaturgan, adabî, siyasî, iktisadî,
  ilmî, tarihî, ictimaî va fannî,
  Şark yuksullari azadlığıga hizmet
  kılguçı rasimlik Özbikça
  San 1 (Noyabr 1923) - [?]
  Bukhara: Buhara Maarif Nazarati
  Uzbek; Arabic characters

  BL:OIOC: 1 (11.1923)   [14499.t.27]

MAARİF VA OKUTGUCİ CURNALİ: ayda bir
  tapkar çıkarıla turgan
  ta'lim-tarbiyavî, ictimâ'î [sic],
  ilmî va fanni Özbikça [curnali] /
  Özbikistan Ma'ârif Komisarligi
  Taşkent, [192-?]-[192-?]
  Publication history not known. The
  issuing body was based at Samarkand
  Uzbek; Arabic characters

  BL:OIOC: 1925:2 (3.1925), 1925:9/10
  (12.1925)   [14499.tt.29]

MAARİF VEKÂLETİ İHSÂİYÂT MECMUASI
  [1] (1310-1311 [1894-1895]) - [6]
  (1340-1341 [1924-1925])
  Istanbul, [189-?]-1927
  Published in cumulations

  BL:OIOC: [6] (1924-1925)   [14495.k.1]

MAARİF VEKÂLETİ MECMUASI
  Sayı 1 (1 Mart 1341 [1925]) - Sayı 17
  ([date?], 1929)
  Istanbul
  Issues 1-16 are in Arabic characters

  BL:OIOC: 9 (9.1926) - 15 (4.1928)
  [14498.b.10]

MAARIFET
  See: MARİFET

MADEN İSTATİSTİKLERİ = Mining
  statistics / Başbakanlık Devlet
  İstatistik Enstitüsü
  Ankara, [19--?]-
  In Turkish and English
  Annual; some earlier issues cumulated

  BL:HSS: 1982 -; lacking 1985, 1989
  [S.Q.170/50]
  DU:DC: 1961/1968; 1963/1970; 1974/1975,
  1976/1977; 1979/1980; 1982-
  [25/4/INDUSTRY/EXTRACTIVE]
  SU:IDS: 1979 -; lacking 1985
  [SERIALS/OFFICIAL/TURKEY]

MADENCİ: aylık dergi / Türkiye Maden
  İşçi Sendikaları Federasyonu yayın
  organı
  Yıl 1, sayı 1 (Nisan 1970) -
  Ankara

  DU:DC: 1:2 (5.1970) - 6:72 (3.1976);
  lacking 5:52, 6:67 - 6:70
  [25/3/TRADE UNIONS]

MAGTIMGULI ADINDAKİ ÊDEBİYAT
  İNSTİTUTINIŇ İŞLERİ = Trudy
  instituta literatury imeni Makhtumkuli
  Goyberliş 1 ([date?]) - [?]
  Aşgabat: Türkmenistan SSR Ilımlar
  Akademiyasınıň neşiryatı, [195-
  ?]-[19--?]
  Articles in Turkmen or Russian
  Annual?

  BL:OIOC: 4 (1960) - 5 (1961)
  [ITA.1988.a.164]
  LO:SOAS: 4   [Per.10.208849]

MAHASİN
  See: MEHASİN

MAHFİL: dinî, edebî, ictimâî ve
  şimdilik şehrî mecmua-i islamiyedir
  Aded 1 (Zilkade 1338 [August 1920]) -
  Aded 68 (Ramazan 1344 [March 1926])
  [İstanbul]
  In Arabic characters

  BL:OIOC: 1 (8.1920) - 68 (3.1926);
  lacking 39, 46, 47, 49   [14480.d.180]
  LO:SOAS: 25 - 28   [L.E.Per.21549]
  CA:UL: 1 - 67 (11.1926)   [Q.830.b.8]
  OX:BOD: 1 - 24   [Per.Turk.d.1465]

MALATYA İL YILLIĞI
[1] (1967) - [2] (1973)
Ankara

OX:BOD: [1] (1967)   [Turk.d.3324/44]

MALÎ İSTATİSTİKLER
See: MALİYE İSTATİSTİKLERİ

MALİYE ENSTİTÜSÜ TERCÜMELERİ /
İstanbul Üniversitesi İktisat
Fakültesi Maliye Enstitüsü
1. seri (1965) - [?]
Istanbul
Irregular

DU:UL: 1 (1965) - 4 (1969)   [Per./PL
328]

MALİYE İSTATİSTİKLERİ: Devlet
Maliyesi / Başbakanlık İstatistik
Genel Müdürlüğü
1926-1944 - [?]
Ankara, 1947-[19--?]
Title of first issue: Malî
istatistikler

BL:HSS: 1926/1944; 1939/1949
[S.Q.170/18]

MALUM PAŞA: halk için haftalık siyasî
mizah gazetesi
Yıl 1, sayı 1 (8 Eylûl 1947) - Yıl 1,
sayı 6 (11 Ekim 1947)
Istanbul

BL:OIOC: 1:1 (8.9.1947) - 1:6
(11.10.1947)   [OR.FICHE445]

MALUMÂT: menâfi-i Mülk ve Devlete hadim
haftalık gazete
Aded 1 (11 Mayıs 1311 [24 May 1885]) -
19. cild, aded 423 (5 Şubat 1319 [18
Feb. 1904])
Istanbul
Weekly magazine on news and cultural
affairs
Added title in French (no French
contents) : Illustration turque Malumat

BL:OIOC: 1 (24.5.1885) - 19:423
(18.2.1904)   [14498.a.81]
LO:SOAS: 1 - 16   [L.E.Per.162887]
CA:UL: 1 - 30   [T.830.a.6]
OX:BOD: 1 - 24 (5.12.1887)
[Turk.c.173]

MA'MURET ÜL-AZİZ VİLÂYETİ SALNAMESİ
Defa 1 (1298 [1880-1881]) - Defa 9 (1325
[1907-1908])
Elazığ
Ten issues published: two Defa 1s, dated
1298 and 1301
Most issues are entitled: Salname-i
Vilâyet-i Ma'muret ül-Aziz

CA:UL: 9 (1907)   [S.828.01.b.35]
OX:BOD: 9   [Turk.e.1470]

MANİSA İL YILLIĞI
[1] (1967) - [2] (1973)
Izmir, 1968-1973

OX:BOD: [1] (1968)   [Turk.d.3324/45]

MANUFACTURING INDUSTRY EMPLOYMENT AND
PROUCTION BY QUARTERS AND SECTORS
See: ÜÇ AYLIK DÖNEMLER VE SEKTÖRLER
İTİBARİYLE İMALAT SANAYİİ,
İSTİHDAM VE ÜRETİM

MANUFACTURING INDUSTRY PRODUCTION INDEXES
See: İMALAT SANAYİİ ÜRETİM
İNDEKSİ

MANUFACTURING INDUSTRY (QUARTERLY)
EMPLOYMENT-PRODUCTION-EXPECTATION
See: DÖNEMLER İTİBARİYLE İMALAT
SANAYİİ, İSTİHDAM-ÜRETİM-EĞİLİM

MANZARA: havadis-i medeniye, mebhis-i
fenniye ve edebiye, hıfzıssıha, seyahat,
teracim-i ahval ve roman gibi hususat-ı
mütenevvia'dan bahseder
1. sene, sayı 1 (1 Mart 1303 [14 Mar.
1887]) - 1. sene, sayı 16 (8
Teşrinisani 1303 [21 Nov. 1887])
Istanbul
Subtitle varies
Fortnightly

OX:BOD: 1:1 (14.3.1887) - 1:16
(21.11.1887)   [Per.Turk.d.2854]

MARAŞ İL YILLIĞI
[1] (1967) - [2] (1973)
Maraş

OX:BOD: [1] (1967)   [Turk.d.3324/46]

MARDİN İL YILLIĞI
[1] (1967) - [2] (1973)
Ankara

OX:BOD: [1] (1967)   [Turk.d.3324/47]

MARİFET: Türkçe ve Fransızca olarak
haftada bir defa neşrolunur fennı ve
edebî risaledir
1. sene, aded 1 (5 Mart 1314 [18 Mar.
1898]) - 1. sene, aded 16 (27 Ağustos
1314 [9 Sep. 1898])
[İstanbul]
French t.p.: Maarifet: la seule revue
hebdomadaire Turco-Française
All issues comprise two sections, with
different contents, in Ottoman and in
French

BL:OIOC: 1:1 (18.3.1898) - 1:16
(9.9.1898)   [14498.a.108]
OX:BOD: 1:1 - 1:16   [Turk.d.1847 (3)]

MARKO PAŞA
See: HÜR MARKO PAŞA

MARRIAGE STATISTICS
See: EVLENME İSTATİSTİKLERİ

MATERIAL'NAÎA KUL'TURA AZERBAÎDZHANA
See: AZĔRBAYCANIN MADDİ
MĔDĔNİYYĔTİ

MATERIALY PO ISTORII AZERBAÎDZHANA
See: AZĔRBAYCAN TARİHİNĔ DAİR
MATERİALLAR

MAVERA: aylık edebiyat dergisi
Yıl 1, sayı 1 (Aralık 1976) - Yıl 13,
sayı 156 (Aralık 1989)
Ankara
Cultural and current affairs magazine

BL:OIOC: 1:1 (12.1976) - 48 (11.1980);
62; 73 - 75; 100 -   [14498.cc.44]
OX:BOD: 48 - 96 (1.1984)
[Per.Turk.d.3097]

MĔ'ARİF / Tatarstan Mĕ'arif Halk
Kamisariyatı tarafından ayga bir tabkar
çıgarıla turgan ilmî pedagogiya
curnalı
1925, no.1 ('İnvar 1925) - [?]
Kazan
Tatar; Arabic characters

BL:OIOC: 1925:6/7 (6-7.1925); 1927:1-2
(1-2.1927)   [14499.eee.4]

MĚARÎF ÎŞCÎSÎ: siyasî, ictimaî,
edebî, hěmkarlar, pedagoji, ilmî
mecmuadır; ayda bir çıkar / Azěrbaycan
Měarif Îşcileri Îttifakı
No. 1 (Nisan 1925) - [?]
Baku
In Azeri
Nominally monthly; mainly cumulated
bi-monthly

BL:OIOC: 6/7 (9-10.1925); 10 (2.1926),
14/15 (6-7.1926); 25 (5.1927), 30/31
(10-11.1927); 35 (3.1928)   [14499.t.35]

MĚARÎF VĚ MĚDĚNÎYĚT: ědebî,
ilmî, fěnnî aylık mecmuadır /
Azěrbaycan Ěděbiyyat Cěmiyyětiniñ
iştirakiyle Měarif Komisarlığı
tarafından něşr idilir
Sayı 1 (Yanvar 1923) - [?]
Baku: A. K. F. Měrkězi Komitěsi
Azeri; Arabic characters

BL:OIOC: 2.14/15 (2/3.1924), 2:18
(6.1924); 3:22 (10.1925); 4:24 (1.1926)
- 4:26 (3.1926), 4:30 (7.1926)
[ITA.1986.c.13]
LO:SOAS: 2:12 (12.1923) - 2:14/15
(2-3.1924); 3:22 (10.1925)
[Per.10.L.136622]

MECHEROUTIETTE
See: MEŞRUTÎYET

MECHROUTIYET
See: MEŞRUTÎYET

MECHVERET
See: MEŞVERET

MECMUA-Î ÂSÂR: manzum ve mensur eski ve
yeni tarzda yazılmış bilcümle âsâr-ı
nefise ve makbule'yi havi mecmua-i
edebiyedir
Yıl 1, sayı 1 (1299 [1882]) - Yıl 2,
sayı 12 (1300 [1883])
Istanbul
Monthly; issues dated by year only

CA:UL: 1:1   [Gibb.d.241]
OX:BOD: 1:1 (1882) - 2:12 (1883)
[Turk.f.226]

MECMUA-Î EBUZZÎYA: fünun ve maariften
bahseder ve her şehr-i Arabî
ibtidasiyle onbeşinde neşrolunur
mecmua-i mevkutedir
Cild 1, cüz' 1 (15 Ramazan 1297 [31
August 1880]) - 31. sene, cild 15, cüz'
159 (2 Ramazan 1330 [15 August 1912])
Istanbul: Ebüzziya Tevfik
Not published between 1305 [1888-9] and
1312 [1895-6]
French added titles: Médjmou-a-i
Ebuzzia; Revue Ebuzzia
Initially nominally fortnightly;
nominally weekly from no. 94 onwards

BL:OIOC: (a) 1:1 (31.8.1880) - 31:15:159
(15.8.1912) (microfiche); (b) 1:1 -
18:78 (hard copy)   [(a) OR.MICROFICHE
85; (b) 14485.b.2]
LO:SOAS: 1:1 - 13:15:159
[Per.10.63302]
CA:UL: (a) 1:1 - 31:15:159; (b) 1:1 -
?:48; (c) 9, 37, 49 - 53, 61   [(a)
Q.830.c.17; (b) Gibb.c.239; (c)
L.830.c.17]
OX:BOD: (a) 1:1 - 31:15:159; (b) 54-55
   [(a) Turk.e.1530; (b) Per.Turk.d.38]
OX:MEC: 1:1 - 31:15:159   [APT Mec]

MECMUA-Î EDEBÎYE [2. SERÎ]: edebî,
fennî, sınaî, ticarî gazetedir
1. cild, aded 1 (12 Teşrinievvel 1316
[25 Oct. 1900]) - 1. cild, aded 52 (18
Teşrinisâni 1317 [1 Dec. 1901])
Istanbul
Second series, comprising 85 issues,
published 1317-18 [1901-2]
Weekly

BL:OIOC: 1:1 (25.10.1900) - 1:52
(1.12.1901)   [14499.k.1]

MĚCMUA-Î ĚVRÂK-I NĚFÎSĚ
See: ĚVRÂK-I NĚFÎSĚ

MECMUA-Î FÜNUN / eser-i Cemiyet-i
Îlmiye-i Osmaniye
1. sene, numero 1 (Muharrem 1279
[June-July 1862]) - 5. sene, numero 47
(Safer 1284 [July-Aug. 1867])
Istanbul
Initially monthly

BL:OIOC: 1:1 (7.1862) - 1:12 (6.1863)
[ITA.1988.a.41]
CA:UL: (a) 1:1 - 3:33; (b) 1:13 - 2:22
[(a) T.830.c.11; (b) S.828.d.86.6]
OX:MEC: 1:1 - 5:46   [APT Mec 2]

MECMUA-Î ÎBRETNÜMA: edebî dergi; işbu
mecmua beher mah-ı Arabî evahirinde bir
defa çıkar / eser-i Cemiyet-i Kitabet
Numero 1 ([Şevval?] 1281 [1865] -
Numero 16 (Muharrem 1283 [May-June
1866])
Istanbul

BL:OIOC: 11 (12.1865)   [ITA.1988.a.395]

MECMUA-Î KEMAL: üç ayda bir neşrolunur
risale-i si-mahedir / müessis, Ali
Kemal
Sene 1, cüz' 1 (1 Haziran 1901 [14 June
1901])
Cairo
General cultural magazine. All
contributions are by Ali Kemal
Only one issue published

BL:OIOC: 1:1 (14.6.1901)   [14480.d.237]
OX:BOD: 1:1   [Turk.d.2385]

MECMUA-Î LÎSAN: onbeş günde bir
neşrolunur elsine, tarih, edebiyat ve
saire'den bâhis Osmanlı gazetesidir
Cilt 1, sayı 1 (4 Haziran 1314 [17 June
1898]) - [2. seri], cilt 1, sayı 47 (19
Ağustos 1316 [1 Sep. 1900])
Istanbul
Series 1 comprises 7 issues
Includes contributions in French

OX:BOD: 1:1 (17.6.1898) - [2]:1:47
(1.9.1900)   [Per.Turk.d.1847 (1)]

MECMUA-Î MAÂRÎF: onbeş günde bir
çıkar
1. nüsha (15 Cumâdâssâni 1284 [14
Oct. 1867]) - [?]
Istanbul
Publication history not known.
Lithographed. No apparent connection
with the Mecmua-i Maârif published in
1284 [1868] by Cemiyet-i Îlmiye-i
Osmaniye

BL:OIOC: 1 (14.10.1867)   [14498.a.7]

MECMUA-İ MUALLİM
1. sene, nüsha 1 (30 Eylül 1303 [13
Oct. 1887]) - 2. sene, nüsha 58 (3
Teşrinisani 1304 [16 Nov. 1888])
Istanbul
A literary journal
Weekly

BL:OIOC: 1:1 (13.10.1887) - 2:58
(16.11.1888) [14498.a.82]
LO:SOAS: 1:1 - 2:58 [L.E.Per.137107]
CA:UL: (a) 1 - 58; (b) 1 - 53 [(a)
Gibb.a.243; (b) L.830.a.6]
OX:BOD: 1:1 - 2:58 [Turk.c.69]

MEDENİET CĔNE TÜRMİS
See: PARASAT

MÉDJMOU-A-I EBUZZIA
See: MECMUA-İ EBUZZİYA

MEDRESE İTİKADLARI: Cuma günleri
neşrolunur usbuî İslâm ceridesidir
Numero 1 (27 Ağustos 1329 [9 Sep.
1913]) - Numero 18 (13 Eylül 1329 [26
Sep. 1913])
Istanbul
Subtitle for nos.1-7 begins: Pazar
ertesi günleri

BL:OIOC: 1 (9.9.1913) - 18 (26.9.1913)
[14415.d.144]

MEHASİN: her Rumî ayın birinci günü
neşrolunur hanımlara mahsus gazetedir
Numero 1 (Eylül 1324 [1908]) - Numero
12 (Teşrinisani 1325 [1909])
Istanbul
General interest and fashion magazine
for ladies

BL:OIOC: 1 (9.1908) - 12 (11.1909)
[14498.cc.57]
OX:BOD: 1 - 12 [Turk.d.1020]

MEHNAT VA TURMUŞ: oyda bir çikadigan
ictimoiy-şiyosiy, adabiy-badiiy, suratli
curnal / Üzbekiston Kompartiyasi
Markaziy Komitetining curnali
No. 1 ([month?] 1942) -
Tashkent
In Uzbek

BL:OIOC: 1970:1-12 [14499.tt.35]

MEHTAB: edebî, fennî, ictimaî teceddüd
ve inkılâb-ı fikriye'ye hadim ceride-i
üsbûiyedir
Yıl 1, sayı 1 (10 Temmuz 1327 [23 July
1911]) - Yıl 1, sayı 15 (20
Teşrinievvel 1327 [2 Nov. 1911])
Istanbul

OX:BOD: 1:1 (23.7.1911) - 1:15
(2.11.1911) [Per.Turk.d.1019]

MEHTAP
See: MEHTAB

MEKHNAT VA TURMUSH
See: MEHNAT VA TURMUŞ

MEKTEB: onbeş günde bir defa perşembe
günleri neşrolunur, edebî ve hikemî,
fennî risaledir
1. yıl, 1. cilt, sayı 1 (26 Temmuz 1307
[8 Aug. 1891]) - [3. seri], 5. cilt,
sayı 72 (30 Kanunusani 1313 [12 Feb.
1898])
Istanbul
Published in three series, 211 issues

OX:BOD: 1:1 (8.8.1897) - 2:99; 2:3:1 -
2:3:26 (15.3.1894) [Turk.d.985]

MEKTEP
See: MEKTEB

MEMLEKET
Sene 1, aded 1 ([date?], Şubat 1335
[1919]) - [?]
Istanbul
Daily

BL:OIOC: 1:50 (31.3.1919) - 1:140
(29.6.1919) (damaged, lacking several
issues); 10.7.1919 [OR.MIC.11705
(O.P.254)]

MEMLEKETİMİZİN UMUMİ İKTİSADİ
DURUMU HAKKINDA RAPOR / Türkiye İş
Bankası
Ankara, [196-?]-
10 issues annually

DU:DC: 3.1962-12.1965; lacking 11.1963,
7-8.1964, 11.1965
[25/4/ECONOMY/GENERAL]

MERAM: vatan ve milletin menafiine hadim
dinî, siyasî, felsefî, edebî
mecmuadır
Numero 1 (30 Teşrinievvel 1324 [12 Nov.
1908]) - Numero 10 (29 Kanunusani 1324
[11 Feb. 1909])
[Istanbul]
Subtitle varies
Frequency varies between weekly and
fortnightly

BL:OIOC: 1 (12.11.1908) - 10 (11.2.1909)
[14489.b.195]
CA:UL: 1 - 10 [Q.830.c.18]
OX:MEC: 1 - 10 [APT Mer]

MERHUM PAŞA: haftalık siyasi mizah
gazetesi
Yıl 1, sayı 1 (26 Mayıs 1947) - Yıl 1,
sayı 4 (1 Kasım 1947)
Istanbul
Continuation of: Lala Paşa

BL:OIOC: 1:1 (26.5.1947) - 1:4
(1.11.1947) [OR.FICHE 446]

MĔ'RUZĔLĔR = Doklady / Azĕrbaycan SSR
Elmlĕr Akademiyası
1 ([date?], [1945?]) -
Baku
ISSN 0002-3078
Articles in Azeri or Russian
Quarterly

BL:HSS: 10:1 (1.1954) - [Ac.1109.d.]
LO:SOAS: 1960:1 - [Per.10.143924]
OX:BOD: 1945:2; 1946:1, 3-5; 1947:1-3;
1950:1, 9-11; 1951:1-8; 1952:2, 4-6, 9;
1953:4-5, 7-12; 1954:5-12; 1955:1-12;
1956:1-11; 1957:1 - [Per.3974.d.867]

MEŞALE: onbeş günde bir çıkar sanat ve
edebiyat mecmuası
Numero 1 (1 Temmuz 1928) - Numero 8 (15
Teşrinievvel 1928)
Istanbul
In Ottoman (i.e. Arabic characters),
excepting two pages in nos. 7 and 8

BL:OIOC: 1 (1.7.1928) - 8 (15.10.1928)
[14480.d.239]
OX:BOD: 1 - 8 [Per.Turk.d.3164]

MEŞRUTİYET: bilâ tefrik-i cins ü
mezheb bilumum Osmanlıların müzavat-ı
hukukuna ve menâfi'-i siyasiye ve
iktisadiye'lerinin müdafaasına hâdim
bir ceridedir
1. sene, numero 1 ([date?], 1326 [1910])
– 3. sene, numero [?] ([date?], 1328
[1912])
Paris
Added title: Mechroutiyet; later:
Mecheroutiette
Approximately monthly

BL:OIOC: 1:3 (1.4.1910); 2:19
(15.3.1911), 2:29 (1.11.1911)
[ORB.45/9]

MEŞVERET / Osmanlı İttihad ve Terakki
Cemiyetinin vasıta-i neşriyatıdır
1. sene, numero 1 (1 Kanunuevvel 1312
[14 Dec. 1896]) – 3. sene, numero 30 (6
Mayıs 1898)
Paris
Incorporating: Mechveret: organe de la
Jeune Turquie, supplément français
Irregular; sometimes fortnightly

BL:OIOC: 1:3 (14.4.1910); 2:19
(28.3.1911); 2:29 (14.11.1911)
[ORB.45/9]

METEOROLOJİ RASATLARI
See: YILLIK METEOROLOJİ BÜLTENİ

METÜ. JOURNAL OF THE FACULTY OF
ARCHITECTURE
See: ODTÜ. MİMARLIK FAKÜLTESİ
DERGİSİ

METU. STUDIES IN DEVELOPMENT
See: ODTÜ. GELİŞME DERGİSİ

MEYDAN
Yıl 1, sayı 1 ([date?], 1964) – [?]
Istanbul
Weekly newspaper

BL:OIOC: 260 (61.1970) – 467
(25.12.1973); 479 (26.3.1974) – 518
(24.12.1974); lacking 497 (30.7.1974)
[14498.a.68]

MİHNAT = Trud: ayda ikki martaba çıkadi
/ Uzbekistan Halk Mihnat Kamisarligi,
Kasabalar Şurasi va Baş İctimaî
Istrahavaniyanıñ fikir tarkatguçisi
1 ([date?], 1926) – [?]
Tashkent
Uzbek (Arabic characters) and Russian

BL:OIOC: 2:1 (1.1927) – 2:4 (8.3.1927);
2:7/8 (1.5.1927)   [14499.tt.23]

MİHRAB: ahlâkî, ictimaî, felsefî,
tarihî, edebî mecmuadır; şimdilik
onbeş günde bir neşrolunur
Sene 1, sayı 1 (15 Teşrinisani 1339
[1923]) – Sene 2, sayı 28 (1 Nisan 1341
[1925])
Istanbul

LO:SOAS: 1:1 – 1:2   [Per.10.188715]
OX:BOD: 1:1 (15.11.1923) – 2:28
(1.4.1925)   [Per.Turk.d.3552]

MİHRAP
See: MİHRAB

MİKRASIATIKON ĒMEROLOGİON O "ASTĒR"
1913
[Istanbul]
Yearbook for Turkish-speaking Greeks
Apparently only one issue published
Karamanlitic: Ottoman in Greek
characters

BL:OIOC: 1913   [14498.cc.24]

MİLİTAN: devrimci sanat ve kültür
kavgasında aylık dergi
Sayı 1 (Ocak 1975) – Yıl 2, sayı 18
(Haziran 1976)
Istanbul

BL:OIOC: 3 (3.1975) – 2:17 (5.1976);
lacking 4   [14498.cc.38]

MİLLET MECLİSİ TUTANAK DERGİSİ
See: T.B.M.M. TUTANAK DERGİSİ

MİLLĔTLĔR
No. 1 (Fĕvral 1956) –
Beijing: Millĕtlĕr baspası
Illustrated magazine for minority
peoples in China
Uygur; Arabic characters (roman from ca.
1974 to 1982). Also published in
Chinese, Kazakh, Korean, Mongolian, and
Tibetan
Monthly

BL:OIOC: 1956:1-; lacking 1956:7-12;
1958:3-1961:4; 1966:4; 1966:8-1974:1;
1976:7, 9-10; 1982:1   [15037.a.36/4]
OX:BOD: 1964:1 – 1986:2; lacking 1966:4
[Per.Turk.c.128]

MİLLETLERARASI MÜNASEBETLER TÜRK
YILLIĞI = The Turkish yearbook of
international relations
1 (1960) –
Ankara: Dış Münasebetler Enstitüsü,
Siyasal Bilgiler Fakültesi, Ankara
Üniversitesi
Mainly in English or French; some
articles in Turkish

BL:OIOC: 1 (1960) – 9 (1968)
[14498.a.71]
LO:SOAS: 1 –   [Per.57.156615]
OX:BOD: 1 –   [Per.Turk.d.635]

MILLI BAIRAK
See: MİLLİ BAYRAK

MİLLİ BAYRAK: yarak şarkdagı İdel-Ural
Türk-Tatarlarınıñ atnalık gĕzitĕsi
vĕ birinçi kurultaynıñ tercüman-i
efkârıdır
1nçi yıl, san 1 (1nçi Noyabr 1935) –
6nçi yıl, san 26 (266) (20 İyun 1941)
Mukden
English added title: Milli Bairak: the
national organ of Idel-Oural
Turko-Tatars in the Far East
In Tatar; Arabic characters
Weekly

BL:OIOC: 1:1 (1.11.1935) – 6:266
(20.6.1941); lacking 13.11.1936,
4-25.11.1939, 8-22.12.1939,
5.1-17.5.1940   [OR. MIC. 11989 (O.P.
469)]

MİLLİ EĞİTİM İSTATİSTİKLERİ /
Başbakanlık İstatistik Genel
Müdürlüğü
[19--?] – 1942-1943
Ankara, [19--?]-1945
Succeeded after 1945 by several separate
titles

BL:HSS: 1942/1943   [S.Q.170/16]

MİLLÎ EĞİTİM İSTATİSTİKLERİ,
  İLKÖĞRETİM = National education
  statistics, primary education /
  Başbakanlık Devlet İstatistik
  Enstitüsü
  Ankara, [19--?]-
  In Turkish and English; previously in
  Turkish only
  Currently annual; previously cumulated

  BL:HSS: 1944/1945, 1945/1946
  [S.Q.170/15]
  DU:DC: 1960/1961, 1961/1965, 1965/1967;
  1980/1981 -   [25/4/EDUCATION]
  SU:IDS: 1981/1982 - 1985/1986
  [SERIALS/OFFICIAL/TURKEY]

MİLLÎ EĞİTİM İSTATİSTİKLERİ,
MESLEK, TEKNİK VE YÜKSEK ÖĞRETİM
  See: MİLLÎ EĞİTİM
  İSTATİSTİKLERİ, MESLEKİ VE TEKNİK
  ÖĞRETİM

MİLLÎ EĞİTİM İSTATİSTİKLERİ,
  MESLEKİ VE TEKNİK ÖĞRETİM =
  National education statistics,
  vocational and technical secondary
  education / Başbakanlık Devlet İstatik
  Enstitüsü
  (1943-1944) -
  Ankara, 1946-
  Some issues combined with other
  educational statistics
  In Turkish and English; previously in
  Turkish only
  Annual; generally cumulated

  BL:HSS: 1944/1945, 1945/1946
  [S.Q.170/16]
  DU:DC: 1961/1965, 1965/1967, 1967/1973;
  1980/1981 -   [25/4/EDUCATION]
  SU:IDS: 1980/1981 - 1985/1986
  [SERIALS/OFFICIAL/TURKEY]

MİLLÎ EĞİTİM İSTATİSTİKLERİ,
  ÖRGÜN EĞİTİM = National education
  statistics, formal education /
  Başbakanlık Devlet İstatistik
  Enstitüsü
  1986/1987 -
  Ankara, 1988-
  Continuation of: Millî eğitim
  istatistikleri, ilköğretim, ...
  meslekî ve teknik öğretim, and ...
  ortaöğretim
  In Turkish and English
  Annual; sometimes cumulated

  SU:IDS: 1986/1987 -
  [SERIALS/OFFICIAL/TURKEY]

MİLLÎ EĞİTİM İSTATİSTİKLERİ,
  ORTAÖĞRETİM = National education
  statistics, general secondary education
  / Başbakanlık Devlet İstatistik
  Enstitüsü
  (1943-1944) -
  Ankara, 1946-
  In Turkish and English; previously in
  Turkish only
  Nominally annual; generally cumulated

  BL:HSS: 1944/1945 - 1945/1946
  [S.Q.170/17]
  DU:DC: 1961/1965; 1965/1967; 1980/1981 -
  [25/4/EDUCATION]
  SU:IDS: 1980/1981 - 1985/1986
  [SERIALS/OFFICIAL/TURKEY]

MİLLÎ EĞİTİM İSTATİSTİKLERİ,
  YAYGIN EĞİTİM = National education
  statistics, adult education se
  Başbakanlık Devlet İstatistik
  Enstitüsü
  Ankara, [19--?]-
  In Turkish and English
  Currently annual

  DU:DC: 1980/1981 -   [25/4/EDUCATION]
  SU:IDS: 1980/1981 -
  [SERIALS/OFFICIAL/TURKEY]

MİLLÎ EĞİTİM İSTATİSTİKLERİ,
  YÜKSEK ÖĞRETİM = National education
  statistics, higher education /
  Başbakanlık Devlet İstatistik
  Enstitüsü
  Ankara, [19--?]-
  Previously sometimes combined with other
  education statistics
  Currently in Turkish and English;
  previously in Turkish only
  Generally biennial

  DU:DC: 1970/1974; 1981/1982 -
  [25/4/EDUCATION]
  SU:IDS: 1967/1970; 1978/1979 - 1982/1983
  [SERIALS/OFFICIAL/TURKEY]

MİLLÎ EĞİTİM VE KÜLTÜR: üç aylık
  ilmî araştırma ve inceleme dergisi
  Sayı 1 (1 Aralık 1978) - Yıl 8, sayı
  37-37 [i.e. 37-38] - 39 (Mayıs 1986)
  Ankara

  OX:BOD: 1:1 (2nd ed., 9.1980) -
  37/[38]/39 (5.1986)   [Per.Turk.d.3224]

MİLLÎ GÜVENLİK KONSEYİ TUTANAK
DERGİSİ
  See: T.B.M.M. TUTANAK DERGİSİ

MİLLÎ KÜLTÜR: üç aylık dergi /
  Kültür ve Turizm Bakanlığı
  Yıl 1, cilt 1, sayı 1 (Ocak 1977)-
  Ankara
  Quarterly; initially monthly

  BL:OIOC: 1:1:1 (1.1977) - 1:11
  (11.1977); 52 (3.1986) -   [14498.a.89]
  LO:SOAS: 2:3 - 3:7; 37 -
  [Per.10.L.445989]
  OX:BOD: 1:12   [Per.Turk.d.2947]
  OX:MEC: 2:3-12; 3:1-7; 37 (?.1981) -
  [APT Mil]
  CA:OS: 75 (8.1990) -; lacking some
  issues   [enquire for location]

MİLLÎ KÜTÜPHANE HABERLERİ: aylık
  bülten
  Yıl 1, sayı 1 (Ocak 1957) - Yıl 16, sayı
  [?] ([date?] 1973)
  Ankara

  BL:OIOC: 1:1 (1.1957) - 3:31 (7.1959);
  lacking 2:15   [O.P.547; OR.MIC.11748]
  BL:HSS: 2:15 (3.1958); 3:32 (8.1959);
  2:35 (11.1959) - 4:41 (5.1960); 4:45
  (9.1960); 5:51 (3.1961) - 5:54 (6.1961);
  5:56/57 (8-9.1961); 6:61 (1.1962) - 6:62
  (2.1962); 15:1 (1.1971) - 15:7 (7.1971);
  15:10 (10.1971) - 16:1 (1.1972); 16:3
  (3.1973)   [S.Q.154]
  DU:UL: 1:3 (3.1957); 2:13 (1.1958)
  [Per./PL18]

MİLLÎ KÜTÜPHANE PERİYODİKLER
  BÖLÜMÜ AYLIK BÜLTENİ
  Yıl 1, sayı 1 (Ocak 1953) - [?]
  Ankara

  DU:UL: 4:47 (11.1956)   [Per./PL18]

MİLLÎ MECMUA: ilmî, edebî, iktisadî,
harsî mecmuadır
1. sene, nu. 1 (1 Teşrinisani 1339
[1922]) - Cilt 14, yıl 14, sayı 162
(Mart 1955)
Istanbul
Numerous subtitles through publication
history
Frequency: 1922-1933, twice monthly ;
1952 - October 1953, monthly ; irregular
thereafter

BL:OIOC: 1:1 (1.11.1922) - 14:14:162
(3.1955) (some in photostat)
[14498.a.86]
OX:BOD: 1:1 - 14:14:162
[Per.Turk.c.187]

MİLLÎ NEVSAL: her sene Mart ibtidasında
neşrolunur ve herşeyden bahseder Türk
salnamesi
Sene 1 (1338 [1922]) - Sene 4 (1341
[1925])
Istanbul: Kanaat

BL:OIOC: 1 (1922) - 4 (1925) (a); 3-4
(b)   [(a) 14498.a.69; (b) 14495.d.29]
CA:UL: 1 - 4   [T.830.d.1]

MİLLÎ TETEBBÜLER MECMUASI: din, ahlâk,
hukuk
Cilt 1, sayı 1 (Mart-Nisan 1331 [1915])
- Cilt 2, sayı 5 (Kanunuevvel 1331
[1915])
Istanbul
Bi-monthly

BL:OIOC: 1:1 (3-4.1915) - 2:5 (12.1915)
[14498.1.39]
CA:UL: 1:1 - 2:5   [Moh.16.b.3]
OX:BOD: 1:1 - 2:5   [Turk.d.261]
OX:MEC: 1:1 - 2:5   [APT Mil 1]

MİLLÎ YUL
See: YAÑA MİLLÎ YUL

MİLLİYET
1. sene, no. 1 (11 Şubat 1926) - 10.
sene, no. 3282 (22 Nisan 1935)
Istanbul
Daily newspaper
Later issues have additional title: Tan

BL:OIOC: 9:3226 (1.2.1935) - 10:3253
(28.2.1935)   [OR.MIC.11876 (O.P.641)]

MİLLİYET
Yıl 1, sayı 1 (3 Mayıs 1950) -
Istanbul
Daily newspaper

BL:OIOC: (a) 1.1.1962 - 31.12.1984;
lacking 1.9.1963 - 6.9.1963, 1.9.1965 -
23.9.1965, 26.9.1965 - 3.10.1965,
23.12.1965 - 12.12.1969, 30.6.1970 -
17.7.1970, 1.5.1971 - 3.5.1971,
1.8.1971, 1.11.1982, 26.11.1983 -
8.1.1984; (b) 5.5.1960 - 6.5.1960; (c)
2.1.1985 - 30.6.1986   [(a)
OR.MIC.11459; (b) OR.MIC.12769; (c)
O.P.1130]
DU:UL: 1.10.1965 -   [not callmarked]

MİMAR SİNAN / Türkiye Hür ve Kabul
Edilmiş Masonları Büyük Locasının
tarihi, çağdaş ve gerçekçi açıdan
araştırma ve yayın organıdır
Yıl 1, sayı 1 (Ekim 1966) - Sayı 68
(Haziran 1988)
Istanbul
Quarterly

BL:OIOC: 1:1 (10.1966) - 1981:42
[14439.d.213]
OX:BOD: 1:1 - 61 (?.1986); 68 (6.1988)
[Per.Turk.d.3313]

MINING STATISTICS
See: MADEN İSTATİSTİKLERİ

MİR'ÂT
See: AYNA

MİR'AT-I ÂLEM [2. SERİ]: şuunât-ı
medeniye, mebâhis-i fenniye ve edebiye,
seyahât ve terâcim-i ahvâl gibi
hususat-ı mütenevvia'dan bahseder /
Encümen-i Hâdim-i Terakki-i Maarif
Cild 1, aded 1 (25 Haziran 1300 [8 July
1884]) - Cild 2, nusha 2 ([undated],
1303 [1887 or 1888])
Istanbul
Vol. 1 comprises 12 issues
Irregular; issues not dated after vol.
1, no. 7 (8.5.1885)

BL:OIOC: 1:1 (8.7.1884) - 2:2 (1887 or
1888)   [14498.d.16]
OX:BOD: 1:1 - 1:12   [Turk.c.86]

MİRSAD: siyasattan maada herşeyden
bahseder ve haftada bir defa neşrolunur
1. sene, numero 1 (14 Mart 1307 [27 Mar.
1891]) - Cild 2, numero 25 (29 Ağustos
1307 [11 Sep. 1891])
[Istanbul]

BL:OIOC: 1:1 (27.3.1891) - 2:25
(11.9.1891)   [14480.d.238]
OX:BOD: 1:1 - 2:25   [Per.Turk.c.205]

MİZAN [1. SERİ]: yalnız perşembe
günleri neşrolunur Türk gazetesidir
Sayı 1 (22 Muharrem 1304 [21 Oct. 1886])
- Sayı 184 (19 Temmuz 1315 [31 July
1899])
Istanbul

OX:BOD: 1 (21.10.1886) - 52 (?.?.1887)
[Turk.b.6]

MİZAN [2. SERİ] / Osmanlı İttihad ve
Terakki Cemiyetinin vasıta-i
neşriyatıdır
1. sene, numero 1 (14 Kanunuevvel 1896)
- 1. sene, numero 29 (19 Temmuz 1897)
Paris; Geneva
Published first at Paris (nos. 1-18),
then at Geneva
Added title: Mizan (La Balance)
Weekly; but issues 27-29 all have the
same date

BL:OIOC: 1:1 (14.12.1896) - 1:29
(19.7.1897)   [14498.d.8]

MIZRAP: müzik/kültür/turizm/aktüalite
magazin, aylık dergi
Sayı 1 (Ekim 1982) - Yıl 5, sayı 57-58
(Haziran-Temmuz 1987)
Istanbul

CA:UL: 2:17 (2.1984) -   [Picken
Collection (unplaced)]
OX:BOD: 1 (10.1982) - 5:57/58 (6-7.1987)
[Per.Turk.d.3229]

MOLLA NASREDDIN
See: MOLLA NÊSRÊDDİN

MOLLA NÊSRÊDDİN
No. 1 ([7 Aprel 1906]) - [Sene [?], no.
[?] ([date?] 1931)
Tbilisi; Tabriz; Baku
Illustrated satirical weekly
Published at Tiflis (Tbilisi) (1906-17);
Tabriz (1921); and Baku (1922-1931)
Russian added title: Molla Nasreddin
Azeri; Cyrillic characters

LO:SOAS: 1 [7.4.1906] - 2:49
(30.12.[1907] (reprint in book form,
Baku 1988)   [Per.10.L.209851]

LE MONDE DENTAIRE
See: DİŞÇİLİK ÂLEMİ

58

MONTHLY BULLETIN OF PRICE INDEXES
    See: TOPTAN EŞYA VE TUKETİCİ
    FİYATLARI AYLIK İNDEKS BÜLTENİ

MONTHLY BULLETIN OF STATISTICS
    See: AYLIK İSTATİSTİK BÜLTENİ

MONTHLY FOREIGN TRADE STATISTICS
    See: AYLIK DIŞ TİCARET
    İSTATİSTİKLERİ

MONTHLY STATISTICAL AND EVALUATION
BULLETIN
    See: İSTATİSTİK VE DEĞERLENDİRME
    BÜLTENİ

MONTHLY STATISTICAL BULLETIN
    See: AYLIK İSTATİSTİK BÜLTENİ

MOTORLU KARA TAŞITLARI İSTATİSTİKLERİ
    = Road motor vehicles statistics /
    Başbakanlık Devlet İstatistik
    Enstitüsü
    Ankara, [19--?]-
    Turkish and English
    Annual; some cumulated issues

    SU:IDS: 1976/1980 -
    [SERIALS/OFFICIAL/TURKEY]

MOUHIT
    See: MUSAVVER MUHİT

MÜDAFAA-İ MALİYE VE İKTİSADİYE:
    Türkçe ve Fransızca neşrolunur
    haftalık Osmanlı gazetesi = La Défense
    financière et économique /
    administration, Yéni Osmanli
    Kitabhanessi
    Numero 1 (24 Şubat 1329 [8 Mar. 1914])
    - Numero 11 ([date?] 1330 [1914])
    Istanbul
    In Ottoman and (issues 6-11) French

    BL:OIOC: 1 (8.3.1914) - 11 (?.?.1914)
    [14498.cc.44]

MUĞLA İL YILLIĞI
    [1] (1967) - [2] (1973)
    Ankara, 1968-1973

    OX:BOD: [1] (1967)   [Turk.d.3324/48]

MUHÂDARÂT
    See: MUHÂDARÂT, MUKTATAFÂT

MUHÂDARÂT, MUKTATAFÂT: efâhim-i
    islamiye aşarını havi risaledir
    1. cild, cüz 1 (1 Rebiyülevvel 1300
    [Jan.-Feb. 1883]) - 2. cild, cüz 2
    (Cemaziyeluhra 1301 [Mar.-Apr. 1884])
    Istanbul
    Nominally fortnightly, but irregular;
    some issues cumulated

    BL:OIOC: 1:1 (1-2.1883) - 2:2 (3-4.1884)
    [ORB.30/229]
    OX:BOD: 1:1 - 1:24 (12.1883)
    [Turk.e.5034]

MUHÂMÂT: ayda bir defa neşrolunur
    nazariyat ve mukarrerat-i mehakim ve
    kavanin-i mer'iyeden bâhis mecmuadir
    Sayı 1 (10 Temmuz 1327 [23 July 1911]) -
    [2. seri,] sayı 24 (18 Eylül 1339
    [1923])
    Istanbul
    44 issues published in first series

    OX:BOD: [1]:1 (23.7.1911) - [2]:24
    (18.9.1923)   [Per.Turk.d.1459]

MUHARRİR: edebiyat, sanayi, bedâyi,
    terâcim-i ahvâl, tarih, coğrafya,
    seyahat ve saire'den bahseder ve oniki
    nüshası bir senelik itibar olunur
    mecmuadır
    Cild 1, cüz' 1 (Muharrem 1293 [Jan. -
    Feb 1876]) - Cild 1, cüz' 8 (Safer 1295
    [Feb. 1878])
    Istanbul
    Irregular; nominally monthly

    OX:BOD: 1:1 (1-2.1876) - 1:8 (2.1878)
    [Per.Turk.d.3550]

MUHBİR = Le Mukhbir / Yeni Osmanlılar
    Cemiyeti
    Nüsha 1 ([date?] 1284 [1867]) - Nüsha
    37 (12 Safer 1285 [3 June 1868])
    London
    In Ottoman and French
    Weekly

    BL:OIOC: 12 (14.11.1867) - 37 (3.6.1868)
    [14498.d.7]

MUKAYESELİ HUKUK ARAŞTIRMALARI DERGİSİ
    = Revue de recherches juridiques
    comparées / İstanbul Üniversitesi
    Mukayeseli Hukuk Enstitüsü
    Yıl 1, sayı 1 (1957) - [?]
    Istanbul
    Articles in Turkish or French
    Irregular; initially annual

    LO:SOAS: 1:1 (1957) - 2:2 (1958)
    [Per.32.135338]

LE MUKHBIR
    See: MUHBİR

AL-MUKHBIR AL-YABÂNÎ
    See: YAÑÎ YAPON MUHBİRİ

MÜLKİYE: her ayın ibtidasında
    neşrolunur mecmuadır / Mülkiye
    Mezunları İttihad ve Teavün Cemiyeti
    Yıl 1, sayı 1 (1 Şubat 1324 [14 Feb.
    1909]) - Yıl 4, sayı 30 (1 Ağustos 1327
    [14 Aug. 1911])
    Istanbul

    OX:BOD: 1:1 (14.2.1909) - 4:30
    (14.8.1911)   [Turk.d.1474]

MUŞ İL YILLIĞI
    [1] (1967) - [2] (1973)
    Elazığ, 1968-1973

    BL:OIOC: [1] (1967)   [14498.a.44]
    OX:BOD: [1]   [Turk.d.3324/49]

MUSAVVER DEVR-İ CEDİD: siyasî, fennî,
    edebî, içtimaî, haftalık musavver
    Osmanlı gazetesidir
    Cilt 1, sayı 1 (4 Mayıs 1325 [17 May
    1909]) - Cilt 1, sayı 10 (6 Temmuz 1325
    [19 July 1909])
    Istanbul

    OX:BOD: 1:1 (17.5.1909) - 1:4 (7.6.1909)
    [Per.Turk.d.1462(3)]
    OX:MEC: 1:1 - 1:10 (19.7.1909)   [APT
    Mus 3]

MUSAVVER EDEB: haftalık edebî, fennî,
    siyasî gazetedir
    Cilt 1, sayı 1 (27 Haziran 1325 [10 July
    1909]) - Cilt 1, sayı 6 (6 Ağustos 1325
    [19 Aug. 1909])
    Istanbul

    OX:BOD: 1:1 (10.7.1909) - 1:6
    (19.8.1909)   [Turk.d.1462 (1)]

MUSAVVER EŞREF: haftalık edebî ve
mizahî Osmanlı gazetesidir
1. yıl, sayı 1 (3 Eylül 1325 [16 Sep.
1909]) - 1. yıl, sayı 25 (18 Şubat 1325
[3 Mar. 1910])
Istanbul
Continuation of: Eşref. Issues are also
numbered 26 [for 27] to 51

OX:BOD: 1:1 (16.9.1909) - 1:25
(3.3.1910)   [Turk.d.2221]

MUSAVVER FEN VE EDEB: menafi-i mülk ve
devlet'e hadim Osmanlı risalesi
Yıl 1, cild 1, sayı 1 (11 Mart 1315 [24
Mar. 1899]) - Yıl 1, cild 1, sayı 18 (15
Temmuz 1315 [28 July 1899])
Istanbul

OX:BOD: 1:1:1 (24.3.1899) - 1:1:17
(21.7.1899)   [Turk.c.103(2)]

MUSAVVER MUHİT: her hafta perşembe
günleri neşrolunur, siyasî, edebî,
ilmî, felsefî gazetedir
Cild 1, sayı 1 (23 Teşrinievvel 1324 [5
Nov. 1908]) - Cild 2, sayı 52 ([date?]
1325 [1909])
Istanbul
Added title: Mouhit: illustration
hebdomadaire

LO:SOAS: 1:1 (5.11.1908) - 1:22
(8.4.1909)   [L.E.Per.305843]
CA:UL: 1:1 - 1:22   [Q.830.a.2]

MUSAVVER NEVSAL-İ SERVET-İ FÜNUN
See: NEVSAL-İ SERVET-İ FÜNUN

MUSAVVER NEVSAL-İ SERVET-İ FÜNUN
1. sene (1310 [1895-1896]) - 5. sene
(1314 [1898-1899])
Istanbul

CA:UL: 4 (1897) - 5 (1898)
[Gibb.c.290.a-b]

MUSAVVER SALNAME-İ SERVET-İ FÜNUN /
Servet-i Fünun gazetesi namına
müessestir
1 (1325 [1909-1910]) - 4 (1328
[1912-1913])
Istanbul, 1326 [1910 or 1911] - 1329
[1913 or 1914]

OX:BOD: 1 (1910) - 4 (1913)
[Turk.d.1074]
OX:MEC: 1 - 3 (1912)   [APT Sal 1]

THE MUSIC MAGAZINE
See: MUSİKİ MECMUASI

MUSİKİ MECMUASI: 3 aylık müzikoloji
dergisi
Sene 1, no. 1 (1 Mart 1948) -
Istanbul
Previously published by: İleri Türk
Musiki Konservatuarı
Some issues entitled: İleri musiki
mecmuası, or: Yeni musiki mecmuası.
Subtitle varies. Added title: The music
magazine
Previously monthly

BL:OIOC: 14:173 (7.1962) -
[14498.cc.16]
LO:SOAS: 219 (?.1966) - 223 (?.1966);
229 (?.1967) - 251 (?.1969); 254
(?.1970) - 278 (?.1972)
[Per.10.L.197294]
CA:UL: (a) 1 - 21 (?.1949); (b) 17:???
(?.1965) -   [(a) Picken 42.1; (b)
Picken 42.11]
OX:BOD: 1:1 (1.3.1948) -
[Per.Turk.d.3357]

MUSİKİ VE NOKTA [1. SERİ]: eğitici
aylık musikî mecmuası
Sayı 1 (Kasım 1969) - Sayı 35 (Eylül
1972)
Istanbul

OX:BOD: 1 (11.1969) - 35 (9.1972)
[Per.Turk.d.3321]

MUSİKİ VE NOKTA [2. SERİ]: eğitici
aylık musikî mecmuası
Sayı 1 (Ocak 1983) -
Istanbul

OX:BOD: 1 (1.1983) -   [Per.Turk.d.3321]

MUSTAKİL BOLU SANCAĞI SALNAMESİ
Defa 1 (1334 [1915-1916])
Istanbul
Only one issue published

LO:SOAS: 1 (1916)   [E.Per.280662]

MUSUL VİLÂYETİ İÇİN SALNAME
See: MUSUL VİLÂYETİ SALNAMESİ

MUSUL VİLÂYETİ SALNAME-İ RESMİSİ
See: MUSUL VİLÂYETİ SALNAMESİ

MUSUL VİLÂYETİ SALNAMESİ
1. defa (1308 [1890-1891]) - Defa 5
(1330 [1912])
Mosul
Some issues entitled: Musul vilâyeti
için ... salname; or: Musul vilâyeti
salname-i resmîsi
Irregular; nominally annual

BL:OIOC: 4 (1907-1908)   [14496.e.13]
DU:UL: 3 (1894)   [PL 367]

MÜTEVAKKİT
See: VAKİT

MUVAKKAT
See: VAKİT

NAFOSAT: ictimoiy-ommaviy, badiy-bezakli
oynoma / muassis, Üzbekiston
Respublikasi Madaniyat vazirligi
Sayı 1 (1 Mart 1971)-
Ankara
ISSN 0235-9715
Published down to 1991 by Üzbekiston KP
Markaziy Komiteti
Title down to 1991: Üzbekiston, with
Russian title Uzbekistan

BL:OIOC: 1961:1 (229) - 1969:12 (336);
1992:2 (590) -; lacking 1965:7, 1966:9,
1967:5,10,12   [14499.tt.2]
DU:UL: 1 (1.3.1971)-31; 135-447
(21.10.1979); lacking a few issues
[Per./PL 1]
OX:BOD: 1(1.3.1971) - 199 (6-12.1.1975)
[Per.Turk.d.1932]

NARODNOE KHOZİAİSTVO AZERBAİDZHANA
See: İGTİSADİYYAT VƏ HƏYAT

NASH KRAİ
See: ÜLKEMİZ

NATIONAL EDUCATION STATISTICS, ADULT
EDUCATION
See: MİLLİ EĞİTİM
İSTATİSTİKLERİ, YAYGIN EĞİTİM

NATIONAL EDUCATION STATISTICS, FORMAL
EDUCATION
See: MİLLİ EĞİTİM
İSTATİSTİKLERİ, ÖRGÜN EĞİTİM

NATIONAL EDUCATION STATISTICS, GENERAL
SECONDARY EDUCATION
See: MİLLİ EĞİTİM
İSTATİSTİKLERİ, ORTAÖĞRETİM

NATIONAL EDUCATION STATISTICS, HIGHER
EDUCATION
  See: MİLLÎ EĞİTİM
  İSTATİSTİKLERİ, YÜKSEK ÖĞRETİM

NATIONAL EDUCATION STATISTICS, PRIMARY
EDUCATION
  See: MİLLÎ EĞİTİM
  İSTATİSTİKLERİ, İLKÖĞRETİM

NATIONAL EDUCATION STATISTICS, VOCATIONAL
AND TECHNICAL SECONDARY EDUCATION
  See: MİLLÎ EĞİTİM
  İSTATİSTİKLERİ, MESLEKÎ VE TEKNİK
  ÖĞRETİM

NATIONAL INCOME OF TURKEY
  See: TÜRKİYE MİLLÎ GELİRİ

NÂZIM HİKMET: Nâzım'ın uğradığı
  haksızlıklarla mücadele için çıkan
  fikir ve politika dergisi
  [Sayı 1] (11 Mayıs 1950) - Yıl 1, sayı
  10 (4 Temmuz 1950)
  İstanbul
  Generally weekly

  BL:OIOC: [1] (11.5.1950) - 1:10
  (4.7.1950) [OR.FICHE 447]

NĔCAT: indilik hĕftĕdĕ bir dĕfa
  şĕnbĕ günari [i.e. günlĕri]
  nĕşrolunacak siyasî, ĕdĕbî ve
  ictimaî müslüman gazetĕsidir =
  Nidzhat' (Spasenie)
  Ĕvvĕlinci [1.] sĕnĕ, numra 1 (20
  Noyabr 1910) - [?]
  [Baku]
  Publication history not known; possibly
  only one issue
  Added title: Nidzhat' (Spasenie)
  Azeri in Arabic characters; with a
  section in Russian

  BL:OIOC: 1:1 (20.11.1910) [ORB.30/342]

NEÇME: siyasî, edebî, ictimaî, haftada
  üç defa neşrolunur ceride-i
  resmiyedir
  Sene 1, numero 1 ([date?] 1918) - [?]
  Kirkuk

  BL:OIOC: 3:490 (20.4.1921) - 4:656
  (23.6.1922); lacking 494-502, 505-508,
  513-514, 519-524, 530, 536, 540-541,
  544-545, 547, 553, 559-562, 566,
  584-589, 599, 614, 618-623, 627-628,
  641-642, 648, 654 [OR.MIC.11877
  (O.P. 680)]

NEDİM: haftalık edebî mecmua
  Yıl 1, sayı 1 (16 Kanunusani 1919) - 1.
  sene, 2. cild, sayı 18 (5 Haziran 1335
  [1919])
  İstanbul
  In early issues, Nedim is preceded by
  Şair on the t.p.

  BL:OIOC: 1:1 (16.1.1919) - 1:2:18
  (5.6.1919) [14498.a.122]

NESİN VAKFI EDEBİYAT YILLIĞI
  1976-
  İstanbul
  Yearbook with articles on culture and
  literature, reprinted from journals
  1976-1977 issues published by Tekin

  BL:OIOC: 1976-1978; 1980-1984
  [14480.d.123]
  OX:BOD: 1977-1981; 1983- [Turk.e.4365]

NEVSAL-İ AFİYET: salname-i tıbbî /
  Besim Ömer
  1. kitab (1315 [1899]) - 4. kitab (1322
  [1906])
  İstanbul: Matbaa-i Ahmed İhsan
  Irregular

  BL:OIOC: 4 (1906) [ORB.30/705]

NEVSAL-İ MALUMÂT
  1. sene (1317 sene-i hicriyesi
  [1899-1900]) - [Sayı 2] (1319 sene-i
  hicriyesi [1901-1902])
  İstanbul: Mehmed Tahir

  OX:BOD: 1 (1899) [Turk.d.2363]

NEVSAL-İ MARİFET
  See: REBİ'-İ MARİFET

NEVSAL-İ MİLLÎ
  1. sene (1330 [1914])
  İstanbul: Frat Asar-ı Müfide
  Kitaphanesi
  Non-official yearbook
  Only one issue published

  BL:OIOC: 1 (1914) [14498.c.13]
  OX:BOD: 1 [Turk.d.2539]

NEVSAL-İ SERVET-İ FÜNUN
  See: MUSAVVER NEVSAL-İ SERVET-İ FÜNUN

NEVSAL-İ SERVET-İ FÜNUN
  1. sene (1310 [1894-1895]) - 5. sene
  (1314 [1898-1899])
  İstanbul, 1311 [1895] - 1314 [1898]
  Some issues entitled: Musavver Nevsal-i
  Servet-i Fünun; or: Musavver Salname-i
  Servet-i Fünun

  OX:BOD: 1 (1895) - 5 (1899)
  [Turk.d.2179]

NEVŞEHİR İLİ YILLIĞI
  [1] (1967) - [2] (1973)
  Ankara, 1968-1973

  BL:OIOC: [1] (1967) [14498.a.56]
  LO:SOAS: [1] [Per.10.L.279251]
  OX:BOD: [1] [Turk.d.3324/50]

NEYYİR-İ HAKİKAT: mesail-i
  içtimaiye'den ve siyasiye'den ve ulum-u
  ahlâkiye ve medeniye'den bâhis ve
  selâmet-i mülk-i millet'e hâdim,
  hürriyet-i kâmile'yi hâiz, haftada
  iki defa neşrolunur Osmanlı gazetesidir
  / Osmanlı İttihad ve Terakki Cemiyeti
  1. sene, numero 1 ([date?] 1324 [1908])
  - 4. sene, numero 317 ([date?] 1327
  [1911])
  Manastır (Bitola, Macedonia)

  BL:OIOC: special issue of 10.7.1324
  (22.7.1907), published 1325 (1909)
  [ITA.1986.a.395]

NIDZHAT' (SPASENIE)
  See: NECAT

NİĞDE İL YILLIĞI
  [1] (1967) - [2] (1973)
  Ankara

  BL:OIOC: [1] (1967) [14498.a.38]
  OX:BOD: [1] [Turk.d.3324/51]

NİLÜFER
  1. sene, numero 1 (Rebiyülevvel 1305
  [Nov.-Dec. 1887]) - 5. sene, numero 60
  (Safer 1309 [Sep.-Oct. 1891])
  Bursa
  Monthly; initially fortnightly

  CA:UL: 1:1 - 5:60 [T.830.a.1]
  OX:BOD: 1:1 (11-12.1887) - 5:60
  (9-10.1891) [Per.Turk.c.207]
  OX:MEC: 1:1 - 5:60 [APT Nil]

NİZAMİ ADINA AZĚRBAYCAN ĚDĚBİYYATI
  MUZEYİNİN ĚSERLĚRİ = Trudy Muzeia
  Azerbaidzhanskoi Literatury imeni
  Nizami
  1 cild (1961) –
  Baku: Elm
  Articles in Azeri or Russian
  Irregular

  BL:OIOC: 1 (1961) – 5 (1987)
  [14499.o.12]
  LO:SOAS: 1 – 3 (1968)   [Per.10.268496]
  OX:BOD: 1 – 4 (1978)   [Per.Turk.e.1226]

NİZAMİ ADINA ĚDĚBİYYAT VĚ DİL
  İNSTİTUTUNUN ĚSĚRLĚRİ: dilçilik
  seriyası = Trudy Instituta Literatury i
  Iazyka im. Nizami: seriia
  iazykoznaniia
  1 cild (1946) –
  Baku: Elm
  Articles in Azeri or Russian
  Occasional publication

  BL:HSS: 1-17; lacking 4, 6, 12
  [P.901/340]

NOKTA: haftalık haber dergisi
  Yıl 1, sayı 1 (15 Şubat 1982) –
  Istanbul

  OX:BOD: 2:1 (28.2.1983) –
  [Per.Turk.d.3307]

NORTH CAUCASIA
  See: ŞİMALİ-KAFKASYA

NOT / T.C. Ziraat Bankasının haber ve
  fikir dergisi
  Sayı 1 (Aralık 1957) – Yıl 6, sayı 39
  (Temmuz 1973)
  Ankara
  Quarterly

  DU:DC: 32 (7.1971) – 39 (7.1973)
  [25/4/BANKING]
  OX:MEC: 11 (12.1963) – 39 (7.1973);
  lacking 20, 27-28   [APT Not]

NÜFUS ETÜTLERİ ENSTİTÜSÜ BÜLTENİ
  [2. SERİ]: üç ayda bir yayımlanır /
  Hacettepe Üniversitesi Nüfus Etütleri
  Enstitüsü
  Cilt 1, sayı 1 (Mart 1973) –
  Ankara: Hacettepe Üniversitesi Nüfus
  Etütleri Enstitüsü
  Supersedes: Nüfus haberleri (quarterly,
  Hacettepe Üniversitesi Nüfus Etütleri
  Enstitüsü)

  BL:HSS: 1:1 (3.1973) – 1:3 (9.1973)
  [S.Q.86]
  DU:DC: 1:1 – 1:3   [25/4/POPULATION]

NÜFUS YAYINLARI BÜLTENİ / Hacettepe
  Üniversitesi Nüfus Etütleri
  Enstitüsü
  Cilt 1, sayı 1 (Nisan 1969) –
  Ankara
  Quarterly

  DU:DC: 1:2 (7.1969) – 2:3 (7-9.1970)
  [25/4/POPULATION]

NÜFUSBİLİMİ DERGİSİ = The Turkish
  journal of population studies /
  Hacettepe Üniversitesi Nüfus Etütleri
  Enstitüsü
  Yıl 1, sayı 1 ([date?] 1979) –
  Ankara
  Contributions in Turkish or English
  Annual

  SU:IDS: 2/3 (1980/1981) –
  [SERIALS/NON-OFFICIAL/72]

O T A M
  See: OTAM

OBSHCHESTVENNYE NAUKI V UZBEKISTANE
  See: ŪZBEKİSTONDA İCTİMOİY FANLAR

ODLU YURT: Millî Azerbaycan fikriyatını
  tervic eden aylık mecmua
  Yıl 1, sayı 1 (Şubat [?], 1929) – Yıl
  3, sayı 29 (Haziran 1931)
  Istanbul

  LO:SOAS: 1:4 (28.5.1929) – 3:29
  (6.1931); lacking 1:6 (8.1929), 1:11
  (1.1930), 2:17 (6.1930) – 2:18 (7.1930),
  2:21 (10.1930) – 2:22 (11.1930), 2:26
  (3.1931)   [Per.10.93079]

ODTÜ. GELİŞME DERGİSİ = METU. studies
  in development
  1 (Güz 1970) –
  Ankara: Orta Doğu Teknik Üniversitesi
  İdari Bilimler Fakültesi, 1971–
  Irregular. Several special issues

  BL:OIOC: 1 (autumn 1970) – 3 (spring
  1971); 10 – 11; 13 – 15; 7:13 – 9:25;
  13:1/2 –; special issues dated 1978,
  1980 – 1982   [14498.cc.30]
  BL:DSC: 7:13 (1980) –   [5750.365000]
  DU:DC: 1 –; special issues: 1975, 1977,
  1979-1980   [25/4/ECONOMY/GENERAL]
  SU:IDS: 1 –; lacking 21 (autumn 1978)
  [SERIALS/NON-OFFICIAL/72]

ODTÜ. MİMARLIK FAKÜLTESİ DERGİSİ =
  METÜ. Journal of the Faculty of
  Architecture
  Cilt 1, sayı 1 (Bahar 1975) –
  Ankara
  Articles in Turkish or English
  Semi-annual

  DU:DC: 1:1 (spring 1975) – 7:1 (spring
  1981)   [25/4/EDUCATION]

OINA
  See: AYNA

OKU İŞLERİ: ictimaî, siyasî vě
  těrbiyěvi aylık curnal / Kırım Měarif
  Komisarlığı něşri
  Numero 1 (Mayıs 1925) – [?]
  Akmescid; Simferopol'
  Crimean Tatar; Arabic characters

  BL:OIOC: 1 (5.1925) – 2:10/11
  (2/3.1926); 3:1/2 (19/20) (1/2.1927)
  [14499.t.24]

OKUL-AİLE BİRLİĞİ BELLETEN
  1 (Temmuz 1947) – 4 (Nisan 1948)
  Ankara: Millî Eğitim Bakanlığı
  Quarterly

  BL:OIOC: 1 (7.1947) – 4 (4.1948)
  [14498.c.9.]

OLAYLARA BAKIŞ: aylık siyasi dergi
  Sayı 1 ([Eylül?] 1982) – Sayı 31 (20-27
  Nisan 1984)
  Istanbul

  OX:BOD: 14 (11.1983) – 31 (20-27.4.1984)
  [Per.Turk.d.3218]

ÖLÜM İSTATİSTİKLERİ (İL VE İLÇE
MERKEZLERİNDE) = Death statistics (in
province and district centers) /
Başbakanlık Devlet İstatistik
Enstitüsü
Ankara, [19--?]-
Continuation of: Vilâyet (later
Vilâyet ve kaza) merkezlerindeki
ölümler, and of: İl ve ilçe
merkezlerindeki ölümler
Title sometimes begins: Hayatî
istatistikler ...
Currently in Turkish and English
Formerly irregular; currently annual,
with some cumulated issues

    BL:HSS: 1952-1956; 1957-1958; 1957-1959
    [S.Q.170/30]
    CA:UL: 1980/1981 -   [enquire in
    Official Publications Dept.]
    DU:DC: 1952/1956 - 1957/1958; 1962 -
    1973; 1977-   [25/4/POPULATION]

ÖNASYA: aylık Türkoloji fikir ve
aktualite mecmuası
Özel sayı no. 1 (Eylûl 1965) - Yıl 7,
Cilt 7, sayı 78 (Şubat 1972)
Istanbul
Issues 1-28 lack subtitle

    BL:OIOC: 1 (10.1965) - 7:76 (12.1971)
    [14498.a.34]

ONBİRİNCİ TEZ KİTAP DİZİSİ
1 (Kasım 1985) -
Istanbul: Uluslararası Yayıncılık
A political journal
Quarterly

    OX:BOD: 1 (11.1985) -
    [Per.Turk.d.3529]

[ONDOKUZUNCU] 19 MAYIS / Samsun Halkevi
dergisi
Samsun
Dates of publication not known
Mainly quarterly

    LO:SOAS: 56 (19.5.1942); 5:60
    (29.10.1942); 6:64 (29.10.1943) - 7:65
    (19.1.1944)   [Per.10.L.45928]

[ONSEKİZ] 18 VE DAHA YUKARI GROS
TONİLATOLUK DENİZ TAŞITLARI
İSTATİSTİKLERİ = Statistics of
vessels 18 gross tonnages [sic] and over
/ Başbakanlık Devlet İstatistik
Enstitüsü
1986 -
Ankara
In Turkish and English
Annual

    BL:HSS: 1989   [SQ.170/67]
    SU:IDS: 1986 -
    [SERIALS/OFFICIAL/TURKEY]

ORDU İL YILLIĞI
[1] (1967) - [2] (1973)
Ankara

    OX:BOD: [1] (1967)   [Turk.d.3324/52]

ORDU SALNAMESİ
[1] (1330 [1914-1915])
Istanbul
Only one issue published
Ottoman; in separate Arabic characters
(Enver Paşa system)

    DU:UL: [1] (1914-1915)   [PL 331]
    OX:BOD: [1]   [Turk.e.4299]

ORGANİZASYON / Istanbul Üniversitesi
İşletme Fakültesi Yönetim ve
Organizasyon Enstitüsü dergisi
Yıl 1, sayı 1 ([Kasım 1976]) - Yıl 2,
sayı 8 ([Temmuz 1980])
Istanbul
Issues not dated. Irregular; nominally
quarterly

    SU:IDS: 1:1 [11.1976] - 2:8 [7.1980]
    [SERIALS/NON-OFFICIAL/72]

ORHUN: aylık Türkçü mecmua
1 (5 Teşrinisani 1933) - 16 ([date?]
1944)
Istanbul
Continued from 1950 to 1952, and from
1962 to 1963, by: Orkun
Originally monthly; then irregular

    BL:OIOC: 2 (11.1933) - 9 (7.1934)
    [14498.cc.36]

ORKUN
See also: SANAT, BİLİM VE KÜLTÜRDE
ORKUN

ORKUN [1. SERİ]: haftalık Türkçü dergi
1. sayı (6 Ekim 1950) - 68. sayı (18
Ocak 1952)
Istanbul
Continuation of: Orhun

    BL:OIOC: 1 (6.10.1950) - 68 (18.1.1952)
    [ITA.1989.a.237]
    OX:BOD: 1 - 68   [Per.Turk.d.3361]

ORKUN [2. SERİ]: aylık fikir, ülkü ve
sanat dergisi
Yıl 1, sayı 1 (Şubat 1962) - Yıl 2,
sayı 23 (25 Aralık 1963)
Istanbul

    BL:OIOC: 1:1 (2.1962) - 2:23
    (25.12.1963)   [ITA.1989.c.4]

ORMAN BAKANLIĞI AYLIK BÜLTENİ / Orman
Bakanlığı tarafından ayda bir
yayınlanır
Yıl 1, sayı 1 ([Nisan 1965?]) - [?]
Ankara
Publisher named as Orman Bakanlığı
Orman Genel Müdürlüğü until Year 9,
no. 107 (Feb. 1974)
Previous titles: Bülten / Orman
Bakanlığı; Haber bülteni / Orman
Bakanlığı

    BL:HSS: (a) 6:68 (11.1970); 7:70
    (1.1.1971) - 9:113 (8.1974); 9:115
    (10.1974) - 11:137 (8.1976); 14:163/164
    (11-12.1978) - 14:167/168 (3-4.1979);
    special issues 1 (1974), 3 (1976); (b)
    11:139 (9.1976) - 13:161/162
    (9-10.1978); special issues 4 (1977), 5
    (1978)   [(a) S.Q.42/8; (b) S.Q.19/2]

ORMAN HAZİNELERİ / Kıbrıs Orman Kurumu
Cilt 1, no. 1 ([date?], 1944) - [?]
Lefkoşa
Quarterly?

    BL:OIOC: 7:1 (summer 1950)
    [ITA.1986.a.419]

ORMAN VE MAADİN MECMUASI [2. SERİ]
Aded 1 (31 Temmuz 1305 [13 Aug. 1889]) -
aded 12 ([date?], 1305 [1889 or 1890])
Istanbul
First series (2 vols., 24 issues) was
published in 1300-1302 (1884-1887)

    BL:OIOC: 1 (13.8.1889) - 12 (?.1889 or
    1890)   [ITA.1987.a.529]

ORMANCILIK ARAŞTIRMA ENSTİTÜSÜ YILLIK
   BÜLTENİ = Annual report of the Turkish
   Forest Institute
   1 (1952) - 26 (1977)
   Ankara
   Added titles in English, French, German,
   and Spanish
   With summaries in English only

   DU:DC: 24 (1975) - 26 (1977)
   [25/2/FORESTS]

ORMANCILIK İSTATİSTİK ALBÜMÜ =
   Forestry statistics / Ormancılık Genel
   Müdürlüğü
   Ankara: [19--?]-[19--?]
   Turkish and English
   Annual

   SU:IDS: 1960 - 1961; 1964 - 1966
   [SERIALS/OFFICIAL/TURKEY]

ORTA DOĞU: siyasi, ekonomik ve sosyal
   Türk dergisi
   1. sene, sayı 1 (Nisan 1961) -
   Ankara
   Monthly

   OX:MEC: 1:1 (4.1961) - 1:12 (5.1962);
   2:17 (3.1963) - 6:51 (7.1966); 7:57
   (1.1967) - 14:142 (2.1974); lacking a
   few issues   [APT Not]
   CA:OS: 1 (?.1961) - 1:? (10.1961);
   1.1962 - 3:1962; 9.1965 - 2.1974
   [enquire for shelfmark]

OSMANLI: bu gazete umum-u Osmanlıların
   hukuk-u magsuba ve zayialarını taharrî
   ve taleb eyler ve delalet ve
   irşâdâtta bulunacak namuslu
   Osmanlıların tercümanıdır
   1. sene, numero 1 (1 Kanunuevvel-i
   Efrencî 1897) - 1. sene, numero 8 (1
   Haziran-ı Efrencî 1898)
   Cairo
   Added title: The Osmanlı
   In Ottoman and Arabic; one page per
   issue in English
   Monthly; first four issues fortnightly

   BL:OIOC: 1:1 (1.12.1897) - 1:8
   (1.6.1898)   [14498.d.11 (1)]

OSMANLI: onbeş günde bir neşrolunur /
   İttihad ve Terakki Cemiyetinin vasıta-i
   neşriyâtı
   1. sene, numero 1 (1 Kanunuevvel 1897) -
   8. sene, numero 142 (8 Kanunuevvel 1904)
   Geneva; London; Folkestone; Cairo
   Published mainly in Folkestone or
   Geneva; also at Cairo and London
   French added title: Osmanli: journal
   bi-mensuel, organe de la Jeune Turquie /
   dirigé par le Comité d'Union et de
   Progrès

   BL:OIOC: (1) 14498.d.15; (2) Or.
   microfiche 24
   OX:BOD: 1:1 - 6:119   [Or. microfiches
   56]

OSMANLI ARAŞTIRMALARI = The Journal of
   Ottoman studies
   1 [1980] -
   İstanbul: Enderun
   Articles in Turkish, English, French, or
   German
   Irregular

   BL:OIOC: 1 [1980] -   [14498.cc.55]
   LO:SOAS: 1 -   [Per.10.437942]
   CA:UL: 1 -   [P.617.c.66]

OSMANLI ARŞİVİ BÜLTENİ / T.C.
   Başbakanlık Devlet Arşivleri Genel
   Müdürlüğü Osmanlı Arşivi Daire
   Başkanlığı
   1 (1990) -
   Istanbul
   Announced as four-monthly

   BL:OIOC: 1 (1990)   [ITA.1993.a.275]

OSMANLI HİLAL-İ AHMER CEMİYETİ
   SALNAMESİ
   [1] (1329 [1913-1914] - 1331
   [1915-1916])
   Istanbul, 1329 [1913]
   Only one issue published

   CA:UL: [1] (1913-1916)
   [S.828.01.b.124]
   DU:UL: [1]   [PL.375.3]

OSMANLI TARİH VE EDEBİYAT MECMUASI:
   mülk ve millet'e nafi' tarih, edebiyat,
   fünun, iktisadiyat ve şüun-i saire'ye
   müteallık mebahis-i müfide'yi hâvi
   mecmua-i şehrîdir
   Sene 1, aded 1 (31 Mart 1334 [1918]) -
   Sene 3, aded 31 (30 Eylül 1336 [1920])
   İstanbul: [s.n.], 1334 [1918] - 1336
   [1920]
   Continued by: Tarih ve edebiyat

   BL:OIOC: 1:1 (31.3.1918) - [2]:1:5
   (31.12.1919)   [OR. MICROFICHE 92]
   LO:SOAS: 1:1 - 3:31   [E.Per.285360]
   CA:UL: 1:1 - 3:31   [Q.830.c.15]
   OX:BOD: 1:1 - 3:31   [Per.Turk.d.3553
   (hard copy); Or. microfiches 57
   (microfiche)]
   OX:MEC: 1:1 - 3:31   [APT Tar 3]

OTAM / Ankara Üniversitesi Osmanlı Tarihi
   Araştırma ve Uygulama Merkezi dergisi
   Yıl 1, sayı 1 (Haziran 1990) -
   Ankara
   Semi-annual

   BL:OIOC: 1:1 (6.1990) -
   [ZOR.1991.a.68]
   LO:SOAS: 1:1 -   [Per.10.611042]

OULOUM GAZATASSY
   See: ULUM GAZETESİ

ÖZGÜR HALK: aylık siyasi-kültürel
   dergi
   Yıl 1, sayı 1 ([Kasım?] 1989) -
   Istanbul: Ses

   LO:SOAS: 2:7 (15.5.1991) -
   [Per.57.L.619982]

ÖZGÜR İNSAN: aylık dergi
   Sayı 1 (Haziran 1972) - Yıl 6, sayı 54
   (Nisan 1978)
   Ankara: Cumhuriyet Halk Partisi
   Journal of C.H.P. ideology

   DU:DC: 6:44 (6.1977) - 6:54 (4.1978)
   [25/3/GENERAL]

PANCAR: aylık çiftçi dergisi
   1 (Ekim 1951) - 322 (Ekim 1983)
   Ankara: Türkiye Şeker Fabrikaları

   BL:OIOC: 19:210 (1970) - 22:243 (1972)
   except 225, 237; 241, 242; 25 (1975) :
   286-289, 291   [14498.cc.66]
   BL:HSS: 5:55 (?.1956) - 19:209 (2.1970),
   lacking many issues; 21:2 (?.1973) -
   25:285 (6.1976), lacking 4 issues
   [S.Q.30/8]

PAPİRÜS
1 (Bahar 1980) - 2 [1981]
İstanbul
Left-wing journal of literature and
ideas

BL:OIOC: 1 - 2   [14480.d.188]

PARA KREDİ: aylık ekonomi haber yorum
dergisi
Yıl 1, sayı 1 (Ocak 1981) -
İstanbul

DU:UL: 1:1 (1.1981) - 2:14 (2.1982)
[Per./PL328]

PARASAT / Kazakstan Kompartiyası
Ortalık Komitetinin ay sayın
şıgatın kogamdık-sayasi,
edebi-körkem cene sretti curnalı
1 ([date?] 1958) -
Alma-Ata
ISSN 0236-1361
Title down to 9.1990: Medeniet cene
türmıs
In Kazakh

BL:OIOC: 1984:4 -   [14499.tt.40]

PERAKENDE FİYAT İSTATİSTİKLERİ:
seçilmiş şehirlere ve maddelere göre
yıllık ortalama fiyatlar = Retail price
statistics: annual average prices by
selected cities and items / Başbakanlık
Devlet İstatistik Enstitüsü
Ankara, [19--?]-
Currently in Turkish and English
Annual

DU:DC: 1982/1983   [25/4/PRICES]
SU:IDS: 1948/1970; 1971/1979; 1982 -
[SERIALS/OFFICIAL/TURKEY]

PEREVODCHIK
See: TERCÜMAN

PĚRVAZ: jiliga bir ketim neşir
kilinidigan edebiy-bediiy,
ictimaiy-seyasiy toplam
1983 -
Alma-Ata: Jazuşı
Added title in Russian: Vysota
Uygur; Cyrillic characters

OX:BOD: 1983 -   [Per.Turk.d.3560]

PERVİN: edebî, ilmî risale-i usbuiyedir
1. sene, aded 1 (24 Kanunuevvel 1325 [6
Jan. 1910]) - 1. sene, aded 5 (21
Kanunusani 1325 [3 Feb. 1910])
İstanbul

BL:OIOC: 1:1 (6.1.1910) - 1:5 (3.2.1910)
[14498.a.116]

PETKİM DERGİSİ: iki ayda bir
yayımlanır
Sayı 1 (Nisan 1968) -
Yarımca: Petkim (Petrokimya A.Ş.)
Frequency varies; initially quarterly,
later nominally bi-monthly

DU:DC: 2 (16.7.1968) - 11 (1.11.1971);
lacking 5
[25/4/INDUSTRY/MANUFACTURING]

PINAR: aylık kültür ve sanat dergisi
Cilt 1, sayı 1 [1972?] -
İstanbul

BL:OIOC: 7:81 (9.1978)   [14498.cc.96]

PLÂNLAMA / Devlet Plânlama Teşkilâtı
dergisi
Cilt 1, sayı 1 (İlkbahar 1963) - [?]
Ankara
Occasional; initially quarterly

BL:HSS: 1:4 (winter 1963); 7 (5.1968) -
10 (9.1970); special issue (11.1967)
[S.Q.145/9]
LO:SOAS: 2:5 (spring 1964)
[Per.10.210125]
DU:DC: 1:4 - 2:5; 7
[25/4/PLANNING/GENERAL]

POUL MEDJMOUASSI
See: PUL MECMUASI

PRIZYV
See: ÇAĞIRIŞ

PRODUCTION OF MAIN INDUSTRIAL PRODUCTS BY
QUARTERS
See: ÜÇ AYLIK DÖNEMLER İTİBARİYLE
BAŞLICA SANAYİ MADDELERİ ÜRETİMİ

PROLETER DEVRİMCİ AYDINLIK
Sayı 1 15 (Ocak 1970) - Sayı 38 (13
Nisan 1971)
Ankara
Initially monthly, then weekly

OX:BOD: 1 15 (1.1970) - 38 (13.4.1971)
[Per.Turk.d.1726 (1-27); Per.Turk.b.9
(28-38)]

PUL MECMUASI: ayda bir neşrolunur,
fennî, edebî, risale-i mevkutedir
Sayı 1 (19 Ağustos 1313 [1 Sep. 1897])
- Sayı 28 (11 Mart 1315 [24 Mar. 1899])
İstanbul
Added title: Poul medjmouassi: revue
mensuelle scientifique et littéraire

OX:BOD: 1 (1.9.1887) - 26 (11.11.1888)
[Turk.d.1847(2)]

QUARTERLY BULLETIN
See: ÜÇ AYLIK BÜLTEN

RADYO: mecmua, bilhassa radyo teknik ve
neşriyatından bahseder / Başvekâlet
Matbuat Ü. Müdürlüğünce çıkarılır
Cilt 1, sayı 1 (15 Aralik 1941) - Cild
8, sayı 94-95-96 (Ekim-Kasım-Aralık
1949)
Ankara
Title of issuing body varies. Succeeded
from 1950 by: Radyo haftası
Monthly

BL:OIOC: 2:17 (15.4.1943) - 8:94/95/96
(10-12.1949)   [OR.MIC.12954 (O.P. 500)]

RADYO HAFTASI [1. SERİ]
Cilt 1, sayı 1 (27 Mayıs 1950) - Cilt 8,
sayı 16 (14 Kasım 1957)
İstanbul
Magazine on radio personalities and
programmes
Successor of: Radyo
Weekly

BL:OIOC: 1:1 (27.5.1950) - 12:150
(4.4.1953); lacking 1:12; 2:17, 22, 24;
3:25, 29; 6:67, 68; 7:78.79.81, 83;
8:85, 86; 9:114   [14479.b.12]

RASADHANE-İ ÂMİRE'NİN SALNAMESİ
[1] (1289 [1872-1873])
İstanbul, 1288 [1871 or 1872]
Only one issue published

BL:OIOC: [1] (1872-1873)   [14445.d.1]

RASATHANE-İ ÂMİRE'NİN SALNAMESİ
See: RASADHANE-İ ÂMİRE'NİN
SALNAMESİ

REBÎ'-Î MARÎFET
[1. defa] (1297 [1880]) - 11. sene
(1309/1310 [1891-1892])
Istanbul: Ebüzziya Tevfik, 1297 [1880]
- 1310 [1892]
Succeeded by: Takvim-i Ebüzziya
Title of issues 9-11: Nevsal-i marifet
Annual

BL:OIOC: 8 (1887); 10 (1890)
[14496.e.2]
OX:BOD: 11 (1892)   [Turk.d.2697]

RESÎMLÎ AY
Numero 1 (Şubat 1340 [1924]) - 7. sene,
n. 10 (Kânunusani 1931)
İstanbul
A general-interest magazine
Issues 24-36 entitled: Sevimli ay
Initially in Arabic characters ; in
roman characters from March 1929 onwards
Generally monthly

BL:OIOC: 1:1 (2.1924) - 7:10 (11.1931)
[14498.a.95]
OX:BOD: 1:1 - 5:57   [Turk.c.123]

RESÎMLÎ GAZETE: her hafta cumartesi
günleri neşrolunur, herşeyden
bahseder, müstakil ül-efkâr ve
terakkiperver siyasî resimli Türk
gazetesi
Sene 1, numero 1 (8 Eylül 1339 [1923])
- Sene 6, numero 272 (10 Teşrinisani
1928)
Istanbul

BL:OIOC: 1:1 (8.9.1923) - 1:25
(23.2.1924)   [14498.a.60/1]

RESÎMLÎ GAZETE [1. SERÎ]: perşembe
günleri neşrolunur fennî ve edebî
gazete
Sene 1, aded 1 (14 Mart 1307 [27 Mar.
1891]) - Sene 5, aded 234/235 (21 Eylül
1311 [4 Oct. 1895])
Istanbul
Subtitle varies

BL:OIOC: 1:1 (27.3.1891) - 5:234/235
(4.10.1895) (microfiche)
[OR.MICROFICHE 86]
LO:SOAS: 1:1 - 3:156 (23.3.1893)
[Per.10.L.172653]
OX:BOD: (a) 1:1 - 5:209 (5.4.1895) (hard
copy); (b) 5:209 - 5:234/235
(microfiche)   [(a) Per.Turk.d.1111;
(b) Or. microfiches 60]

RESÎMLÎ İSTANBUL
1. sene, numara 1 (8 Haziran 1325 [21
June 1909]) - 1. sene, numara 25 (23
Teşrinisani 1325 [6 Dec. 1909])
Istanbul
Title of issues 1-12: Haftalık resimli
İstanbul
Weekly

LO:SOAS: 1:1 (21.6.1909) - 1:25
(6.12.1909)   [Per.10.L.172652]
OX:BOD: 1:1 - 1:25   [Turk.c.174]
OX:MEC: 1:1 - 1:25   [APT Res 8]

RESÎMLÎ KÎTAB: her ayın onbeşinde
neşrolunur edebî, siyasî, fennî,
felsefî ve ictimâî mecmua-i
musavverdir
Cild 1, nu. 1 (Eylül 1324 [1908]) -
Cild 9, nu. 51 (Şubat 1329 [1914])
Istanbul
French added title: Ressimli kitab

BL:OIOC: 1:1 (9.1908) - 5:49 (6-7.1913)
; lacking 3:19 - 3:24   [14498.a.80]
LO:SOAS: 1:1 - 7:42; 8:43,46
[Per.10.137072]
OX:BOD: 1:1 - 5:49   [Turk.d.1362]
OX:MEC: 1:1 - 5:51 (10.1913)   [APT
Res 2]

RESÎMLÎ ŞARK
Yıl 1, sayı 1 (Kânunusani 1931) - [Yıl
4], no. 48 (İlkkânun 1934)
Izmir
A lightweight cultural and general
interest magazine
Monthly

BL:OIOC: 1:1 (1.1931) - 4:48 (12.1934)
[14498.a.93]
LO:SOAS: 1:1 - 4:38 (2.1934)
[Per.10.L.26409]

RESÎMLÎ TARÎH MECMUASI
Sayı 1 (Ocak 1950) - Cilt 7, sayı 84
(Aralık 1956)
İstanbul
Magazine devoted to Turkish history
Monthly

BL:OIOC: 1:1 (1.1950) - 7:84 (12.1956)
[14498.cc.71]
LO:SOAS: 1:1 - 7:84   [Per.10.289668]

RESÎMLÎ YIL
Yıl 1, sayı 1 (28 Şubat 1925)
Istanbul

OX:BOD: 1:1 (28.2.1925)   [Turk.c.123/2]

RESMÎ GAZETE
See: T.C. RESMÎ GAZETE

RESPUBLIKA ÉLYAZMALARI FONDUNUN
ÉSÉRLÉRÎ
See: ÉLYAZMALAR HÉZÎNÉSÎNDÉ

RESSIMLI KITAB
See: RESÎMLÎ KÎTAB

RETAIL PRICE STATISTICS
See: PERAKENDE FÎYAT ÎSTATÎSTÎKLERÎ

REVIEW OF HISTORICAL RESEARCH
See: TARÎH ARAŞTIRMALARI

REVIEW OF HISTORICAL RESEARCH
See: TARÎH ARAŞTIRMALARI DERGÎSÎ

REVIEW OF THE FACULTY OF POLITICAL SCIENCE
See: ANKARA ÜNÎVERSÎTESÎ SÎYASAL
BÎLGÎLER FAKÜLTESÎ DERGÎSÎ

REVIEW OF THE TURKISH ORIENTAL SOCIETY
See: TÜRK ŞARKÎYAT DERNEĞÎ
DERGÎSÎ

REVNAK: vazifesi, maarif ve edebiyata
müteallık her gûna mebahis ve lataifi
şamil olup, teracim-i ahval ile
makalat-i müfide ve nafia'yı hâvi
olacaktır
Sayı 1 (1290 [1874 or 1875]) - Sayı 11
(1292 [1876 or 1877])
Istanbul
Issues dated by year only
Irregular

OX:BOD: 1 (1874 or 1875) - 11 (1876 or
1877)   [Per.Turk.d.2383]

REVUE DE GÉOGRAPHIE TURQUE
See: TÜRK COĞRAFYA DERGÎSÎ

REVUE DE LA FACULTÉ DES SCIENCES
ÉCONOMIQUES
See: İSTANBUL ÜNÎVERSÎTESÎ
ÎKTÎSAT FAKÜLTESÎ MECMUASI

REVUE DE LA FACULTÉ DES SCIENCES
FORESTIÉRES DE L'UNIVERSITÉ D'ISTANBUL
See: İSTANBUL ÜNÎVERSÎTESÎ ORMAN
FAKÜLTESÎ DERGÎSÎ

REVUE DE LA FACULTÉ DES SCIENCES
POLITIQUES
See: ANKARA ÜNÎVERSÎTESÎ SÎYASAL
BÎLGÎLER FAKÜLTESÎ DERGÎSÎ

REVUE DE RECHERCHES JURIDIQUES COMPARÉES
See: MUKAYESELİ HUKUK ARAŞTIRMALARI
DERGİSİ

REVUE DE SOCIOLOGIE
See: SOSYOLOJİ DERGİSİ

REVUE DE TURCOLOGIE
See: TÜRKBİLİK REVÜSÜ

REVUE DES ÉTUDES D'AZERBAIDJAN
See: AZERBAYCAN YURT BİLGİSİ

REVUE DES SCIENCES JURIDIQUES
See: HUKUKİ BİLGİLER MECMUASI

REVUE DU DÉPARTEMENT DE FRANÇAIS DE
L'ÉCOLE SUPÉRIEUR DES LANGUES
ÉTRANGÈRES DE L'UNIVERSITÉ D'ISTANBUL
See: DİLBİLİM

REVUE DU TOURING & AUTOMOBILE CLUB DE
TURQUIE
See: TURİNG

REVUE EBUZZIA
See: MECMUA-İ EBUZZİYA

REVUE TURQUE D'ANTHROPOLOGIE
See: TÜRK ANTROPOLOJİ MECMUASI

REVUE TURQUE DES SCIENCES SOCIALES ET
ÉCONOMIQUES
See: İŞ

RİZE İL YILLIĞI
[1] (1967) - [2] (1973)
Ankara, 1968-1973

BL:OIOC: [1] (1967)   [14498.a.23]
OX:BOD: [1]   [Turk.d.3324/53]

ROAD MOTOR VEHICLES STATISTICS
See: MOTORLU KARA TAŞITLARI
İSTATİSTİKLERİ

ROAD TRAFFIC ACCIDENTS STATISTICS
See: TRAFİK KAZALARI İSTATİSTİKLERİ

RÖLÖVE VE RESTORASYON DERGİSİ /
sahibi, Vakıflar Genel Müdürlüğü
Yıl 1, sayı 1 (1974) -
Ankara
With English summaries
Occasional

BL:OIOC: 1 (1974) - 6 (1987)
[14498.a.96]L:OIOC
OX:BOD: 1:1 - 5 (1982)
[Per.Turk.c.180]

ROMEN DİLİ = Limba Română / İstanbul
Edebiyat Fakültesinin, Roman dilleri
Enstitüsüne bağlı Romen dil ve
edebiyatı Seminerinin yardımcı kitabı
Yıl 1, sayı 1 (1.III.1943) - Yıl 1, sayı
5 (1.VI.1943)
Istanbul
In Turkish; with some Romanian texts

BL:OIOC: 1:1 (1.3.1943) - 1:5 (1.6.1943)
[ITA.1993.a.340]

RÜBAB: hayat-i edebiye namına perşembe
günleri musavver olarak intişar eder,
edebî, içtimai, felsefî mecmua
Cild 1, sayı 1 (26 Kanunusani 1327 [8
Feb. 1912] - Cild 3, sayı 116 (26
Kanunusani 1330 [8 Feb. 1915])
Istanbul
Weekly

OX:BOD: 1:1 (8.2.1912) - 1:40
(24.10.1912)   [Turk.d.1844]

RÜSUMÂT MUHARRERÂT-İ UMUMİYESİ ...
SALNAME
1 (1330 [1914-1915])
Istanbul
Only one issue published

CA:UL: 1 (1914)   [S.828.01.b.140]

RUZNAME-İ AYİNE-İ VATAN
See: İSTANBUL

RUZNAME-İ CERİDE-İ HAVADİS
Sene 1256, numero 1 (1 Cumadessâni 1256
[11 August 1840]) - Sene 1294, numero
5804 ([[date?], 1294 [1877])
Istanbul
Numeration commences from 1 again
following 959 (26.5.1865)
Many issues published under the title:
Ceride-i havadis
Generally daily; sometimes five issues
weekly; initially published every ten
days

BL:OIOC: (a) 708 (3.10.1854) - 755
(9.9.1854); [2]:400 (11.5.1866) -
[2]:500 (1.10.1866); (b) [2]:1
(26.9.1864) - [2]:847 (24.2.1868)
[(a) O.P.954; (b) 14498.a.85]
LO:SOAS: 801 (16.8.1855) - 900
(8.9.1858)   [L.E.Per.137106]

SABAH: her gün neşrolunur
25 Şubat 1291 [9 Mar. 1876] - 7
Teşrinisani 1338 [1922]
Istanbul
Newspaper

BL:OIOC: 10.9.1917 - 16.10.1917;
6.11.1917 - 16.12.1917; 1.1.1918 -
29.6.1918; 14.7.1918 - 17.8.1918;
22.9.1918 - 5.10.1918; lacking numerous
issues   [OR.MIC.11699 (O.P.248)]

SABAH POSTASI: günlük siyasî gazete
Izmir, 1953-[19--?]
Publication dates not known

BL:OIOC: 29.5.1960, 31.5.1960,
25.12.1960   [OR.MIC.12611 (O.P.552/11)]

SAÇAK [2. SERİ]: aylık dergi
Sayı 1 (Şubat 1984) - Sayı 70 (Aralık
1989)
Istanbul
Series 1 published: 1:1 (8.1976) - 4:29
(3.1980)

OX:BOD: 1 (2.1984) - 70 (12.1989)
[Per.Turk.d.3308]

SADÂ: edebî, tarihî, ilmî onbeş
günlük Osmanlı mecmuasıdır
1. sene, numero 1 (9 Teşrinisani 1325
[22 Nov. 1909])
[Istanbul]
Apparently only one issue published

BL:OIOC: 1 (22.11.1909)   [14498.a.113]

SADÂKAT: millet-i necib-i İslâmiye,
devlet-i muazzama-i Osmaniye ile Romanya
hükûmetinin menafi'ine hâdim haftada
bir defa çıkar İslâm gazetesidir
Numero 1 (1 Muharrem 1314/20 Mayıs 1313
[2 June 1897] - Numero 23 ([[date?],
1314/1313 [1897])
Constanta (Rumania)

BL:OIOC: 1 (2.6.1897) - 3 (16.6.1897)
[ORB.40/69]

ŞADIRVAN: haftalık sanat mecmuası
Cilt 1, sayı 1 (1 Nisan 1949) - Sayı 35
(25 Kasım 1949)
[Istanbul]: Vatan

BL:OIOC: 1:1 (1.4.1949) - 35
(25.11.1949)   [14448.f.155]

ŞAİR: haftalık edebî mecmua
  Cilt 1, sayı 1 (12 Kanunuevvel 1918) -
  Cilt 1, sayı 15 (20 Mart 1919)
  İstanbul

  BL:OIOC: 1:1 (12.12.1918) - 1:15
  (20.3.1919)   [ITA.1988.a.885]
  OX:BOD: 1:1 - 1:15   [Per.Turk.d.2265]

ŞAİR NEDİM
  See: NEDİM

SAKARYA İL YILLIĞI
  [1] (1967) - [2] (1973)
  [Istanbul?]

  OX:BOD: [1] (1967)   [Turk.d.3324/54]

ŞALKAR: şĕt ĕldĕgi Kazaktar mĕn
  madĕni baylanıs çasatın /
  ''Kazakstan'' koğamınıñ gazeti
  1977. cil, no. 1 ([date?], 1977) -
  Alma-Ata, 1977-
  Title before 1990: Bizniñ vĕtĕn
  Uygur; in Arabic characters
  Published twice monthly

  BL:OIOC: 1980:1 (?.?.1980) - ; lacking
  1980:13, 1981:8, 1982:14,20,
  1984,2,5,13, 1985:3,10,14,15
  [O.P.1085]
  OX:BOD: 1977:1 (?.?.1977) -; lacking
  some issues   [Per.Turk.b.15]

SALNAME
  See: SALNAME-İ DEVLET-İ ALİYE-İ
  OSMANİYE

SALNAME
  See also: BAĞDAD VİLÂYET-İ
  CELİLESİNE MAHSUS SALNAME

SALNAME
  See also: HÜDAVENDİGÂR VİLÂYETİ
  SALNAMESİ

SALNAME
  See also: SALNAME-İ VİLÂYET-İ
  TRABLUSGARB

SALNAME
  See also: SURİYE VİLÂYETİ SALNAMESİ

SALNAME-İ ADANA
  See: ADANA VİLÂYETİ SALNAMESİ

SALNAME-İ ASKERİ
  Defa 1 (1282 [1865-1866]) - [14] (1326
  (1324) [1908-1909])
  Istanbul, 1282 [1865] - 1324 [1908]
  Not published between 1895 and 1908.
  Some issues dated by malî year

  BL:OIOC: [11] (1892-1893)   [14496.e.1]
  CA:UL: 6 (1892)   [S.828.01.b.105]
  DU:UL: [14] (1908-1909)   [PL331]

SALNAME-İ BAHRİ
  See: BAHRİYE SALNAMESİ

SALNAME-İ CEBEL-İ LÜBNAN
  Defa 1 (1304 [1886-1887]) - Defa 6 (1309
  [1891-1892])
  Beit el-Dine

  OX:BOD: 4 (1889)   [Turk.e.1438]

SALNAME-İ DEVLET-İ ALİYE-İ OSMANİYE
  [1] (Sene 1263 [1847]) - 68. sene
  (1333-1334 [1918])
  İstanbul
  Official yearbook of the Ottoman
  government
  Continued by: T[ürkiye C[umhuriyeti]
  devlet salnamesi
  Early issues entitled: Salname

  BL:OIOC: 1 (1847) - 68 (1915); lacking
  3, 30, 49, 65; two copies of 1, 2, 6,
  21, 22, 32, 36, 57, 64   [14496.c.1]
  LO:SOAS: 1, 3 - 10, 14 -21, 23 - 48, 50
  - 65, 67 - 68   [E.Per.280657]
  CA:UL: (a) 1, 5, 7 - 10, 12 -15, 18, 20
  - 37, 39 - 53, 56 -67; (b) 36 (1881) -
  55 (1899)   [(a) S.828.01.b.1; (b)
  Gibb.d.185-]
  DU:UL: 11, 32, 35, 39 - 40, 43 - 44, 46,
  48, 50 - 53, 55 - 56   [PL324]
  OX:BOD: 1, 4, 9 - 10, 12, 20, 23, 27 -
  28, 30, 32 - 33, 35, 37 - 39, 42 - 45,
  47 - 48, 50 - 64, 66 - 68
  [Per.Turk.e.17]

SALNAME-İ HÜDAVENDİGÂR
  See: HÜDAVENDİGÂR VİLÂYETİ
  SALNAMESİ

SALNAME-İ NEZÂRET-I HARİCİYE
  See: SALNAME-İ NEZÂRET-İ UMUR-I
  HARİCİYE

SALNAME-İ NEZÂRET-İ MAARİF-İ UMUMİYE
  1. sene (1316 [1898-1899]) - 6. sene
  (1321 [1903-1904])
  Istanbul
  Year 5 (1320 [1902-1903]) not published

  BL:OIOC: 4 (1901-1902)   [ORB.30/706]
  CA:UL: 1 (1898-1899)   [S.828.b.135(1)]
  DU:UL: 2 (1899-1900) - 4   [PL374]
  OX:BOD: 3 (1900-1901)   [Turk.e.1484]

SALNAME-İ NEZÂRET-İ UMUR-I HARİCİYE
  Defa 1 (1302 [1884-1885]) - Defa 4 (1320
  [1902-1903])
  Istanbul
  Title of issuing body varies
  Title of issue 1: Salname-i Nezâret-i
  Hariciye. Issue 2: Devlet-i Aliye-i
  Osmaniye Hariciye Nezâret-i Celilesinin
  salnamesi
  Irregular

  BL:OIOC: 1 (1884-1885)   [14496.c.2]
  DU:UL: 1 - 3 (1900-1901)   [PL329]
  OX:BOD: 1 - 4 (1902-1903)
  [Per.Turk.e.810]

SALNAME-İ SELÂNİK
  See: SELÂNİK VİLÂYETİ SALNAMESİ

SALNAME-İ SURİYE
  See: SURİYE VİLÂYETİ SALNAMESİ

SALNAME-İ TRABLUSGARB
  See: SALNAME-İ VİLÂYET-İ TRABLUSGARB

SALNAME-İ TRABZON
  See: TRABZON VİLÂYETİ SALNAMESİ

SALNAME-İ VİLÂYET-İ AYDIN
  See: AYDIN VİLÂYETİ SALNAMESİ

SALNAME-İ VİLÂYET-İ BAĞDAD
  See: BAĞDAD VİLÂYET-İ CELİLESİNE
  MAHSUS SALNAME

SALNAME-İ VİLÂYET-İ BEYRUT
  Defa 1 (1311 [1893-1894] - 1312
  [1894-1895]) - Defa 7 (1326 [1908-1909])
  Beirut
  Irregular

  LO:SOAS: 7 (1908)   [E.Per.280672]
  CA:UL: 7   [S.828.01.b.16]
  DU:UL: 7   [PL.366]

SALNAME-İ VİLÂYET-İ BOSNA
  See: BOSNA VİLÂYETİ SALNAMESİ

SALNAME-İ VİLÂYET-İ CEZAYİR-İ
BAHR-İ SEFİD
  See: CEZAYİR-İ BAHR-İ SEFİD
  VİLÂYETİ SALNAMESİ

SALNAME-İ VİLÂYET-İ DİYARBAKIR
  See: DİYARBAKIR VİLÂYETİ SALNAMESİ

SALNAME-İ VİLÂYET-İ DİYARBEKİR
  See: DİYARBAKIR VİLÂYETİ SALNAMESİ

SALNAME-İ VİLÂYET-İ EDİRNE
  See: EDİRNE VİLAYETİ SALNAMESİ

SALNAME-İ VİLÂYET-İ HALEB
  1. sene (1284 [1876]) - 35. sene (1326
  [1908])
  Aleppo
  Title of issue 34: Haleb Vilayeti
  salnamesi

  BL:OIOC: 34 (1907)   [14498.cc.86]
  LO:SOAS: 13 (1883); 15 (1886); 18
  (1890); 22 (1894); 25 (1897) - 27
  (1899); 30 (1902); 32 (1904) - 33 (1905)
    [E.Per.280658]
  CA:UL: 15   [S.828.01.b.42]
  OX:BOD: 34 (1906)   [Turk.e.822]

SALNAME-İ VİLÂYET-İ KASTAMONİ
  See: KASTAMONU VİLÂYETİ SALNAMESİ

SALNAME-İ VİLÂYET-İ KASTAMONU
  See: KASTAMONU VİLÂYETİ SALNAMESİ

SALNAME-İ VİLÂYET-İ KONYA
  See: KONYA VİLÂYETİ SALNAMESİ

SALNAME-İ VİLÂYET-İ KOSOVA
  1 (1296 [1879-1880)] - 8 (1318
  [1900-1901])
  Priština; Skopje
  Issues 1-5 published at Priština, 6-8
  at Skopje
  Title of issues 4 and 5: Kosova
  Vilâyeti salnamesi

  LO:SOAS: 7 (1896)   [E.Per.280669]
  CA:UL: 7   [S.828.01.b.58]

SALNAME-İ VİLÂYET-İ MA'MURET ÜL-AZİZ
  See: MA'MURET ÜL-AZİZ VİLÂYETİ
  SALNAMESİ

SALNAME-İ VİLÂYET-İ SELÂNİK
  See: SELÂNİK VİLÂYETİ SALNAMESİ

SALNAME-İ VİLÂYET-İ SİVAS
  See: SİVAS VİLÂYETİ SALNAMESİ

SALNAME-İ VİLÂYET-İ SURİYE
  See: SURİYE VİLÂYETİ SALNAMESİ

SALNAME-İ VİLÂYET-İ TRABLUSGARB
  Defa 1 (1286 [1869-1870]) - Defa 12
  [i.e. 13] (1312 [1894-1895])
  Tripoli (Libya)
  Issue 1 entitled: Salname. Issues 2-4
  entitled: Salname-i Trablusgarb

  LO:SOAS: 11 (1885)   [E.Per.280666]

SALNAME-İ VİLÂYET-İ TRABZON
  See: TRABZON VİLÂYETİ SALNAMESİ

SALNAME-İ VİLÂYET-İ TUNA
  Defa 1 (1285 [1868-1869]) - Defa 10
  (1294 [1877])
  Ruse (Rusçuk)

  OX:BOD: 9 (1876)   [Turk.e.4381]

SALNAME-İ VİLÂYET-İ YANYA
  Defa 1 (1288 [1871-1872]) - Defa 8 (1319
  [1901-1902])
  Ioannina
  Title of no. 8: Yanya Vilâyeti
  salnamesi

  LO:SOAS: 8 (1901)   [E.Per.280667]

SÂLNÂME (YILLIK)
  1390/1970
  Istanbul: Aba
  Mainly on Islam and politics
  Only one issue published?

  BL:OIOC: 1970   [14498.a.72]

SAMĞAU: onbirinşi Besçıldıktın
  körkem şeciresi
  1. cıl (1982) - 5. cıl (1986)
  Alma-Ata: Cazuşı
  In Kazakh
  Annual

  OX:BOD: 1 (1982) - 5 (1986); lacking 2
  (1983)   [Per.Turk.d.3954]

SAMSUN İL YILLIĞI
  [1] (1967) - [2] (1973)
  Samsun

  OX:BOD: [1] (1967)   [Turk.d.3324/55]

SANAT / Başbakanlık Kültür
  Müsteşarlığı
  Yıl 1, sayı 1 (Haziran 1973) - 7 (Nisan
  1982)
  Istanbul
  Title of early issues: Kültür ve sanat
  Frequency?

  OX:BOD: 1:1 (6.1973) - 7 (4.1982)
  [Per.Turk.c.191]

SAN'AT / Üzbekiston Kompartiyası Markaziy
  Komitetining curnali
  No. 1 ([month?] 1942) -
  Tashkent
  ISSN 0202-1455
  Magazine on the arts and culture in
  Uzbekistan
  Title until May 1989: Sovet Üzbekistoni
  san'ati
  Monthly

  BL:OIOC: 1979:2 - ; lacking 1979:9,
  1982:1   [14499.tt.37]

SANAT, BİLİM VE KÜLTÜRDE ORKUN: aylık
  dergi
  Sayı 1 (Ağustos 1981) -
  Istanbul
  Initially monthly

  OX:BOD: 1 (8.1981) -   [Per.Turk.d.3322]

SANAT ÇEVRESİ: aylık sanat dergisi
  Sayı 1 (Kasım 1978) - 120 (Ekim 1988)
  Istanbul

  OX:BOD: 1 (11.1978) - 120 (10.1988)
  [Per.Turk.d.3320]

SANAT DÜNYAMIZ
  Yıl 1, sayı 1 (Mayıs 1974) -
  Istanbul: Yapı ve Kredi Bankası
  Four-monthly

  BL:OIOC: 1:1 (5.1974) - 7:21 (1.1981)
  [14498.a.73]
  OX:BOD: 1 -   [Per.Turk.c.133]

SANAT-EDEBİYAT: üç aylık edebiyat
dergisi / SED
1974/1 (Haziran 1974) - 1976/1 (Ocak
1976)
Ankara: Sanat Eleştirmeleri Derneği
Intended title may be: SED: sanat
edebiyat üç aylık araştırma dergisi

BL:OIOC: 1974:1-2 - 1975:2
[14480.d.192]

SANAT EMEĞİ: aylık sanat kültür
dergisi
Sayı 1 (Mart 1978) - Cilt 6, sayı 31
(Eylül 1980)
Istanbul
Militant left-wing cultural journal
Title on t.p.: Devrimci savaşımda Sanat
emeği

BL:OIOC: 1 (3.1978) - 6:31 (9.1980)
[ITA.1989.a.235]

SANAT TARİHİ ARAŞTIRMALARI DERGİSİ:
dört ayda bir çıkar
Cilt 1, sayı 1 (Kasım 1987) -
Istanbul

BL:OIOC: 1:1 (11.1987) -
[ZOR.1988.a.86]
OX:BOD: 1:1 -   [Per.Turk.d.3562]

SANAT TARİHİ YILLIĞI / İstanbul
Üniversitesi Edebiyat Fakültesi Sanat
Tarihi Enstitüsü
1 (1964-1965) -
Istanbul, 1965-

BL:OIOC: 1 (1964/1965) -   [14451.d.16]
LO:SOAS: 1 -   [Per.107.196826]
OX:BOD: 1 -   [Per.Turk.d.1641]

SANAT VE TOPLUM: iki aylık dergi
1 (Temmuz-Ağustos 1978) -
Istanbul
Literary and cultural journal

BL:OIOC: 1 (7-8.1978) - 2 (9-10.1978)
[14480.c.189]

SANAYİ DERGİSİ / Ege Bölgesi Sanayi
Odası
Cilt 1, sayı 1 ([date?], 1963) -
Izmir
New numbering after 132 (Oct.-Dec. 1970)
Original title: Sanayi haberleri
Quarterly; monthly until issue 130 (June
1970)

DU:DC: 7:5 (9.1971); 9.1976 - 9.1983
[25/4/INDUSTRY/GENERAL]

SANAYİ HABERLERİ
See: SANAYİ DERGİSİ

SAODAT: hotin-kızlarning oyda bir
çikadigan ictimoiy-siyosiy,
adabiy-badiiy curnali / Üzbekiston
Kommunistik Partiyasi Markaziy
Komitetining curnali
1925, no. 1 ([date?]) -
Tashkent
ISSN 0134-2223
In Uzbek

BL:OIOC: 1972:1 - 1983:12; lacking
1982:1   [14499.t.32]

ŞARK: mesail-i siyasiye ve mezhebiyeden
maada her şeyden bahseder ve ayda bir
kere neşrolunur
1. sene, 1. cild, 1. cüz' (1 Zilhicce
1297 [17 Nov. 1880]) - 1. cild, 8. cüz'
(1 Receb 1298 [30 May 1881])
Istanbul

BL:OIOC: 1:1 (17.11.1880) - 1:8
(30.5.1881)   [14480.d.240]
OX:BOD: 1:1 - 1:8   [Per.Turk.d.3554]

ŞARK YULDUZİ / Üzbekiston Yozuvçilar
Soyuzining oylik adabiy-badiiy,
ictimoiy-siyosiy curnali
1933, no. 1 ([date?] 1933) -
Tashkent
ISSN 0131-1832
Issuing body varies
In Uzbek

BL:OIOC: 1972:1 -; lacking 1976:1 -
1976:2, 1984:1 - 1984:3, 1984:6
[14499.t.31]
LO:SOAS: 1967:9 -   [Per.10.211000]
OX:BOD: 1985:1 -   [Per.Turk.d.3388]

ŞARKİYAT MECMUASI / İstanbul
Üniversitesi Edebiyat Fakültesi
Şarkiyat Enstitüsü tarafından
çıkarılır
Sayı 1 [1956] - Sayı 7 [1972]
Istanbul
Irregular

BL:OIOC: 1 [1956] - 7 [1972]
[14498.c.14]
LO:SOAS: 1 - 7   [Per.10.109002]
CA:UL: 1 - 7   [P.810.c.166]
OX:BOD: 1 - 7   [Per.Turk.d.315]

ŞAWT TURKISTĀN AL-SHARQĪYAH
See: DOĞU TÜRKİSTAN'IN SESİ

SAYASİY TRİBUNA: Respublikalık
teoryalık cana koomduk-sayasiy curnal
1991, 1 -
Bishkek
Replacement of: Kommunist Kirgizstana,
formerly Kırgızstan Koomunisti
In Kirgiz
Monthly

OX:BOD: 1991:1 -   [Per.Turk.d.1217]

SEBİLÜRREŞAD: siyasî, dinî, edebî,
ahlakî haftalık mecmua
1. sene, aded 1 (14 Agustos [1]324 [27
Aug. 1908]) - Cild 25, aded 641 (5 Mart
1341 [1925])
Istanbul; Kastamonu; Ankara; Kayseri
Published in various cities during the
War of Independence
Title of issues 1-182: Sirât-ı
müstakim. Subtitle varies

BL:OIOC: 1:1 (21.8.1908) - 25:641
(5.3.1925) (hard copy and microfiche)
[14456.ggg.1 (hard copy); OR. FICHE 448
(microfiche)]
LO:SOAS: 1:1 (21.8.1908) - 2:52
(20.8.1909)   [Per.10.L.8488]
CA:UL: 1:1 - 1:26 (5.2.1909) (hard copy
and microfilm)   [L.830.a.14 (hard
copy); P.72 (microfilm)]

SEÇİLMİŞ GAZETE YAZILARI
BİBLİYOGRAFYASI: ayda bir yayımlanır /
T.C. Kültür Bakanlığı Milli
Kütüphane Başkanlığı
Yıl 1, sayı 1 (Şubat 1989) -
Ankara: Milli Kütüphane

BL:OIOC: 1:1 (2.1989) -
[ZOR.1989.a.41]

SED
See: SANAT-EDEBİYAT

ŞEHBAL
[Sene 6], aded 1 (1 Mart 1325 [14 Mar.
1909]) - [Sene 6], aded 100 (10 Temmuz
1330 [23 July 1914])
Istanbul
General-interest illustrated magazine
Added title: Chehbal: illustration de
salon
Fortnightly

LO:SOAS: 1:1 (14.3.1909) - [6]:100
(23.7.1914) [Per.10.L.21613]
OX:MEC: 1:1 - 5:100 [APT Seh]

ŞEKER DERGİSİ / Türkiye Şeker
Fabrikaları A.Ş.
Ankara, [19--?]

BL:OIOC: 1981 (special issue, Atatürk
centenary) [ITA.1986.a.1624]
BL:DSC: 33:120 (1987) - 35:125 (1989)
[8230.000000]

SELÂMET: aylık manevi değerler ve milli
kültür dergisi
1 (Nisan 1962) - Cilt 2, sayı 16 (Temmuz
1963)
Ankara
Journal of Turkish Islamic cultural
history

BL:OIOC: 1. (4.1962) - 2:16 (7.1963)
[ITA.1988.a.2]

SELÂNİK VİLÂYETİ SALNAMESİ
Defa 1 (1287 [1870-1871]) - Defa 20
(1325 [1907-1908])
Thessaloniki
Some issues entitled: Salname-i
Selânik; Salname-i Vilâyet-i Selânik;
Selânik Vilâyetine mahsus salname

LO:SOAS: 19 (1906) [E.Per.280668]
CA:UL: 9 (1886); 14 (1895); 17 (1902)
[828:01.b.70.9-]
OX:BOD: 2 (1871) [Turk.e.1450]

SELÂNİK VİLÂYETİNE MAHSUS SALNAME
See: SELÂNİK VİLÂYETİ SALNAMESİ

SELÇUK / Selçuk Araştırmaları Merkezi
Yıl 1, sayı 1 ([date?], 1985) -
Konya
Irregular

OX:BOD: 2:1 (12.1986) -
[Per.Turk.d.3947]

SELÇUK ÜNİVERSİTESİ EDEBİYAT
FAKÜLTESİ DERGİSİ
Yıl 1981, sayı 1 -
Konya
Includes articles on western literature
Some contributions in European languages
Irregular

BL:OIOC: 1 (1981) [14498.cc.54]
OX:BOD: 1 - [Per.Turk.d.3093]

SELÇUK ÜNİVERSİTESİ EĞİTİM
FAKÜLTESİ DERGİSİ
Sayı 1 (1987) -
Konya
Irregular

OX:BOD: 1 (1987) - [Per.Turk.d.3950]

SELÇUK ÜNİVERSİTESİ İLÂHİYAT
FAKÜLTESİ DERGİSİ
Sayı 1 (1985) -
Konya
Title on cover: İlâhiyat Fakültesi
dergisi
Annual

BL:OIOC: 1 (1985) - [ZOR.1990.a.130]

SELÇUKLU ARAŞTIRMALARI DERGİSİ /
Selçuklu Tarih ve Medeniyeti
Enstitüsü
1 (1969) - 4 [1975]
Ankara, 1970-1975
Irregular

BL:OIOC: 1 (1969) - 4 [1975]
[14498.cc.62]
LO:SOAS: 1 - 4 [Per.10.275403]
CA:UL: 1 - 4 [P.617.c.41]

SEMİNER: felsefe, sosyoloji, psikoloji,
eğitim, antropoloji araştırmaları /
Ege Üniversitesi Sosyal Bilimler
Fakültesi
Sayı 1 (Haziran 1982) -
Izmir
Irregular

OX:BOD: 1 (6.1982) - [Per.Turk.d.3225]

ŞERGŞÜNASLIG İNSTİTUTUNUN ELMİ
ÉSÉRLÉRİ = Uchenye zapiski Instituta
Vostokovedeniía / Azerbaycan SSR
Elmlér Akademiyası Şergşünaslıg
İnstitutu
1 cild [1959] - 4 cild [1963]
Baku
Articles in Azeri or Russian

LO:SOAS: 1 [1959] - 4 [1963]
[Per.10.145158]

SERVET: her gün sabahları neşrolunur
1. sene, aded 1 (1 Haziran 1314 [14 June
1898]) - [?] sene, aded 2088 ([date?],
[1903])
Istanbul

OX:MEC: 1:1 (14.6.1898) - 1:182
(8.12.1898) [APT Ser 1]

SERVET-I-FUNOUN
See: SERVET-İ FÜNUN

SERVET-İ FÜNUN: perşembe günleri
çıkar musavver Osmanlı gazetesidir =
Servet-i-Funoun: illustration ottomane
paraissant le jeudi
1. cild, 1. sene, aded 1 (4 Mart 1307
[17 Mar. 1891] - 64. cild, 36. sene,
aded 1685 (29 Teşrinisani 1928)
Istanbul
Cultural and news weekly
Includes a separate section in French
Weekly; daily during 1908-9

BL:OIOC: (a) 1:1:1 (17.3.1891) -
48:24:1248 (6.5.1914) ; 57:30:1475
(20.11.1923) - 64:36:1685 (29.11.1928)
(microfiche); 53:27:1368, 54:27:1390,
1392, 1396, 1398, 55:28:1408 (22.1.1917
- 29.8.1918) (microfilm) [OR. FICHE
56; OR. MICR. 11875 (O.P. 640)]
LO:SOAS: 1 - 23 [L.E.Per.162886]
CA:UL: 18:929, 934; 19:940, 942, 945,
949-953, 956-957, 962-963, 980; 20:993
[L.830.a.13.18]
OX:BOD: (a) 1:1 - 48:24:1248
(microfilm); (b) 57:33:1475 - 64:36:1685
(microfilm); (c) 59:34:1527 (19.11.1925)
- 64:36:1685 (hard copy) [(a) Or.
microfiches 54; (b) Or. microfiches 55;
(c) Per.Turk.c.204]
OX:MEC: 1:1 - 32:1026 (?.?.1909);
57:1475 (20.11.1923) - ??:1656
(?.?.1927) [APT.Ser.2]

SESLER: aylık toplumsal sanat dergisi
Yıl 1, sayı 1 ([date], [1965?]) -
Skopje: Nova Makedoniya

OX:BOD: 23:219 (10.1987) -
[Per.Turk.e.7281]

SEVERNYİ-KAVKAZ
See: ŞİMALİ-KAFKASYA

71

SEVİMLİ AY
  See: RESİMLİ AY

SEVK VE İDARE DERGİSİ / Türk Sevk ve
  İdare Derneği
  Istanbul, [ca.1965]-
  Monthly

  DU:DC: 11:92 (4.1976) - 13:121 (9.1978);
  lacking 11:94, 12:108
  [25/4/INDUSTRY/GENERAL]

ŞEYDÂ: ruzname´ist Fârsî ve Türkî,
  meslek´eş beyan-ı hakikatest
  Sal-i evvel [1], şümare 1 (29 Şevval
  1329 [22 Oct. 1911] - Sal-i evvel [1],
  şümare 5 (2 Muharrem 1330 [23 Dec.
  1911])
  Istanbul
  Mainly in Persian; parts in Ottoman

  CA:UL: 1:1 (22.10.1911) - 1:5
  (23.12.1911)   [NPR.A.16(1)]

SHAYDÂ
  See: ŞEYDÂ

SİİRT İL YILLIĞI
  [1] (1967) - [2] (1973)
  Ankara, 1968-1973

  BL:OIOC: [1] (1967)   [14498.a.41]
  OX:BOD: [1]   [Turk.d.3324/57]

ŞIMAL OÇKUNLARI: sirek şurak
  çigaturgan dinî, millî, edebî, ve
  ictimaî mecmuadır
  Inçi san ([date?], [1952 or 1953] - [?]
  Helsinki
  Tatar; Arabic characters

  BL:OIOC: 4 (11.1953)   [ITA.1986.a.396]

ŞİMALÎ-KAFKASYA: aylık mecmua =
  Severnyî-Kavkaz: ezhemeşiachnyî
  zhurnal / organ Narodnoi Partii Gortsev
  Kavkaza
  No. 1 (Mayis [sic] 1934) - No. 61-62
  (Mayıs-Haziran 1939)
  Warsaw
  Added titles: Le Caucase du Nord; North
  Caucasia
  Articles in Turkish or Russian

  BL:HSS: 1 (5.1934) - 61/62 (5-6.1939);
  lacking 41 (9.1937), 53/54 (9-10.1938),
  57 (1.1939) - 59 (3.1939)
  [P.P.4842.dhc.]

ŞİNCAŇ MĚDĚNİYİTİ: ķoş ěylıķ
  universal ěděbiy jurnal
  Yıl 1, 1 san ([date?], 1952) -
  Urumchi
  Cultural magazine
  Added title in English: Xinjiang
  civilization
  Uygur; Arabic characters

  BL:OIOC: 38:2-4 (1989)
  [ZOR.1989.a.180]

ŞİNCAŇ SĚNĚTİ: ķoş ěylıķ sěnět
  jurnalı
  1981, 1 -
  Urumchi
  Added title in English: Xinjiang art
  Uygur; Arabic characters

  BL:OIOC: 9:3 (1989) - 9:4 (1989)
  [ZOR.1989.a.181]

ŞİNCAŇ SİFAN DÂŞÖ İLMİY
  JURNILI, İÇTİMÂ'İ PAN ĶISMI:
  pasıllık jurnal / Şincan sifan
  dâşö ilmiy jurnill tahrir hay'iti
  tarıpıdan naşr ķılındı
  Yıl 1, 1 san (1985) -
  Urumchi
  Journal of social sciences and
  humanities
  Uygur, in Arabic characters
  Quarterly; issues dated by year only

  BL:OIOC: 1988:1 -   [ZOR.1989.a.68]

SİNOP İL YILLIĞI
  [1] (1967) - [2] (1973)
  Sinop, 1970-1973

  BL:OIOC: [1] (1967)   [14498.a.24]
  OX:BOD: [1]   [Turk.d.3324/56]

SİRÂT-I MÜSTAKİM
  See: SEBİLÜRREŞAD

SIVAS FOLKLORU: aylık folklor dergisi
  Sayı 1 (Mart 1973) - Sayı 78 (Temmuz
  1979)
  Istanbul
  Scope not confined to the folklore of
  Sivas itself
  Succeeded by: Türk folkloru

  BL:OIOC: 1 (3.1973) - 78 (7.1979)
  [14498.b.20]
  LO:SOAS: 1 - 78   [Per.10.L.496953]
  DU:UL: 61 (2.1978) - 78   [Per./PL264]
  OX:BOD: 1 - 78   [Per.Turk.d.3160]

SİVAS İL YILLIĞI
  [1] (1967) - [2] (1973)
  Sivas, 1968-1973

  BL:OIOC: [1] (1967)   [14498.a.35]
  OX:BOD: [1]   [Turk.d.3324/58]

SİVAS VİLÂYETİ SALNAMESİ
  Defa 1 (1287 [1870-1871]) - Defa 17
  (1325 [1907-1908])
  Sivas
  Some issues entitled: Salname-i
  Vilâyet-i Sivas

  DU:UL: 16 (1903)   [PL366.S5]
  OX:BOD: 16   [Turk.d.1439]

SİYASAL BİLGİLER
  See: SİYASİ İLİMLER MECMUASI

SİYASAL BİLGİLER OKULU DERGİSİ
  See: ANKARA ÜNİVERSİTESİ SİYASAL
  BİLGİLER FAKÜLTESİ DERGİSİ

SİYASİ İLİMLER
  See: SİYASİ İLİMLER MECMUASI

SİYASİ İLİMLER MECMUASI: aylık
  Yıl 1, sayı 1 (Nisan 1931) - 11. yıl,
  cilt 19, sayı 215 (Şubat 1949)
  Ankara
  Titles of earlier issues: Siyasal
  bilgiler; Siyasi ilimler; Aylık siyasi
  ilimler mecmuası

  BL:OIOC: 14:162 (9.1944) - 19:215
  (2.1949)   [14498.c.8]
  LO:SOAS: 6:70 (1.1937); 6:72 (3.1937) -
  9:101 (8.1939); 15:178 (1.1946) - 18:208
  (7.1948)   [Per.57.33220]
  CA:UL: 14:162 - 18:213 (12.1948)
  [L.830.c.7]
  OX:BOD: 14:162 - 18:213   [Turk.d.448]

SOCIOLOGICAL REVIEW
  See: SOSYOLOJİ DERGİSİ

SOSYAL BİLİMLER FAKÜLTESİ DERGİSİ /
[Ege Üniversitesi Sosyal Bilimler
Fakültesi]
1 [1980] - 2 [1981]
İzmir
Covers all humanities subjects
Title of no. 1: E.Ü. Sosyal Bilimler
Fakültesi dergisi
Annual

  BL:OIOC: 1 [1980] - 2 [1981]
  [14498.cc.82]
  OX:BOD: 1 - 2   [Per.Turk.d.3228]

SOSYAL SİGORTALAR KURUMU ÇALIŞMA RAPORU
VE BİLANÇOSU
Ankara, [19--?]-
Title varies slightly
Annual

  DU:DC: 1970; 1976   [25/4/SOCIAL
  SERVICES]
  SU:IDS: 1976 - 1982
  [SERIALS/OFFICIAL/TURKEY]

SOSYOLOJİ DERGİSİ = Sociological review
  = Revue de sociologie = Zeitschrift für
  Soziologie / İstanbul Üniversitesi
  Edebiyat Fakültesi yayınları
  Sayı 1 [(1942)] - Sayı 21-22 (1967-1968)
  İstanbul
  Nos. 1-3 are subtitled: Edebiyat
  Fakültesi Sosyoloji Semineri tetkik ve
  araştırmaları
  Some articles in English or French
  Nominally annual

  BL:OIOC: 1 (1942) - 22 (1968)
  [14498.aa.2]
  LO:SOAS: 1 - 22   [Per.10.65378]
  DU:UL: 1 - 5 (1949)   [Per./PL7]
  OX:BOD: 1 - 22   [Per.Turk.d.2868]

SOSYOLOJİ DÜNYASI / Türk Sosyoloji
  Cemiyetinin resmî dergisi
  Cilt 1, no.1 (Temmuz 1951) - Cilt 1,
  no.3 (Temmuz 1953)
  İstanbul
  Apparently only 3 issues published
  Approximately annual; advertised in 1
  and 2 as being published thrice
  annually, in 3 as ten times

  BL:OIOC: 1:1 (7.1951) - 1:3 (7.1953)
  [14439.d.244]

SOSYOLOJİ KONFERANSLARI / İstanbul
  Üniversitesi İktisat Fakültesi
  Sosyoloji Enstitüsü
  [1] (1960-1961) -
  İstanbul, 1962-
  Annual

  OX:BOD: [1] (1960-1961) -
  [Per.Turk.d.2915]

SOVET EDEBİYATI
  See: GARAGUM

SOVET MAKTABİ / Üzbekiston SSR Maorif
  ministrligining oylik ilmiy-metodik
  curnali
  No. 1 (Dekabr 1918) -
  Tashkent: Üzbekiston Kompartiyasi
  Markaziy Komitetining naşriyoti
  ISSN 0134-2231
  Title of issuing body varies
  In Uzbek

  BL:OIOC: 1988:1 -   [ZOR.1988.a.51]

SOVET ŞARKİ MUSULMONLARİ: Ürta Osiyo
  va Kozogiston Dini Boşkarmasining
  jurnali
  Tashkent
  ISSN 0203-5952
  Uzbek in Arabic characters. Also
  published in English, Arabic, Persian,
  etc.
  Quarterly

  OX:BOD: 1986:1 -   [Per.Turk.d.3455]

SOVET ÜZBEKİSTONİ
  See: ÜZBEKİSTON-CONTACT

SOVET ÜZBEKİSTONİ SAN'ATİ
  See: SAN'AT

SOVETTİK KIRGIZSTAN
  See: KIRGIZSTAN TUUSU

SPOR FAALİYETLERİ VE TESİSLERİ =
  Sports activities and facilities /
  Başbakanlık Devlet İstatistik
  Enstitüsü
  1982 -
  Ankara, 1985-
  In Turkish and English
  Irregular

  BL:HSS: 1982   [SQ.170/54]

SPORTS ACTIVITIES AND FACILITIES
  See: SPOR FAALİYETLERİ VE TESİSLERİ

STATISTICAL POCKET BOOK OF TURKEY
  See: TÜRKİYE İSTATİSTİK CEP
  YILLIĞI

STATISTICAL YEARBOOK OF TURKEY
  See: TÜRKİYE İSTATİSTİK YILLIĞI

STATISTICAL YEARBOOK, TURKEY
  See: BAĞ-KUR İSTATİSTİK YILLIĞI

STATISTICS OF COASTWISE AND INTERNATIONAL
SEA TRANSPORTATION
  See: KABOTAJ VE ULUSLARARASI DENİZ
  TAŞIMASI İSTATİSTİKLERİ

STATISTICS OF ELECTRIC POWER IN TURKEY
  See: TÜRKİYE ELEKTRİK ENERJİSİ
  İSTATİSTİK BÜLTENİ

STATISTICS OF VESSELS 18 GROSS TONNAGES
AND OVER
  See: [ONSEKİZ] 18 VE DAHA YUKARI GROS
  TONİLATOLUK DENİZ TAŞITLARI
  İSTATİSTİKLERİ

STATISTIQUE MENSUEL DU COMMERCE
EXTÉRIEUR, COMMERCE SPÉCIAL
  See: DIŞ TİCARET AYLIK İSTATİSTİK,
  ÖZEL TİCARET

STATISTIQUE MENSUEL DU COMMERCE
EXTÉRIEUR, COMMERCE SPÉCIAL
  See: DIŞ TİCARET AYLIK İSTATİSTİK,
  ÖZEL TİCARET, SERİ 1

STUDIEN ZUR DEUTSCHEN SPRACHE UND
LITERATUR
  See: ALMAN DİL VE EDEBİYATI DERGİSİ

SU ÜRÜNLERİ ANKET SONUÇLARISXSEESU
ÜRÜNLERİ İSTATİSTİKLERİ

SU ÜRÜNLERİ İSTATİSTİKLERİ =
Fishery statistics / Başbakanlık Devlet
İstatistik Enstitüsü
Ankara
Previous title: Su ürünleri anket
sonuçları
Sometimes in English as well as Turkish
Annual; some issues cumulated

LO:SOAS: 1985 -   [L.N.S.539400]
DU:DC: 1968 - 1970/1971; 1976/1979 -
[25/4/INDUSTRY/FISHING]
SU:IDS: 1976/1979 -; lacking 1985
[SERIALS/OFFICIAL/TURKEY]

SUFFE: kültür sanat yıllığı
[1] (1982) -
Istanbul
Annual; 1985-1986 published as one issue

BL:OIOC: [2] (1983) -   [14480.c.156]

SÜHA: siyasiyattan başka herşeyden
bahseder
Sayı 1 1300 [1883 or 1884]) - Sayı 4
1300 [1883 or 1884])
Istanbul
Issues dated by year only

OX:BOD: 1 (1883 or 1884)   [Turk.e.640]

SUICIDE STATISTICS
See: İNTİHAR İSTATİSTİKLERİ

SÛK-U UKÂZ: emtek elsine-i selâse
münaveli üzere mensuh ve mamul olan
mâser-i bedi'iyesine ma'rız olarak her
şehr-i arabî gurresinde berküşâd
olur suhan sergisidir
Sayı 1 (28 Cumadessani 1304 [24 Mar.
1887])
Istanbul
Contents in Ottoman or Arabic

OX:BOD: 1 (24.3.1887)   [Turk.d.2207(2)]

SUMMARY OF MONTHLY FOREIGN TRADE
See: AYLIK DIŞ TİCARET ÖZETİ

ŞÛRÂ: haftalık siyasi gazete
Sayı 1 (25 Muharrem 1398 [5 Jan. 1978])
- sayı 41 (26 Zilka'de 1398 [30 Oct.
1978])
Ankara; Istanbul
Muslim political weekly. BL holdings
include banned issues
Published at Ankara up to and including
issues 16 (4 May 1978); then at Istanbul

BL:OIOC: 1 (5.1.1978) - 41 (30.10.1978)
[ORB.40/1]

ŞÛRÂ
Sene 1, aded 1 (1 Teşrinievvel 1908) -
Sene 10, aded 24 ([date?], 1917)
Orenburg: Vakt naşriyati
Cultural journal
Chaghatay; Arabic characters
Published twice monthly

BL:OIOC: 6:9 (1.5.1913) - 6:11
(1.6.1913); 6:22 (15.11.1913); 7:5
(1.3.1914); 7:13 (1.7.1914); 7:15
(1.8.1914)   [14499.tt.18]

ŞÛRÂ-YI ÜMMET: hükümet-i meşrute
ve ıslâhât-ı umumiye tarfdarlarının
vasıta-i neşriyatıdır
[1. sene, numero 1 (10 Nisan [1]320 [23
Apr. 1902]) - 9. sene, numero 220 (29
Nisan 1326 [12 May 1910])
Cairo; Paris; Istanbul
Published at Cairo, then Paris, then
Istanbul; at least one special issue at
Salonica
Initially fortnightly; later daily,
weekly, then irregular

BL:OIOC: (a) 1:2 (6.5.1902) - 5:95
(6.7.1908); special issue (6.5.1908);
lacking 2:37, 3:52 - 3:54, 4:81; (b) 1:1
(23.4.1902) - 1:21 (11.2.1903); lacking
1:20   [(a) ORB.40/67; (b) 14498.d.13]

SURİYE VİLÂYETİ SALNAMESİ
Defa 1 (1285 [1868-1869]) - Defa 32
(1318 [1900-1901])
Damascus
Title varies: Salname, Salname-i Suriye,
Salname-i Vilâyet-i Suriye, Suriye
Vilâyetine mahsus salname

LO:SOAS: 15 (1883) - 16 (1884); 19
(1887); 24 (1892)   [E.Per.280659]
CA:UL: 15   [S.828.01.b.74]
DU:UL: 17 (1886)   [PL367.S.8]

SURİYE VİLÂYETİNE MAHSUS SALNAME
See: SURİYE VİLÂYETİ SALNAMESİ

SÜS: haftalık edebî hanım mecmuası
Sene 1, numara 1 (16 Haziran 1339
[1923]) - Sene 2, numara 55 (26 Temmuz
1340 [1924])
Istanbul

OX:BOD: 1:1 (16.6.1923) - 2:55
(26.7.1924)   [Per.Turk.c.208]

ŞUYOHLUK / Kabartı-Malkar ASSR-ni
Djazıuçularını Soyuzunu suratlau
literatura al'manahı
1 ([date?], 1958) -
Nal'chik
In Karachay-Balkar
Frequency varies

BL:OIOC: 17 (1962); 35 (1-3.1967)
[14499.r.150]

TAÇ: 3 ayda bir çikan meslek dergisi /
Türkiye Anıt Çevre Turizm Değerlerini
Koruma Vakfı
Cilt 1, sayı 1 (Şubat 1986) -
Istanbul
Journal concerned with architectural
monuments and archaeological sites and
their preservation and restoration

BL:OIOC: 1:1 (2.1986) -
[ZOR.1989.a.32]
OX:BOD: 1:1 -   [Per.Turk.d.3946]

TAKVİM-İ EBÜZZİYA
1. sene (1310 ve 1271 [1892-1893]) - [3]
(1316-1317 ve 1277-1278 [1898-1899])
Istanbul: Tevfik Ebüzziya, 1310 [1892]
- 1316 [1898]
Three issues only. Previously published
as a supplement to: Rebi'-i marifet, and
Nevsal-i marifet.
Nominally annual, then biennial

BL:OIOC: 1 (1892-1893)   [Or.80.b.13]

TAKVÎM-İ VAKÂYİ': Devlet-i Âliye-i
Osmâniye'nin ceride-i resmiyesi
Numero 1 (25 Cemaziyülevvel 1247 [25
July 1831]) - [4. seri], sayı 4608
([date?], 1923)
Istanbul
Official gazette of the Ottoman state
Published in four series

BL:OIOC: [1]:117-195   [14498.a.58]
OX:BOD: [1]:1-40   [Turk.c.85]
OX:MEC: [1]:1-300; [1]:314-420;
[1]:478-612; [1]:691-776; [1]:1866-1950;
[2]:1-64; [3]:281-341   [APT Tak]

TALEBE: onbeşde bir çıkar mekteb
mecmuası
Numero 1 (1 Şubat 1327 [14 Feb. 1912])
- 1. cild, numero 8 (15 Nisan 1328 [28
Apr. 1912])
Izmir
Illustrated magazine for schoolchildren

LO:SOAS: 1:1 (14.2.1912) - 1:18
(28.4.1912)   [Per.10.20596]

TAN
See also: MİLLİYET

TAN: haftada bir çıkar / Kosova Çalışan
Halkı Sosyalist Birliği organı
Yıl 1, sayı 1 ([date?], 1969) -
Priština
Weekly newspaper

BL:HSS: 523 (date?, 1979) - ; lacking
about 60 issues   [S.Q.23/4]

TANİN
19 Temmuz 1324 [1 Aug. 1908] - 29 Eylül
1340 [1924]
Istanbul
Daily newspaper

BL:OIOC: 26.3.1917; 20.9.1917 -
22.9.1917; 3.10.1917 - 20.12.1917;
1.1.1918 - 17.8.1918; 22.9.1918 -
5.10.1918; lacking 42 issues
[OR.MIC.11698 (O.P.247)]

TANRIDAĞ [1. SERİ]: Türkcü, ilmî,
edebî; bu Türklerin dergisidir, Cuma
günleri çıkar
Cilt 1, no. 1 (8 Mayıs 1942) - Cilt 1,
no. 18 (4 Eylûl 1942)
Istanbul
Nationalist cultural review

BL:OIOC: 1:1 (8.5.1942) - 1:18
(4.9.1942)   [14498.a.87]

TANRIDAĞ [2. SERİ]: Tanrıdağı kadar
Türk - Hiradağı kadar Müslüman
siyasi Türkçü dergi
Yıl 1, sayı 1 (5 Kasım 1950) - Yıl 1,
sayı 7 (27 Şubat 1951)
Istanbul
Published fortnightly down to issue 6

BL:OIOC: 1:1 (5.11.1950) - 1:7
(27.2.1951)   [14498.a.87]

TAPU İSTATİSTİKLERİ = Title deed
statistics / Başbakanlık Devlet
İstatistik Enstitüsü
Ankara, [19--?]-
In Turkish and English
Generally annual

DU:DC: 1981/1982 -   [25/4/LAW]
SU:IDS: 1981/1982 - 1983
[SERIALS/OFFICIAL/TURKEY]

TARİF-İ DARÜSSAÂDE: rahnümâ-i
ticaret = L'Indicateur
constantinopolitain: guide commercial
1. sene (1285 [1868]) - 12. sene (1296
[1869])
Istanbul
Text in Ottoman and French: also Greek
and Armenian titles on t.p.

BL:OIOC: 1 (1868)   [14429.b.6]

TARİH ARAŞTIRMALARI = Review of
historical research
1 (1957)
Ankara: Ankara Üniversitesi Dil ve
Tarih-Coğrafya Fakültesi
Only one issue published
Articles in Turkish, English or German

BL:OIOC: 1 (1957)   [14456.d.450;
14456.f.76]
LO:SOAS: 1   [Per.10.138147]
OX:BOD: 1   [Turk.d.1351]

TARİH ARAŞTIRMALARI DERGİSİ = Review
of historical research / Ankara
Üniversitesi Dil ve Tarih-Coğrafya
Fakültesi Tarih Araştırmaları
Enstitüsü
Cilt 1, sayı 1 (1963) -
Ankara
Articles in Turkish or English
Currently biennial ; 1963-1969, annual
though nominally semi-annual ; 1970 to
1978, one issue published

BL:OIOC: 1:1 (1963) -   [14498.cc.19]
LO:SOAS: 1:1 -   [Per.10.167565]
CA:UL: 1:1 -   [P.617.c.16]
DU:UL: 1:1   [Per./PL5]
OX:BOD: 1:1 -   [Per.Turk.d.1323]

TARİH COĞRAFYA DÜNYASI: onbeş günde
bir çıkar
Cilt 1, sayı 1 (15 Nisan 1959) - Cilt 2,
sayı 12 (15 Aralık 1959)
Istanbul

BL:OIOC: 1:1 (15.4.1969) - 2:12
(15.12.1959)   [14498.c.19]

TARİH DERGİSİ
See: İSTANBUL ÜNİVERSİTESİ
EDEBİYAT FAKÜLTESİ TARİH DERGİSİ

TARİH DÜNYASI
Yıl 1, sayı 1 (15 Nisan 1950) - Yıl 3,
sayı 38 (Şubat 1953)
Istanbul
Succeeded from Sept. 1953 by: Yeni tarih
dünyası
Monthly

LO:SOAS: 1:1 (15.4.1950) - 3:38 (2.1953)
[Per.10.296639]
OX:MEC: 1:1 - 3:38   [APT Tar 6]

TARİH ENSTİTÜSÜ DERGİSİ
See: İSTANBUL ÜNİVERSİTESİ
EDEBİYAT FAKÜLTESİ TARİH
ENSTİTÜSÜ DERGİSİ

TARİH HAZİNESİ: tarih ve ilim mecmuası
/ çıkaran, Ülkü Kitap Yurdu
Yıl 1, sayı 1 (15 Kasım 1950) - Yıl 2,
Cilt 2, sayı 17 (Nisan 1953)
Istanbul
Mainly on Ottoman cultural history

BL:OIOC: 1:1 (15.11.1950) - 2:2:17
(4.1953)   [14456.d.459]
LO:SOAS: 1:1 - 1:12   [Per.10.118952]

TARİH-İ OSMANİ ENCÜMENİ MECMUASI
See: TÜRK TARİH ENCÜMENİ MECMUASI

TARİH İNCELEMELERİ DERGİSİ / Ege
  Üniversitesi Edebiyat Fakültesi yayını
  1 ([1983]) -
  Izmir
  Concerned mainly with Turkish and
  Islamic history
  Annual

  BL:OIOC: 1 (1983) -   [14498.cc.80]
  LO:SOAS: 1 -   [Per.10.497098]
  OX:BOD: 1 -   [Per.Turk.d.3094]

TARİH İNSTİTUTUNUN ESERLERİ =
  Trudy Instituta Istorii / Azĕrbaycan
  SSR Ĕlmlĕr Akademiyası
  1 (1951) - 18 (1970)
  Baku
  Titles of nos. 1-10: Tarih vĕ
  Fĕlsĕfĕ Institutunun esĕrlĕri =
  Trudy Instituta Istorii i Filosofii
  Articles in Azeri or Russian
  Irregular; 10 published before 9

  BL:OIOC: 6 (1955); 9 (1955) - 15 (1961)
    [14499.s.3]
  BL:HSS: 2 (1952) - 12 (1957); 14 (1960)
  - 17 (1966)   [Ac.1109.dm.]
  OX:BOD: (a) 1 - 9; (b) 11 (1957) - 18
  (1970)   [(a) 3974.d.1051; (b)
  2233.e.104]

TARİH KONUŞUYOR: aylık tarih mecmuası
  Cilt 1, sayı 1 (Şubat 1964) - Cilt 8,
  sayı 60 (Ocak 1969)
  Istanbul

  BL:OIOC: 1:1 (2.1964) - 8:60 (1.1969)
    [14498.cc.51]
  OX:MEC: 1:1 - 8:60   [APT Tar 5]

TARİH MECMUASI
  See: HAYAT TARİH MECMUASI

TARİH SEMİNERİ DERGİSİ / İstanbul
  Üniversitesi Edebiyat Fakültesi
  Yayınları
  1 [1937] - 2 [1938]
  Istanbul
  French added title (no French contents):
  Travaux du Séminaire d'Histoire

  BL:OIOC: 1 [1937] - 2 [1938]
    [14498.b.11]
  LO:SOAS: 1 - 2   [Per.10.77886]
  DU:UL: 1 - 2   [Per./PL5]
  OX:BOD: 1 - 2   [Turk.d.522]

TARİH VE EDEBİYAT: mülk-i millet'e
  nafi, tarih, edebiyat, fünun,
  iktisadiyat ve şuûn-i saire'ye
  müteallık mebahis-i müfide'yi hâvi
  mecmua-i şehriyedir
  Aded 1 (31 Ağustos 1338 [1922]) - Aded
  5 (31 Kanunuevvel 1338 [1922])
  Istanbul
  Continuation of: Osmanlı tarih ve
  edebiyat mecmuası

  OX:BOD: 1 (31.8.1922) - 5 (31.12.1922)
  (microfiche)   [Or. Microfiches 57]

TARİH VE EDEBİYAT MECMUASI
  See: HAYAT TARİH MECMUASI

TARİH VĔ FĔLSĔFĔ İNSTİTUTUNUN
ESERLERİ
  See: TARİH İNSTİTUTUNUN ESERLERİ

TARİH VE TOPLUM: aylık ansiklopedik dergi
  Sayı 1 (Ocak 1984) -
  Istanbul: İletişim

  BL:OIOC: 1 (1.1984) -   [ZOR.1987.a.78]
  LO:SOAS: 54 (6.1988); 61 (1.1989) -;
  lacking 65 (5.1989)   [Per.10.L.562510]
  OX:BOD: 1 -   [Per.Turk.d.3099]
  CA:OS: 11:65 (5.1989) -   [M.40]

TARİH VESİKALARI
  1. cilt, 1-6ncı sayı (Haziran 1941 -
  Mayıs 1942) - Yeni seri, 1. cild, 3 (18)
  sayı (Mart 1961)
  [İstanbul]: Maarif Vekâleti
  Nomenclature of issuing body changed to
  Maarif Vekilliği, then to Millî
  Eğitim Bakanlığı
  Bimonthly until no.14, then irregular

  BL:OIOC: 1:1-6 (6.1941-5.1942) - New
  series 1:3 (3.1961)   [14498.c.7]
  LO:SOAS: 2 (?.1941) - New series 1:3
    [L.E.Per.48519]
  CA:UL: 1:1 - 3:14 (10.1944); New series
  1:1 - 3:18 (3.1961)   [T.830.b.16]
  OX:BOD: 1:1 - 3:15; New series 1:1 - 1:3
    [Per.Turk.d.396]
  OX:MEC: 1:2 (8.1941) - 3:15 (5.1949);
  New series 1:1 (8.1955) - 1:2 (1.1958)
    [APT Tar 4]

TARIM BAKANLIĞI DERGİSİ
  Sayı 1 (Ekim 1947) -
  Ankara
  Monthly

  BL:OIOC: 1:1 (10.1947) - 3:20/21
  (12.1949)   [14448.d.5]

TARIM İSTATİSTİKLERİ ÖZETİ = The
  summary of agricultural statistics /
  Başbakanlık Devlet İstatistik
  Enstitüsü
  1941-1962
  Ankara, 1963-
  Previous title: Ziraî istatistik
  özetleri
  In Turkish and English
  Nominally annual

  BL:HSS: 1941/1962   [S.Q.170/24]
  LO:SOAS: 1985 -   [L.N.S.310.541824]
  DU:DC: 1956-1959; 1962-1963; 1967-1972;
  1974-   [25/4/AGRICULTURE/GENERAL]
  SU:IDS: 1967; 1969 - 1970; 1973 - 1974;
  1978; 1981 -   [SERIALS/OFFICIAL/TURKEY]

TARIMSAL YAPI VE ÜRETİM = Agricultural
  structure and production / Başbakanlık
  Devlet İstatistik Enstitüsü
  1934-1950 -
  Ankara
  Early issues entitled: Ziraî bünye ve
  istihsal
  In Turkish and English
  Annual since 1960

  BL:HSS: 1934/1950; 1946/1954; 1954/1958;
  1958/1959   [S.Q.171/5]
  DU:DC: 1958/1960 - 1960/1962; 1965 -
  1969; 1972 -
  [25/4/AGRICULTURE/GENERAL]
  SU:IDS: 1967 -
  [SERIALS/OFFICIAL/TURKEY]

TARSUS'UN EKONOMİK RAPORU
  Tarsus: Tarsus Ticaret ve Sanayi Odası,
  [196-?]-
  Annual

  DU:DC: 1971-1972   [25/4/COMMERCE]

TASVİR-İ EFKÂR
  See also: TEVHİD-İ EFKÂR

TATAR TELE HĔM ĔDĔBİYATI / SSSR
  Fĕnnĕr Akademiyase Kazan filialı Tel,
  ĕdĕbiyat hĕm tarih institutı
  hĕzmĕtlĕre
  1 ([196-?]) -
  Kazan
  Russian added title: Trudy po tatarskomu
  iazyku i literature
  In Tatar
  Frequency not known

  BL:OIOC: 2 (1963)   [14499.o.43]

T.B.M.M. TUTANAK DERGİSİ
1. Cild (23 Nisan - 19 Mayıs 1336
[1920]) -
Ankara
Proceedings of the Turkish Grand
National Assembly
Title from 1920 to 1960: T.B.M.M. zabıt
ceridesi. Other past titles include:
Millet Meclisi tutanak dergisi;
Cumhuriyet Senatosu tutanak dergisi;
Millî Güvenlik Konseyi tutanak
dergisi; Danışma Meclisi tutanak
dergisi
Irregular; in general, approximately
monthly

BL:OIOC: 1 (23.4.1920) - 19.5.1920) - 22
(27.7.1922 - 11.9.1922)   [14456.k.88]
BL:HSS: 2:5:11 (1928-1929) - 15/16
(1976-1977); lacking 1960   [S.Q.1/2]

T.B.M.M. ZABIT CERİDESİ
See: T.B.M.M. TUTANAK DERGİSİ

T.C. DEVLET YAYINLARI BİBLİYOGRAFYASI:
ayda bir yayımlanır / Millî Kütüphane
Devlet Yayınları Dokümentasyon Merkezi
Cilt 1, sayı 1 (Ocak 1971) -
Ankara

BL:OIOC: 9:10 (10.1979) -
[14498.cc.50]
LO:SOAS: 9:10 -   [PRA.015.493025]
CA:UL: 9:10 -   [OP.32000.021.01]
OX:BOD: 9:10 -   [Per.Turk.d.3078]

T.C. RESMÎ GAZETE / Başbakanlık
Basın-Yayın ve Enformasyon Genel
Müdürlüğü
Cilt 1, sayı 1 (7 Teşrinievvel 1336
[1920]) -
Ankara
Title of publishing body varies.
Successor to: Ceride-i resmi; Türkiye
Cumhuriyeti resmi gazete
Daily

BL:HSS: 7351 (?.?.1949) - 17135
(?.?.1980); lacking very few issues
[O.G.T.200]
DU:DC: 9624 (?.6.1957) - 11541
(?.8.1963); 12493 (?.1.1967) - 14006
(?.11.1971); lacking scattered issues;
16 mm. microfilm   [25/1/GENERAL]

T.C. TARIM BAKANLIĞI DERGİSİ
See: TARIM BAKANLIĞI DERGİSİ

T.C. TURİZM BAKANLIĞI BÜLTENİ: üç
ayda bir yayınlanır
Sayı 1 (Ekim [?] 1983) -
Ankara

DU:DC: 17 (10.1987) -   [25/4/BANKING]

TEÂVÜN-Ü AKLÂM [1. SERİ]: haftada bir
defa neşrolunur risale-i mevkutedir
1. sene, numero 1 (3 Temmuz 1302 [16
July 1886]) - 1. sene, numero 22
(Kanunuevvel 1302 [mid-Dec. 1886 -
mid-Jan. 1887])
Istanbul

OX:BOD: 1:1 (16.7.1886) - 1:22
(12.1886-1.1887)   [Turk.c.66]

TEÂVÜN-Ü AKLÂM [2. SERİ]: haftada bir
defa neşrolunur, gazete-i fennî ve
edebî
1. sene, numero 1 (4 Mayıs 1303 [17 May
1887]) - 1. sene, numero 47 (22 Mart
1304 [4 Apr. 1888])
Istanbul

OX:BOD: 1:1 (17.5.1887) - 1:47
(4.4.1888)   [Turk.c.66]

TEDRİSÂT-I İBTİDAİYE MECMUASI /
Maarif Nezareti namına Darülmuallimîn
hey'et-i ta'limiyesi tarafından her ayın
onbeşinde neşrolunur
Sene 1, numero 1 ([Şubat] 1325 [1909])
- Sene 2, numero 18 ([Temmuz] 1326
[1910])
Istanbul

BL:OIOC: 1 (2.1909) - 18 (7.1910)
[ITA.1993.a.321]

TEFSİR-İ EFKÂR
See: TEVHİD-İ EFKÂR

TEKİRDAĞ İL YILLIĞI
[1] (1967) - [2] (1973)
Istanbul

BL:OIOC: [1] (1967)   [14498.a.31]
OX:BOD: [1]   [Turk.d.3324/59]

TEKNİK BÜLTEN / Devlet Su İşleri Genel
Müdürlüğü
Ankara, [ca. 1966]-
With summaries in English
Generally quarterly

DU:DC: 21 (2.1971) - 25 (8.1972);
lacking 23   [25/4/ENERGY]

TEMİR KAZIK: ayında bir çığatın
sayasât, çarvaçılık, ılım, adabiyât
curnal
San 1 (Fevral 1923) - [?]
Moscow
Kazakh; Arabic characters

BL:OIOC: 1 (2.1923)   [14499.tt.31]

TERBİYE
See: TERBİYE MECMUASI

TERBİYE / Maârif Vekâleti Talim ve
Terbiye Hey'eti tarafından ayda bir
neşrolunur terbiye ve tedrisât
mecmuasıdır
Sayı 1 (15 Şubat 1927) - Cild 2, sayı
10 (Kanunusâni 1928)
Istanbul

BL:OIOC: 1 (15.2.1927) - 2:8 (12.1927)
[14498.b.12]

TERBİYE MECMUASI: onbeş günde bir neşr
olunur
Sene 1, numero 1 (15 Mart 1330 [28 Mar.
1914]) - [Seri 2] Sene 1, numero 6 (15
Kanunuevvel 1334 [1918])
Istanbul
Second series (not described as such)
begins with Sene 1, numero 1 (29
Ağustos 1334 [1917])
Second series has the title: Terbiye

BL:OIOC: 1:1 (28.3.1914) - [Seri 2], 1:6
(15.10.1918)   [14498.cc.70]

TERBİYE MECMUASI / Fenn-i Terbiye
Encümeni tarafından iki ayda bir
neşrolunur
Sene 1, numero 1 (Kanunusani 1333 [Jan.
1918])
Istanbul
Only one issue published

BL:OIOC: 1:1 (1.1918)   [ITA.1990.a.526]

TERCÜMAN: siyasât ve maarif ve
edebiyat'a müteallık resimli millî
gazetedir = Perevodchik: ezhedel'naīa
gazeta literatury, otechestvennoi,
innostranoi zhizni i politiki
Sene 1, numero 1 ([date?] 1300 [1882]) -
Sene 35, numero [?] ([date?] [1917])
Bakhchisaray (Crimea)
Some issues entitled: Tercüman-i
ahval-i zaman. Subtitle varies
In Ottoman / literary Tatar, and Russian
Weekly

BL:OIOC: 13:37 (1.10.1895); 18:1
(8.1.1901) - 21:45 (17.11.1903)   [OR.
MIC. 12630 (O.P. 217)]

TERCÜMAN: günlük müstakil siyasi
gazete
Yıl 1, sayı 1 ([date?] 1955) -
Istanbul
Title on masthead: Hâdiselere Tercüman

BL:OIOC: 6:1790 (31.5.1960)
[OR.MIC.12615 (O.P.552/15)]

TERCÜMAN-İ AHVAL-İ ZAMAN
See: TERCÜMAN

TERCÜMAN-İ HAKİKAT
Istanbul, 1877-1922
Daily newspaper with cultural
contributions

BL:OIOC: 2.10.1917 - 8.10.1917;
22.1.1918 - 28.6.1918; 28.9.1918 -
30.9.1918; lacking 16 issues from these
    [OR.MIC.11702 (O.P.251)]

TERCÜME
Cilt 1, sayı 1-6 (Mayıs 1940 - Mart
1941) - Cilt 18, sayı 87 (Temmuz-Eylül
1966)
Ankara
Journal devoted to Turkish translations
(sometimes including the original) of
western literary works, and articles on
aspects of translation
Cilt 1-4 published by: Mf.V. (i.e.
Maarif Vekilliği)
Bimonthly until 1954 ; thereafter
quarterly

BL:OIOC: 1:1/6 (5.1940-3.1941) - 18:87
(7/9.1966)   [14498.cc.76]
LO:SOAS: 1:2 (19.7.1949) - 7:37
(19.5.1946); lacking 4:19 (19.5.1943)
 [Per.10.45931]
CA:UL: 1:1 - 3:6; 4:20 - 9:52
[L.830.c.4]

TEVHİD-İ EFKÂR: müstakil ül-efkâr
Osmanlı gazetesi
1. sene, numero 1 (31 Mayıs 1325 [13
June 1909]) - 16. sene, numero 4356 (5
Mart 1925)
Istanbul
Title of publication varies. Some issues
have the following titles: Yeni Tasvir-i
efkâr, Tasvir-i efkâr, İntihab-ı
efkâr, Tefsir-i efkâr
Daily

BL:OIOC: 1:1 (13.6.1909) - 1:90
(29.8.1909) (1); 9:2209 (1.1917) -
9:2520 (22.7.1918) (2)   [O.P.955 (1);
O.P.245 (2)]
OX:BOD: 1:1 - 1:80 (25.12.1909)
[Turk.b.7]
OX:MEC: 1:1 - 1:340 (23.5.1910)   [APT
Tas]

[TEZ-BÜRO İŞ] BÜLTENİ [2. SERİ]:
aylık bülten
Yıl 1, sayı 1 (Temmuz 1971) -
Ankara: Tez-Büro-İş
Series 1 published 1969-1971

DU:DC: 1:1 (7.1971) - 1:2 (8.1971)
[25/3/TRADE UNIONS]

TİCARET: günlük siyasi ticari gazete
Sene 1, no. 1 (20 Nisan 1941) -
Izmir

BL:OIOC: 20:5781 (20.5.1961)   [OR.
MIC. 12618 (O.P. 552/18)]

TİCARET ŞİRKETLERİ VE FİRMA
İSTATİSTİKLERİ = Commercial
companies and firms statistics /
Başbakanlık Devlet İstatistik
Enstitüsü
Ankara, [19--?]-
Turkish and English
Annual

SU:IDS: 1988   [SERIALS/OFFICIAL/TURKEY]

TİL MEÑ EDEBİET İNSTİTUTİNİÑ
EÑBEKTERİ = Trudy Instituta īazyka i
literatury / Kazak SSR Ġılım
Akademiyası Til meñ edebiet institutı
1 (1959) - 3 (1963)
Alma-Ata
Articles in Kazakh or Russian

OX:BOD: 1 (1959) - 3 (1963)
[Per.Turk.d.373]

TIP TARİHİ ARAŞTIRMALARI = History of
medicine studies
[1] (1986) -
Istanbul: İstanbul Üniversitesi
Cerrahpaşa Tıp Fakültesi, 1986 [i.e.
1987]-
1st issue, dated 1986 but published
1987, not numbered
With summaries in English
Irregular

BL:OIOC: [1] (1986) -   [ZOR.1988.a.83]

TITLE DEED STATISTICS
See: TAPU İSTATİSTİKLERİ

TİYATRO VE MUSİKİ: musikîden,
tamaşadan ve sinemadan bahis haftalık
gazetedir
Numero 1 (19 Kanunusani 1928) - Numero
11 (5 Nisan 1928)
Istanbul
In Arabic characters

BL:OIOC: 1 (19.1.1928) - 11 (5.4.1928)
 [14498.a.117]

TOKAT İL YILLIĞI
[1] (1967) - [2] (1973)
Ankara

LO:SOAS: [1] (1967)   [Per.10.L.245339]
OX:BOD: [1]   [Turk.d.3324/60]

TOPLU SÖZLEŞME İSTATİSTİKLERİ =
Collective bargaining agreements /
Başbakanlık Devlet İstatistik
Enstitüsü
1972-1986 -
Ankara, 1980-
Turkish and English
Annual; sometimes cumulated

SU:IDS: 1972/1976; 1980
[SERIALS/OFFICIAL/TURKEY]

TOPLUM VE BİLİM: üçaylık dergi
[1] (Bahar 1977) –
İstanbul
With summaries in English
Quarterly; some cumulated issues

BL:OIOC: 28 (autumn 1985) –
[ZOR.1988.a.211]
LO:SOAS: [1] (spring 1977) –
[Per.10.570820]
OX:BOD: [2] (summer 1977) –
[Per.Turk.e.5218]
OX:MEC: [1] – 7   [APT Top]
CA:OS: 45 (spring 1989) – 48/49 (spring
1990)   [M.29]

TOPRAKSU: teknik dergisi / Köy İşleri
Bakanlığı Topraksu Genel Müdürlüğü
Sayı 1 (Şubat 1961) – Sayı 43 (Aralık
1976)
Ankara
Generally quarterly

DU:DC: 20 (3.1978) – 47 (1.1985);
lacking 21-23, 31, 33, 36, 38
[25/4/AGRICULTURE/GENERAL]

TOPRAKSU BÜLTENİ [1. SERİ] / Köy
İşleri Bakanlığı Genel Müdürlüğü
Sayı 1 (Kasım 1970) – Sayı 53 (Mart
1975)
Ankara
Monthly

DU:DC: 3 (1.1971) – 53 (3.1975); lacking
5-6, 12, 16, 18-20, 28-31, 47
[25/4/AGRICULTURE/GENERAL]

TOPRAKSU BÜLTENİ [2. SERİ] / Köy
İşleri Bakanlığı Topraksu Genel
Müdürlüğü
Sayı 1-2 (Mayıs-Haziran 1976) –
Ankara
Monthly

DU:DC: 1/2 (5-6.1976) – 23/24
(11-12.1978); lacking 9- 10
[25/4/AGRICULTURE/GENERAL]

TOPTAN EŞYA VE TÜKETİCİ FİYATLARI
AYLIK İNDEKS BÜLTENİ = Wholesale and
consumer price indexes monthly bulletin
/ Başbanlık Devlet İstatistik
Enstitüsü
Ocak 1972 –
Ankara
Previous titles: Aylık fiyat indeksleri
bülteni = Monthly bulletin of price
indexes
Bilingual after 1980

DU:DC: 1.1977; 4.1977 – 1.1978; 3.1980;
5.1980 – 6/7.1980; 12.1983 – 1.1984;
3.1984 –   [25/4/PRICES]
SU:IDS: 11:1977 – 12.1977; 2.1978;
9.1979; 11.1979 – 3.1980; 12.1980;
9.1986 – 10.1986; 1.1989
[SERIALS/OFFICIAL/TURKEY]

TOPTAN FİYAT İSTATİSTİKLERİ: ticaret
borsalarında işlem gören maddeler =
Wholesale price statistics: registered
commodities in commodity exchanges /
Başbakanlık Devlet İstatistik
Enstitüsü
1949/1965 –
Ankara, [ca.1966]-
Previous title: Fiyat istatistikleri.
Subtitle varies
Currently in Turkish and English
Annual; generally cumulated

DU:DC: 1949/1965; 1967/1968; 1974/1975;
1983   [25/4/PRICES]
SU:IDS: 1969/1973 –
[SERIALS/OFFICIAL/TURKEY]

TOURISM STATISTICS
See: TURİZM İSTATİSTİKLERİ

TRABZON KÜLTÜR-SANAT YILLIĞI /
Trabzonlular Kültür ve Yardımlaşma
Derneği
[1] ([19]87) –
İstanbul

OX:BOD: [1] (1987)   [Per.Turk.d.3948]

TRABZON VİLÂYETİ SALNAMESİ
Defa 1 (1286 [1869-1870]) – Defa 22
(1322 [1904-1905])
Trabzon
Some issues entitled: Salname-i Trabzon;
Salname-i Vilâyet-i Trabzon; Trabzon
Vilâyetine mahsus salnamedir

LO:SOAS: 22 (1904)   [E Per 280664]
OX:BOD: 15 (1893); 18 (1900)
[Per.Turk.e.812]

TRABZON VİLÂYETİNE MAHSUS SALNAME
See: TRABZON VİLÂYETİ SALNAMESİ

TRAFİK KAZALARI İSTATİSTİKLERİ = Road
traffic accidents statistics /
Başbakanlık Devlet İstatistik
Enstitüsü
1978/1980 –
Ankara, 1982-
Turkish and English
Annual; some cumulated issues

SU:IDS: 1978/1980 –
[SERIALS/OFFICIAL/TURKEY]

TRANSPORTATION AND ROAD TRAFFIC ACCIDENTS
STATISTICS
See: ULAŞTIRMA VE TRAFİK KAZALARI
İSTATİSTİKLERİ

TRANSPORTATION STATISTICS
See: ULAŞTIRMA VE TRAFİK KAZALARI
İSTATİSTİKLERİ

TRAVAUX DU SÉMINAIRE D'HISTOIRE
See: TARİH SEMİNERİ DERGİSİ

TRUD
See: MİHNAT

TRUDY AZERBAĬDZHANSKOGO GEOGRAFICHESKOGO
OBSHCHESTVA
See: AZĚRBAYCAN COĞRAFYA
CĚMİYYĚTİNİN ĚSĚRLĚRİ

TRUDY AZERBAĬDZHANSKOGO GOSUDARSTVENNOGO
NAUCHNO-ISSLEDOVATEL´SKOGO INSTITUTA
PEDAGOGIKI
See: AZĚRBAYCAN DÖVLĚT
ELMİ-TĚDGİGAT PEDAGOKİKA
İNSTİTUTUNUN ĚSĚRLĚRİ

TRUDY INSTITUTA ĬAZYKA I LITERATURY
See: DİL VE ĚDEBİYAT İNSTİTUTININ
İŞLERİ

TRUDY INSTITUTA ĬAZYKA I LITERATURY
See also: TİL MEN̄ EDEBİET
İNSTİTUTININ EN̄BEKTERİ

TRUDY INSTITUTA ĬAZYKOZNANIĬA
See: DİL VE ĚDEBİYAT İNSTİTUTININ
İŞLERİ

TRUDY INSTITUTA ISTORII
See: TARİH İNSTİTUTUNUN ĚSĚRLĚRİ

TRUDY INSTITUTA ISTORII I FILOSOFII
See: TARİH İNSTİTUTUNUN ĚSĚRLĚRİ

TRUDY INSTITUTA LITERATURY I ĬAZYKA IM.
NIZAMI
See: NİZAMİ ADINA ĚDĚBİYYAT VĚ
DİL İNSTİTUTUNUN ĚSĚRLĚRİ

TRUDY INSTITUTA LITERATURY IMENI
MAKHTUMKULI
See: MAGTIMGULI ADINDAKİ ĚDEBİYAT
İNSTİTUTININ İŞLERİ

TRUDY MUZEĬA AZERBAĬDZHANSKOĬ
LITERATURY IMENI NIZAMI
  See: NĬZAMĬ ADINA AZĒRBAYCAN
  ĒDĒBĬYYATI MUZEYĬNĬN ĒSĒRLĒRĬ

TRUDY MUZEĬA ISTORII AZERBAĬDZHANA
  See: AZĒRBAYCAN TARĬHĬNĒ DAĬR
  MATERĬALLAR

TRUDY PO TATARSKOMU ĬAZYKU I LITERATURE
  See: TATAR TELE HĒM ĒDĒBĬYATI

TRUDY RESPUBLIKANSKOGO RUKOPISNOGO FONDA
  See: ĒLYAZMALAR HĒZĬNĒSĬNDĒ

TRUDY SEKTORA FILOSOFII
  See: FĒLSĒFĒ BŌLÜMÜNÜN
  ĒSĒRLĒRĬ

TRUDY SEKTORA VOSTOKOVEDENIĬA /
  Akademiĭa Nauk Kazakhshkoĭ SSR,
  Sektor Vostokovedeniĭa
  Tom 1 [1959]
  Alma-Ata
  Mainly in Russian; some Kazakh

  LO:SOAS: 1 [1959]   [Per.10.141292]
  OX:BOD: 1   [Or.Per.135]

TULÛ': siyasiyâttan başka herşeyden
  bahseder ve her şehr-i Rumî
  ibtidasıyle onbeşinde cüz' cüz'
  neşrolunur risale-i mevkutedir
  1. sene, numero 1 (31 Temmuz 1300 [13
  Aug. 1884]) - 1. sene, numero 9 (31
  Kanunusâni 1300 [13 Feb. 1885])
  Istanbul

  BL:OIOC: 1:1 (13.8.1884) - 1:9
  (13.2.1885)   [14498.c.5]

TURİNG: üç ayda bir yayımlanır = Revue
  du Touring & Automobile Club de Turquie:
  revue trimestrielle / Türkiye Turing ve
  Otomobil Kurumu belleteni
  Sayı 1 ([Nisan 1971?]) - Sayı 76 (355)
  (1987)
  Istanbul
  Initially quarterly; later irregular

  OX:BOD: 63 (342) (7-12.1978) - 76 (355)
  (1987)   [Per.Turk.d.3534]

TURİZM İSTATİSTİKLERİ = Tourism
  statistics / Başbakanlık Devlet
  İstatistik Enstitüsü
  1972 -
  Ankara
  Earlier issues entitled: Türizm
  istatistikleri bülteni = Bulletin of
  tourism statistics
  In Turkish and English
  Annual

  DU:DC: 1970; 1980 -   [25/4/TOURISM]
  SU:IDS: 1972; 1976; 1980 -;
  [SERIALS/OFFICIAL/TURKEY]

TURİZM İSTATİSTİKLERİ AYLIK BÜLTENİ
  / Başbakanlık Devlet İstatistik
  Enstitüsü
  Ankara, [19--?]-

  DU:DC: 1972:1, 3-4, 6-9, 11-12
  [25/4/TOURISM]

TURİZM İSTATİSTİKLERİ BÜLTENİ
  See: TURİZM İSTATİSTİKLERİ

TÜRK ANTROPOLOJİ MECMUASI = Revue turque
  d'anthropologie / Türk antropoloji ve
  Etnoloji Derneği tarafından yılda bir
  neşrolunur
  1. yıl, sayı 1 ([1925?]) - [?]
  Ankara
  Mainly in Turkish; some contents in
  French

  LO:SOAS: 15:19/22 (9.1939)
  [Per.10.L.109107]

TÜRK ARKEOLOJİ DERGİSİ / Kültür
  Bakanlığı Eski Eserler ve Müzeler
  Genel Müdürlüğü tarafından
  yayımlanır
  Sayı 6 (1956) -
  Istanbul
  Continuation (hence the numbering of the
  first issue) of: Türk tarih, arkeologya
  ve etnografya dergisi
  Some articles are in English, French or
  German
  Occasional

  BL:OIOC: 6 (1956) - 25 (1980)
  [14448.f.16]
  LO:SOAS: 8 (1958) -; lacking 10
  [Per.10.L.138013]
  OX:BOD: 6 -   [Per.Turk.d.408]

TÜRK COĞRAFYA DERGİSİ = Revue de
  géographie turque
  Yıl 1, sayı 1 [1943] -
  Ankara: Türk Coğrafya Kurumu
  Early issues lack French title
  Some articles summarized in English,
  French or German
  Frequency varies

  BL:OIOC: 1:1 [1943] - 13:17 (1957)
  [14498.c.16]
  LO:SOAS: 1:1 - 1:3 (1947); 18 (1963) -
  19 (1964)   [Per.10.L.138013]
  CA:UL: 1:1 - 13:17   [T.617.c.1]

TÜRK DİLİ [1. SERİ]:
  Türkçe-Fransızca belleten / Türk Dil
  Kurumu
  Sayı 1 (Nisan 1933) - No. 33 (İlkkânun
  1938)
  Ankara
  Earliest issues published by: Türk Dili
  Tetkik Cemiyeti
  Subtitle varies
  Some contributions in French
  Generally bi-monthly; initially
  irregular

  BL:OIOC: 1 (4.1933) - 33 (12.1938)
  [14498.b.16]
  LO:SOAS: 1 - 33   [Per.10.33383]
  DU:UL: 1 - 33; lacking a few issues
  [Per./PL2]
  OX:BOD: 1 - 33; lacking 6/7 (6-7.1934)
    [Per.Turk.d.633]

TÜRK DİLİ [2. SERİ]:
  Türkçe-Fransızca belleten / Türk Dil
  Kurumu
  Seri 2, Sayı 1-2 (Sonkânun 1940) - Seri
  2, sayı 18-20 (1943)
  Ankara
  Entirely in Turkish
  Irregular

  BL:OIOC: 1/2 (1.1940) - 18/20 (1943)
  [14498.b.16]
  LO:SOAS: 1/2 - 18/20   [Per.10.33383]
  DU:UL: 1/2 - 18/20   [Per./PL2]
  OX:BOD: 1/2 - 18/20   [Per.Turk.d.582]

TÜRK DİLİ [3. SERİ]: belleten / T.D.K.
Yayın Kolu tarafından üç ayda bir
yayınlanır
Seri 3, sayı 1-3 (Haziran 1945) - Seri
3, sayı 14-15 (Ocak 1950)
Ankara: Türk Dil Kurumu

BL:OIOC: 1/3 (6.1945) - 14/15 (1.1950)
[14498.b.16]
LO:SOAS: 1/3 - 14/15 [Per.10.33383]
DU:UL: 1/3 - 14/15 [Per./PL2]
OX:BOD: 1/3 - 14/15 [Per.Turk.d.3158]

TÜRK DİLİ [4. SERİ]: aylık dil ve
edebiyat dergisi / Türk Dil Kurumu
Cilt 1, sayı 1 (Ekim 1951) -
Ankara
Index exists for vols. 1-24 (1951-1971)

BL:OIOC: 1:1 (10.1951) - [14498.b.16]
LO:SOAS: 1:1 -; lacking 30 - 34
[Per.10.33383]
CA:UL: 1:1 - [L.830.c.39]
DU:UL: 1:1 -; lacking a few issues
[Per./PL 2]
OX:BOD: 1:1 - [Per.Turk.d.342]

TÜRK DİLİ ARAŞTIRMALARI YILLIĞI
BELLETEN / Türk Dil Kurumu
yayınlarından
[1] (1953) -
Ankara
Some articles in English or German
Biennial since 1973-1974, despite title

BL:OIOC: [1] (1953) - [14498.bb.3]
LO:SOAS: [1] - [Per.10.96286]
CA:UL: [1] - [L.830.c.28]
DU:UL: [1] - [11] (1963); [16] (1968) -
[17] (1969) [Per./PL2]
OX:BOD: [1] - [Per.Turk.d.356]

TÜRK DİLİ VE EDEBİYATI ARAŞTIRMALARI
DERGİSİ / Ege Üniversitesi Sosyal
Bilimler Fakültesi
1 (1982) -
Izmir
Occasional; initially annual

BL:OIOC: 4 (1985) [ZOR.1989.a.110]
LO:SOAS: 1 (1982) - [Per.10.475864]
OX:BOD: 1 - [Per.Turk.d.2985]

TÜRK DİLİ VE EDEBİYATI DERGİSİ
See: İSTANBUL ÜNİVERSİTESİ TÜRK
DİLİ VE EDEBİYATI DERGİSİ

TÜRK DÜNYASI ARAŞTIRMALARI
Yıl 1, Cilt 1, sayı 1 (Haziran 1979) -
İstanbul: Türk Dünyası Araştırmaları
Vakfı
Bi-monthly

BL:OIOC: 3; 7 - 24; 26 - [14498.cc.74]
LO:SOAS: 6 -; lacking many issues
[Per.10.507790]
DU:UL: 2:10 (10.2.1981) - 29 (4.1984);
lacking a few issues [Per./PL1]
OX:BOD: 1 (6.1979) - [Per.Turk.d.3085]

TÜRK DÜNYASI TARİH DERGİSİ: aylık
tarih dergisi
1. yıl, sayı 1 (15 Ocak 1987) -
Istanbul: Türk Dünyası Araştırmaları
Vakfı

BL:OIOC: 1:1 (1.1987) - [ZOR.1987.a.7]
OX:BOD: 1:1 - [Per.Turk.d.3523]

TÜRK DÜŞÜNCESİ: aylık fikir ve sanat
mecmuası
Cilt 1, sayı 1 (Aralık 1953) - Cilt 11,
sayı 12 (63) (Nisan 1960)
İstanbul

BL:OIOC: 1:1 (12.1953) - 11:12 (4.1960)
[14498.cc.88]

TÜRK EDEBİYATI: aylık fikir ve sanat
dergisi
Sayı 1 (Ocak 1972) -
Istanbul

BL:OIOC: 152 (6.1986) -
[ZOR.1987.a.59]
OX:BOD: 1 (1.1972) - [Per.Turk.d.3211]

TÜRK EDEBİYATI: yeni Türk edebiyatının
bir yılını elinizin altına getiren
antoloji
1 (1963) - 10 (1972)
Istanbul: De Yayınevi
Subtitle varies

BL:OIOC: 1 (1963) - 10 (1972)
[ITA.1989.a.236]
CA:UL: 1 (1963) - 10 (1972)
[P.830.d.1]

TÜRK ETNOGRAFYA DERGİSİ / Kültür
Bakanlığı Eski Eserler ve Müzeler
Genel Müdürlüğü tarafından
yayınlanır
Sayı 1 (1956) -
Ankara
Nomenclature of issuing body varies
Added t.p. in English: Turkish review of
ethnography
Irregular

BL:OIOC: 1 (1956) - 16 (1977)
[14448.f.17]
LO:SOAS: 1 - [Per.10.L.117438]
CA:UL: 1 - [T.617.b.3]
DU:UL: 1 - 11 (1968) [Per./PL 7]
OX:BOD: 1 - [Per.Turk.d.313]

TÜRK FOLKLOR ARAŞTIRMALARI: ayda bir
defa çıkar halkbilgisi dergisi
Yıl 1, sayı 1 (Ağustos 1949) - Yıl 31,
no. 366 (Ocak 1980)
Ankara

LO:SOAS: 1:1 (8.1949) - 31:366 (1.1980);
lacking 8:97 (8.1957) - 9:102 (1.1958)
[Per.10.96052]
OX:BOD: 1:1 - 31:366 [Per.Turk.d.1049]

TÜRK FOLKLORU: aylık halkbilim dergisi
1 (Ağustos 1979) - 90 (Ocak 1987)
Istanbul
Successor of: Sıvas folkloru
Original subtitle: aylık folklor dergisi

BL:OIOC: 1 (8.1979) - 90 (1.1987)
[ITA.1989.a.233]
LO:SOAS: 1 - 90 [Per.10.L.432303]
DU:UL: 1 - 90 [Per./PL264]
OX:BOD: 1 - 90 [Per.Turk.d.3161]

TÜRK FOLKLORU ARAŞTIRMA YILLIĞI
See: TÜRK FOLKLORU ARAŞTIRMALARI

TÜRK FOLKLORU ARAŞTIRMALARI / Kültür
ve Turizm Bakanlığı Millî Folklor
Araştırma Dairesi yayınları
1974 -
Ankara, 1975-
Titles of earlier issues: Türk folkloru
araştırmaları yıllığı (1974-1976);
Türk halkbilim araştırmaları yıllığı
(1977-?)
Annual

BL:OIOC: 1974 - 1977; 1982 -
[14498.b.19]
LO:SOAS: (a) 1975 - 1977; (b) 1981 -
[(a) Per.10.350052; (b) Per.10.456144]
CA:UL: 1974 - [Picken.53.1-]
OX:BOD: 1981 - [Per.Turk.d.2984]

TÜRK FOLKLORU BELLETEN
[1] (1986) -
İstanbul: Türk Folkloru Yayınları
Semi-annual?

BL:OIOC: [1] (1986) -   [14498.cc.98]
OX:BOD: [1] -   [Per.Turk.d.3527]

TÜRK FOLKLORUNDAN DERLEMELER / Kültür
ve Turizm Bakanlığı Millî Folklor
Araştırma Dairesi
1986/1 -
Ankara
Appears at least once annually

LO:SOAS: 1986:1 -   [Per.10.539352]
OX:BOD: 1986:1 -   [Per.Turk.d.3526]

TÜRK HALK KÜLTÜRÜ ARAŞTIRMALARI =
Turkish folk culture researches /
Kültür Bakanlığı Halk Kültürünü
Araştırma Dairesi
1990/1 -
Ankara
Articles in Turkish; brief synopses in
English
Quarterly

BL:OIOC: 1990:1 -   [ZOR.1992.a.24]

TÜRK HALK MÜZİĞİ VE OYUNLARI: 3 ayda
bir çıkar
Cilt 1, yıl 1, sayı 1 ([date?] 1982) -
Cilt 2, yıl 3, sayı 10
(Nisan-Mayıs-Haziran 1984)
Ankara

OX:BOD: 1:2:5 (1-2-3.1983) - 2:3:10
(4-5-6.1984); lacking 1:2:7 (7-8-9.1983)
[Per.Turk.d.3311]

TÜRK HALKBİLİM ARAŞTIRMALARI YILLIĞI
See: TÜRK FOLKLORU ARAŞTIRMALARI

TÜRK HARB-İŞ / Türkiye Harb-İş
Federasyonu yayın organı
Yıl 1, sayı 1 (23 Nisan 1970) - Yıl 8,
sayı 1956 (Haziran 1977)
Ankara
Monthly; initially fortnightly

DU:DC: 1:6 (18.5.1972) - 3:34 (6.1974);
lacking 5 issues   [25/3/TRADE UNIONS]

TÜRK HUKUK TARİHİ DERGİSİ / T[ürk]
Hukuk K[urumu] Türk Hukuk Tarihi
Enstitüsü tarafından çıkarılır
Cilt 1 (1941-1942)
Ankara, 1944
Only one issue published

BL:OIOC: 1 (1941-1942)   [14458.fff.281]
LO:SOAS: 1   [Per.32.289667]

TÜRK HUKUK VE İKTİSAT TARİHİ MECMUASI
/ İstanbul Darülfünun Türkiyat
Enstitüsü tarafından neşredilir
Cilt 1 (1931) - Cilt 2 (1939)
İstanbul

BL:OIOC: 1 (1931)   [14458.fff.58]
LO:SOAS: 1 - 2 (1939)   [Per.10.29471]
CA:UL: 1 - 2   [Q.617.c.2]
DU:UL: 1 - 2   [Per./PL5]
OX:BOD: 1 - 2   [Per.Turk.d.431]

TÜRK-İŞ: aylık dergi / Türkiye İşçi
Sendikaları Konfederasyonu
Cilt 1, sayı 1 (Mart 1963) -
Ankara

DU:DC: 8 (10.1963); 10-12; 15-17; 21;
30; 48; 50; 52; 62-105; 107-112 (5.1974)
[25/3/TRADE UNIONS]

TÜRK KÜLTÜRÜ: aylık dergi / Türk
Kültürünü Araştırma Enstitüsü
Sayı 1 (Kasım 1962) -
Ankara

BL:OIOC: 1 (11.1962) - 21:248 (12.1983);
lacking 11:126 (4.1973), 12:130-132
(8-10.1974), 13:135 (1.1975), 15:170
(12.1976), 16:171-172 (1-2.1977), 17:6-7
(4-5.1977), 15:183-184 (1-2.1978)
[14498.cc.9]
LO:SOAS: 13 (1.1963) -; lacking some
issues   [Per.10.227304]
CA:UL: 1 - 13:135 (1.1975); lacking
106-107   [L.830.c.72]
OX:BOD: 1 -   [Per.Turk.d.1728]
OX:MEC: 1 - 6:66 (4.1968)   [APT Tur 1]

TÜRK KÜLTÜRÜ ARAŞTIRMALARI
Yıl 1, sayı 1 (1964)-
Ankara: Türk Kültürünü Araştırma
Enstitüsü

LO:SOAS: 1:1 (1964) - 22 (1984)
[Per.10.490830]
CA:UL: 1:1 -   [P.617.c.36]
OX:BOD: 1:1 -   [Per.Turk.d.1888]

TÜRK KÜLTÜRÜNDE DAĞARCIK [2. DİZİ]:
sanat ve fikir dergisi
1 (Şubat [19]84) - 3-4-5 (Haziran
[19]84)
İstanbul
Nominally monthly

OX:BOD: 1 (2.1984) - 3/4/5 (6.1984)
[Per.Turk.d.3230]

TÜRK KÜTÜPHANECİLER DERNEĞİ AYLIK
HABER BÜLTENİ
Yıl 1, sayı 1 (Ocak 1953) -
Ankara

BL:OIOC: 5:51 (3.1957) - 7:80 (8.1959)
[O.P.546]

TÜRK KÜTÜPHANECİLER DERNEĞİ
BÜLTENİ = Bulletin de l'Association de
Bibliothécaires Turcs
Cilt 1, sayı 1 [1952] - 35. cilt, 4.
sayı (Sonbahar 1986)
Ankara
Continued by: Türk kütüphaneciliği
Quarterly; 1952-1955, semi-annual; 1956,
3 issues

BL:OIOC: 1:1 [1952] - 35:4 (autumn 1986)
[14498.cc.1]
LO:SOAS: 12:1 (1963) - 35:4
[Per.10.168312]
OX:BOD: 1:1 - 35:4   [Per.Turk.d.722]

TÜRK KÜTÜPHANECİLİĞİ / Türk
Kütüphaneciler Derneği bülteni
1. cilt, 1. sayı (Kış 1987) -
Ankara
Continuation of: Türk Kütüphaneciler
Derneği bülteni
Quarterly

BL:OIOC: 1:1 (winter 1987) -
[ZOR.1988.a.52]
LO:SOAS: 1:1 -   [Per.10.549841]

TÜRK MUSİKİSİ KLASİKLERİ: Türk
mûsikîsi nota dergisi; iki ayda bir
çıkar / Nevzad Atlığ
Fasikül 1 (Mart-Nisan 1987) -
İstanbul: Türk Dünyası Araştırmaları
Vakfı

OX:BOD: 1:1 (3-4.1987) -
[Per.Turk.c.199]

TÜRK SAN'ATI TARİHİ ARAŞTIRMA VE
  İNCELEMELERİ / İstanbul Güzel
  Sanatlar Akademisi Türk San'atı Tarihi
  Enstitüsü
  1 [1963]
  Istanbul
  Articles on Turkish art, architecture
  and cultural history

  BL:OIOC: 1 [1963]   [14448.e.17]

TÜRK ŞARKİYAT DERNEĞİ DERGİSİ
  Cild 1, cüz 1 [1964]
  Istanbul
  Added title in English: Review of the
  Turkish Oriental Society
  In Turkish; with English summaries

  BL:OIOC: 1:1 [1964]   [14498.cc.20]

TÜRK SESİ: hakkın ve hakikatın sesidir,
  aylık müstakil siyasi gazete
  Yıl 1, sayı 1 (Haziran 1959) - Yıl 1,
  sayı 2 (Temmuz 1959)
  London

  BL:OIOC: 1:1 (6.1959) - 1:2 (7.1959)
  [OR.MIC.11990 (microfilm); O.P.914
  (hard copy)]

TÜRK TARİH, ARKEOLOGYA VE ETNOGRAFYA
DERGİSİ
  See: TÜRK ARKEOLOJİ DERGİSİ

TÜRK TARİH, ARKEOLOGYA VE ETNOGRAFYA
  DERGİSİ / Maarif Vekâleti tarafından
  neşrolunur
  Sayı 1 (Temmuz 1933) - Sayı 5 (1949)
  Istanbul
  Nomenclature of issuing body varies
  Irregular

  BL:OIOC: 1 (1933) - 5 (1949)
  [14498.c.12]
  LO:SOAS: 1 (1933) - 4 (1940)
  [Per.10.31564]
  CA:UL: 1 - 5   [T.617.b.1]
  OX:BOD: 1 - 5   [Per.Turk.d.408]

TÜRK TARİH ENCÜMENİ MECMUASI [1.
  SERİ]
  Cild 1, cüz' 1 (1 Nisan 1326 [1910]) -
  [Cild 5], 17-18. sene, numero 19 (96) (1
  Haziran 1928)
  Istanbul
  Issues 1-77 (1910-1924) published by
  Tarih-i Osmanî Encümeni and indexed by
  H.E. Eldem
  Some issues entitled: Tarih-i Osmanî
  Encümeni mecmuası
  In Ottoman
  Bi-monthly

  BL:OIOC: 1:1 (1.4.1910) - 5:96
  (1.6.1928)   [14456.f.9]
  LO:SOAS: 1:1 - 5:96; lacking 13-24
  [Per.10.30448]
  OX:MEC: 1:1 - 5:96   [APT Tar 1]

TÜRK TARİH ENCÜMENİ MECMUASI [2.
  SERİ]
  Cilt 1, sayı 1 (Haziran-Ağustos 1929) -
  Cilt 1, sayı 5 (Haziran 1930 - Mayıs
  1931)
  Ankara
  Continued by: Belleten
  Nominally quarterly

  BL:OIOC: 1:1 (6-8.1929) - 1:5
  (6.1930-5.1931)   [14456.f.9]
  LO:SOAS: 1:1 - 1:5   [Per.10.30448]
  OX:BOD: 1:1 - 1:5   [Per.Turk.d.252;
  also Per.Turk.d.252*]
  OX:MEC: 1:1 - 1:5   [APT Tur 1]

TÜRK TIB TARİHİ ARKİVİ = Archives
  d'histoire de la médecine turque =
  Archiv für Geschichte der türkischen
  Medizin / İstanbul Üniversitesi
  tarafından neşrolunur
  Yıl 1, sayı 1 (Mart 1935) - Cilt 6, sayı
  21-22 (Eylül-Kananuevvel 1943)
  Istanbul
  Journal of medical and cultural history
  Includes articles in French

  BL:OIOC: 1:1 (3.1935) - 6:21/22
  (9-10.1943)   [ITA.1988.a.66]
  LO:SOAS: 1:1 - 4:13 (1939)
  [Per.10.47713]
  CA:UL: 6:21/22   [Moh.756.c.1 item 5]

TÜRK YILI / Türk Ocakları Merkez Heyeti
  tarafından neşrolunmuştur
  [1] (1330 [1914-1915]) - [2] (1928)
  Istanbul

  OX:BOD: [2] (1928)   [Turk.d.980]

TÜRK YURDU
  [1. seri], Yıl 1, sayı 1 (24
  Teşrinisani 1327 [7 Dec. 1911]) - [5.
  seri], Cilt 7, 58. yıl, sayı 1-2
  (Ocak-Şubat 1968)
  Istanbul
  Printed in Arabic letters 1911-1928 ;
  thereafter in roman
  Series 1 and 4 published monthly, series
  2, 3 and 5 fortnightly

  BL:OIOC: 1:1:1 (7.12.1911) - 7:58:1/2
  (1-2.1968); lacking 270 (8.1957)
  [14498.cc.73]
  LO:SOAS: 1:1:1 - 1:14:161; 2:1:1 -
  2:6:33; 3:1:1 - 3:2:11; 5:1:271 -
  5:6:339   [Per.10.139455]
  DU:UL: 209 (3.1929) - 218 (12.1929), 271
  (3.1959)   [Per./PL 1]
  OX:BOD: 49:271 (3.1959) - 50:297
  (6-7.1961)   [Turk.d.726]
  OX:MEC: 1-72; 81-161; 1-33; 234-267;
  lacking a few issues   [APT Tur 3]

TÜRKBİLİK REVÜSÜ = Revue de
  Turcologie / fondée à Paris par le
  Prof. Rıza Nour
  No.1 (Février 1931) - No.8 (1 Février
  1938)
  Alexandria: Société des Publications
  Égyptiennes
  Articles in Ottoman, French, or
  roman-script Turkish

  BL:OIOC: 1 (2.1931) - 7 (2.1937)
  [14498.a.1]
  LO:SOAS: 1 (2.1931) - 8 (1.2.1938)
  [Per 10 26341]
  OX:BOD: 1 - 8 (microfiche); 2 (2.1936)
  (hard copy)   [Or. microfiches 61;
  Per.Turk.d.2025]

TÜRKISCHE MONATSSCHRIFT FÜR
GEISTESWISSENSCHAFTEN
  See: İŞ

TURKISH ATOMIC ENERGY COMMISSION ACTIVITY
REPORT OF THE RADIOACTIVE FALLOUT
LABORATORY
  See: BAŞBAKANLIK ATOM ENERJİSİ
  KOMİSYONU NÜKLEER KİMYA
  LABORATUVARININ RADYOAKTİF YAĞIŞ
  DEĞERLENDİRMELERİ HAKKINDA FAALİYET
  RAPORU

TURKISH BIBLIOGRAPHY OF ARTICLES
  See: TÜRKİYE MAKALELER
  BİBLİYOGRAFYASI

TURKISH FOLK CULTURE RESEARCHES
  See: TÜRK HALK KÜLTÜRÜ
  ARAŞTIRMALARI

THE TURKISH JOURNAL OF COLLECTABLE ART
  See: ANTİKA

THE TURKISH JOURNAL OF POPULATION STUDIES
See: NÜFUSBİLİMİ DERGİSİ

TURKISH NATIONAL BIBLIOGRAPHY
See: TÜRKİYE BİBLİYOGRAFYASI

TURKISH REVIEW OF ECONOMIC AND SOCIAL
SCIENCES
See: İŞ

TURKISH REVIEW OF ETHNOGRAPHY
See: TÜRK ETNOGRAFYA DERGİSİ

THE TURKISH YEARBOOK OF INTERNATIONAL
RELATIONS
See: MİLLETLERARASI MÜNASEBETLER TÜRK
YILLIĞI

TÜRKİSTAN: ilmî içtimaî, iktisadî ve
kültürel aylık dergidir
Sayı 1 (Nisan 1953) - Yıl 1, Cilt 1,
sayı 6 (Eylül 1953)
Istanbul
Chiefly concerned with Central Asia and
émigrés in Turkey

BL:OIOC: 1 (4.1953) - 1:1:6 (9.1953)
[14498.aa.1]
LO:SOAS: 1 - 1:1:6   [Per.10.94650]

TURKISTĀN AL-SHARQĪYAH
See: DOĞU TÜRKİSTAN

TÜRKİYA EDEBİYAT MECMUASI: ayda bir
neşrolunur, ilim ve edebiyata hâdim
musavver mecmua
Sene 1, sayı 1 (1 Eylül 1339 [1923]) -
Sene 2, sayı 1 ([date?], 1341 [1925])
Istanbul
Monthly; first two issues fortnightly

BL:OIOC: 1:1 (1.9.1923) - 1:6 (5.1924)
[OR. FICHE 448]

TÜRKİYAT MECMUASI / İstanbul
Üniversitesi Türkiyat Enstitüsü
tarafından neşredilir
1. cild (Ağustos 1925)-
Istanbul
Vols.1 and 2 published by: İstanbul
Darülfünunu Türkiyat Enstitüsü
Irregular

BL:OIOC: 1 (8.1925) -   [14498.aa.3]
LO:SOAS: 1 -   [Per.10.21168]
CA:UL: 1 -   [P.617.c.21]
OX:BOD: 1 -   [Per.Turk.d.207]

TÜRKİYE BİBLİOĞRAFYASI
See: TÜRKİYE BİBLİYOGRAFYASI

TÜRKİYE BİBLİYOGRAFYASI = Turkish
national bibliography / T.C. Kültür ve
Turizm Bakanlığı, Millî Kütüphane
Müdürlüğü
1928-1933 -
Ankara: Millî Kütüphane
Müdürlüğü, 1933-
Title of issuing body varies
Title up to 1935: Türkiye
bibliyoğrafyası. Parallel titles vary
Monthly. Previously monthly, quarterly
or cumulated

BL:OIOC: 1928/1933 -; lacking 1976:4,
1979:2-4, 1981:11-12, 1982:4-5, 1985:8-
12   [15007.g.1]
LO:SOAS: 1928/1933 -
[Ref.PRA.015.50556]
CA:UL: 1928/1933 -   [P.830.c.130]
SU:IDS: 1965:1 -; lacking some issues
[SERIALS/NON-OFFICIAL/601(72)]

TÜRKİYE BÜYÜK MİLLET MECLİSİ
TUTANAK DERGİSİ
See: T.B.M.M. TUTANAK DERGİSİ

TÜRKİYE CUMHURİYETİ DEVLET SALNAMESİ
[1] (1925-1926) - 5 (1929-1930)
Ankara: Matbuat Müdüriyet-i Umumiyesi,
1926-1930
Official yearbook of the Republic of
Turkey
Supersedes: Salname-i Devlet-i Aliye-i
Osmaniye
Title of nos. 4-5: Türkiye Cumhuriyeti
Devlet yıllığı

BL:OIOC: [1] (1925/1926) - 3 (1927/1928)
[14498.cc.45]
LO:SOAS: [1] - 3   [E.Per.280657/1]
CA:UL: [1], 3   [S.828.01.b.2]
DU:UL: [1] - 4 (1928/1929)   [PL324]
OX:BOD: [1], 3   [Per.Turk.d.236]

TÜRKİYE CUMHURİYETİ DEVLET YILLIĞI
See: TÜRKİYE CUMHURİYETİ DEVLET
SALNAMESİ

TÜRKİYE CUMHURİYETİ MAARİFİ
[1] (1940/1941) - [?]
Ankara: Maarif Vekilliği
Biennial

BL:OIOC: 14482.e.3

TÜRKİYE CUMHURİYETİ RESMİ GAZETE
See: T.C. RESMİ GAZETE

TÜRKİYE DEFTERİ: aylık edebiyat-siyaset
dergisi
Sayı 1 (Nisan 1971) - Sayı 20 (Haziran
1975)
Istanbul

BL:OIOC: 1 (4.1971) - 20 (6.1975)
[14498.cc.65]

TÜRKİYE EDEBİYAT MECMUASI
See: TÜRKİYA EDEBİYAT MECMUASI

TÜRKİYE EKONOMİSİ İSTATİSTİK
RAKAMLARI İLE / İstanbul Ticaret Odası
Istanbul, [ca.1970]-
Also published in English
Annual

BL:HSS: 1972   [S.Q.40/8]
DU:DC: 1972 (plus 1971-1979, 1981 in
English)   [25/4/ECONOMY/GENERAL]

TÜRKİYE ELEKTRİK ENERJİSİ
İSTATİSTİK BÜLTENİ = Statistics of
electric power in Turkey / Elektrik
İşleri Etüt İdaresi Genel
Direktörlüğü
Ankara
Dates of publication not known
In Turkish and English
Annual

DU:DC: 1968   [25/4/ENERGY]

TÜRKİYE ELEKTRİK İSTATİSTİKLERİ
YILLIĞI = Annual bulletin of electrical
statistics of Turkey / Türkiye Elektrik
Kurumu
Ankara, [197-?]-
Turkish and English

SU:IDS: 1979 - 1981/1982
[SERIALS/OFFICIAL/TURKEY]

TÜRKİYE İKTİSAT GAZETESİ / Türkiye
Ticaret Odaları, Sanayi Odaları ve
Ticaret Borsaları Birliği neşir organı
1. yıl, no. 1 (5 Ocak 1953) –
Ankara
A newspaper with the same title was
published at Istanbul from 1921 to 1926
by Türkiye Ticaret Birliği
Weekly

BL:OIOC: 9:422 (20.4.1961)
[OR.MIC.12617 (O.P.552/17)]
DU:DC: 1026 (15.3.1973) – 1154
(11.9.1975); lacking 1029, 1031-1034,
1036-1037, 1039-1040, 1044, 1046-1047,
1051-1056, 1060   [25/4/COMMERCE]

TÜRKİYE İSTATİSTİK CEP YILLIĞI =
Statistical pocket book of Turkey /
Başbakanlık Devlet İstatistik
Enstitüsü
Ankara, [ca. 1937]-
Previous titles: Küçük istatistik
yıllığı, İstatistik cep yıllığı; also
various titles for English-language
version
Currently in Turkish and English;
formerly published in each language
separately
Biennial; previously generally annual

LO:SOAS: 1970 –; lacking 1978
[NS.310.278526]
DU:DC: 1939/1940 – 1941/1942; 1946; 1949
-1951; 1969; 1976; 1978; 1980; 1984 –
(some in English)   [25/1/GENERAL]
SU:IDS: 1978 –
[SERIALS/OFFICIAL/TURKEY]

TÜRKİYE İSTATİSTİK YILLIĞI =
Statistical yearbook of Turkey /
Başbakanlık Devlet İstatik Enstitüsü
1 (1928) –
Ankara
Title of issuing body varies
Former title: İstatistik yıllığı.
French parallel title: Annuaire
statistique
In Turkish and English; formerly in
Turkish and French
Biennial; formerly generally annual

BL:HSS: 1 (1928) – 21 (1953); 1959 –
1960/1962   [S.Q.904.g.]
LO:SOAS: 1952-1953; 1959-1965; 1968;
1971-   [LNS.310.191000]
CA:UL: 1959 –   [O.P.22000.310.01]
DU:DC: 2 (1929); 4 (1930/1931); 6
(1932/1933); 8 (1935/1936) – 9
(1936/1937); 15 (1942/1945) – 16 (1948);
18 (1950) – 19 (1955); 1959 – 1964/1965;
1968; 1973-   [25/1/GENERAL]
OX:BOD: 1959   [Per.Turk.d.596]
SU:IDS: 1968 –
[SERIALS/OFFICIAL/TURKEY]

TÜRKİYE JEOLOJİ KURUMU BÜLTENİ
Cilt 1, sayı 1 (Ekim 1947) – Cilt 24,
sayı 2 (1981)
Ankara
Some translations and, earlier, articles
in English, French or German
Irregular

BL:OIOC: 1:1 (10.1947)   [14448.c.22]

TÜRKİYE KÖMÜR İŞLETMELERİ KURUMU
EREĞLİ KÖMÜRLERİ İŞLETMESİ
MÜESSESESİ İSTATİSTİK YILLIĞI
See: TÜRKİYE TAŞKÖMÜRÜ KURUMU
GENEL MÜDÜRLÜĞÜ İSTATİSTİK
YILLIĞI

TÜRKİYE KÜLTÜR VE SANAT YILLIĞI /
Yazarlar Birliği
[1] (1984) –
Ankara

BL:OIOC: [1] (1984) –   [14480.d.177]
LO:SOAS: [1] – [3] (1986)
[Per.10.490955]
OX:BOD: [1] –   [Per.Turk.d.3277]

TÜRKİYE MAKALELER BİBLİYOGRAFYASI =
Bibliography of articles in Turkish
periodicals / Millî Kütüphane
Müdürlüğü'nce üç ayda bir
yayınlanır
1952, 1-3 (Ocak-Mart) –
Ankara
Earlier added titles: Bibliographie des
articles parus dans les périodiques
turcs ; Turkish bibliography of articles

BL:OIOC: 1984:1 –   [14498.bb.2]
LO:SOAS: 1952:1 –   [PRA.015.91990]
CA:UL: 1952:1 –   [L.850.c.256]
DU:UL: 1952:5 – 1983:1; lacking a few
issues   [Per./PL 40]
OX:BOD: 1984 –   [Per.258691.d.19]
SU:IDS: 1967:1 –; lacking some issues
[SERIALS/NON-OFFICIAL/751(72)]

TÜRKİYE MİLLİ GELİRİ = National
income of Turkey / Devlet İstatistik
Enstitüsü
Ankara, 1957-
Sometimes published in two series:
Toplam harcamaları ve yatırımları;
Kaynak ve yöntemler
Title varies slightly
Annual

DU:DC: 1956 – 1960; 1963; 1965; 1967 –
1970; 1972 – 1973; 1977
[25/4/NATIONAL INCOME AND EXPENDITURE]

TÜRKİYE SORUNLARI DİZİSİ
See: DÜNÜN VE BUGÜNÜN DEFTERLERİ
TÜRKİYE SORUNLARI DİZİSİ

TÜRKİYE TARIMSAL ÜRETİM DEĞERİ =
Agricultural production value of Turkey
/ T.C. Ziraat Bankası
[1957?] –
Ankara
In Turkish and (from 1973) English also
Annual

BL:HSS: 1982 –   [SQ.173/2]
DU:DC: 1963 –
[25/4/AGRICULTURE/GENERAL]
SU:IDS: 1975 –; lacking 1977
[SERIALS/OFFICIAL/TURKEY]

TÜRKİYE TAŞKÖMÜRÜ KURUMU GENEL
MÜDÜRLÜĞÜ İSTATİSTİK YILLIĞI
Zonguldak, [19--?]-
Title of issuing body varies
Previous titles: Ereğli kömür havzası
istatistikleri; Türkiye Kömür
İşletmeleri Kurumu Ereğli Kömürleri
İşletmesi Müessesesi istatistik
yıllığı

DU:DC: 1960-
[25/4/INDUSTRY/EXTRACTIVE/COAL]

TÜRKİYE VE BÜYÜK BRİTANYA
1-inci Tab, no. 1 (Teşrinievel [sic]
1940) – Vol. 28, no. 129 ([date?], 1970)
London: British Industrial Publicity
Overseas Ltd., 1940-1970
English title: Turkey and Britain
Bimonthly?

BL:OIOC: 1:1 (10.1940) – 25:125
(7-9.1965)   [14498.c.1]
CA:UL: 1:1 – 28:129 (?.1970)
[L.617.b.1]

TÜRKİYE YAZILARI
Sayı 1 (Nisan 1977) - Sayı 71 (Şubat
1983)
Ankara
Cultural and literary magazine
Monthly

BL:OIOC: 18 (9.1978)   [ITA.1988.a.529]

TÜRKİYE YILLIĞI / Başbakanlık
Basın-Yayın Genel Müdürlüğü
1944-1945 -
Ankara, 1945-
Official yearbook of the Republic of
Turkey
Supersedes: Türkiye Cumhuriyeti Devlet
Salnamesi. Title of issuing body varies
Early issues entitled: Türkiye
Cumhuriyeti Devlet Yıllığı
Occasional English editions published
under the title: Turkey yearbook
Apparently irregular

BL:OIOC: 1944/1945   [14498.cc.2]
DU:DC: 1944/1945   [25/1/GENERAL]

TÜRKİYE YILLIĞI
1962 - 1965
Istanbul
An unofficial yearbook

BL:OIOC: 1962-1965   [14456.gg.32]

TÜRKİYE ZİRAAT MECMUASI:
ziraat-veteriner-orman / Türkiye Ziraî
Donatım Kurumu
Cilt 1, sayı 1 (Mart 1952) - Cilt 9,
sayı 62 (Ekim 1960)
Ankara
Quarterly; monthly in some years

DU:DC: 46 (12.1958) - 47 (2.1959)
[25/4/AGRICULTURE/GENERAL]

TÜRKİYE'DE İKTİSADİ DURUM
See: TÜRKİYE'DE UMUMİ İKTİSADİ
DURUM

TÜRKİYEDE METEOROLOJİ RASATLARI
See: YILLIK METEOROLOJİ BÜLTENİ

TÜRKİYE'DE UMUMİ İKTİSADİ DURUM /
Türkiye İş Bankası
Ankara, [19--?]-
Title prior to 1963: Türkiye'de
iktisadi durum
Annual

DU:DC: 1962 - 1984
[25/4/ECONOMY/GENERAL]

TÜRKİYEMİZ: 4 aylık sanat dergisi
Sayı 1 (Haziran 1970) -
İstanbul: Akbank
Includes English summaries of all
articles

BL:OIOC: 2 (10.1970) -   [14498.cc.26]
LO:SOAS: 1 (6.1970) - 16:49 (6.1986)
[Per.107.527255]
OX:BOD: 14:42 (1984) -
[Per.Turk.d.3096]

TÜRKLÜK: ayda bir çıkar milliyetçi
kültür mecmuası
1 ([Nisan] 1939) - 3. cild, sayı 14-15
(Kasım 1940)
Istanbul
Not published between 1 Feb. and 31
March 1940

BL:OIOC: (a) 1 (4.1939) - 3:13
(30.4.1940); (b) 1   [(a) 14498.a.120;
(b) 14498.a.8]
LO:SOAS: 1 - 2:7 (10.1939)
[Per.10.136627]
OX:BOD: 1 - 2:12 (1940)
[Per.Turk.d.1034]

TÜRKLÜK ARAŞTIRMALARI DERGİSİ /
Marmara Üniversitesi Fen-Edebiyat
Fakültesi
Sayı 1 (1984) -
Istanbul, 1985-
Irregular

BL:OIOC: 1(1984) -   [ZOR.1989.a.4]

TÜRKLÜK BİLGİSİ ARAŞTIRMALARI =
Journal of Turkish studies
1 (1977) -
Cambridge, Mass.
Mainly in English
Annual

BL:OIOC: 1 (1977) -   [14498.a.74]
LO:SOAS: 1 -   [Per.10.L.377168]

TÜRKMEN MEDENİYETİ / Türkmen Medeniyet
İnstituutı tayından çıkarılyan
ıktısadı içtimakı [sic], sıyası, ılmı
ve edebi aylık çurnal-dır
No.1 ([date?] 1928) - [?]
Ashkhabad
Turkmen; modified roman characters
Nominally monthly; bi-monthly in 1930

BL:OIOC: [3]:4/5 (4-5.1930) - [3]:8/9
(8-9.1930)   [14499.tt.13]
LO:SOAS: [2]:11 (11,1929) - [3]:3
(3.1930)   [L.E.Per.23330]

TÜRKMENİSTAN ILIMLAR AKADEMİYASINIŇ
HABARLARI, GUMANİTAR ILIMLARI =
Izvestiia Akademii Nauk Turkmenistan,
gumaniternye nauki:
nauchno-teoreticheskii zhurnal
1960, no. 1 (Iiun' 1960) -
Aşgabat: Ilım
Former titles: Türkmenistan SSR Ilımlar
Akademiyasının Habarları, cemgietçilik
ılımların seriyası = Izvestiia
Akademii Nauk Turkmenskoi SSR, seriia
obshchestvennykh nauk
Articles in Turkmen or Russian
Bimonthly

BL:OIOC: 1970:1 - ; lacking 1974:5,
1984:2   [14499.tt.34]
BL:HSS: 1960:1 -   [Ac.1161/2]
LO:SOAS: 1967:2 -; lacking 1971:6,
1975:6, 1987:6   [Per.10.199838]

TÜRKMENİSTAN SSR ILIMLAR
AKADEMİYASINIŇ HABARLARI,
CEMGIETÇİLİK ILIMLARIN SERİYASI
See: TÜRKMENİSTAN ILIMLAR
AKADEMİYASINIŇ HABARLARI, GUMANİTAR
ILIMLARI

TÜRKMENİSTANIN HALK MAGARIFI / TSSR
Magarıf ministrliginiň ayda bir gezek
çıkyan ılmı-metodik curnalı
No. 1 ([month?], 1931) -
Ashkhabad
Subtitle varies slightly
In Turkmen

BL:OIOC: 1969:6-   [14499.t.23]

TÜRKOLOJİ DERGİSİ / Ankara
Üniversitesi Dil ve Tarih-Coğrafya
Fakültesi Türk Dili ve Edebiyatı
Araştırmaları Enstitüsü
Cilt 1, sayı 1 (1964) -
Ankara
Irregular

BL:OIOC: 1:1 (1964) - 3:1 (1968)
[14472.hh.82]
LO:SOAS: 1:1 -   [Per.10.211621]
CA:UL: 1:1 -   [L.830.c.63]
DU:UL: 1:1 - 3:1   [Per./PL 4]
OX:BOD: 1:1 - 6:1 (1974)
[Per.Turk.d.1642]

TÜRKÜN
See: ULUDAĞ

ÜÇ AYLIK BÜLTEN = Quarterly bulletin /
T.C. Merkez Bankası
Ankara, [19--?]-
Early issues entitled: Aylık bülten =
Bulletin mensuel
In Turkish and English; earlier issues
in Turkish and French
Quarterly; formerly monthly; many
cumulated issues

BL:HSS: 1981:1 - 1984:4; 1992:1 -
[S.Q.35]
LO:SOAS: (a) 1959:5 1960:4; 1961:1 -
1978.12; (b) 1979:1 (1-3.1979) -
[(a) Per.77.195124; (b) Per.77.L.430101]
DU:DC: 1971:3-9; 1972:1-5, 9-11;
1973:1-4: 1974:1-4, 8; 1977:3-5;
1981:10-12   [25/4/BANKING]
SU:IDS: 1967/10-11 (10-11.1967) -
[SERIALS/NON-OFFICIAL/72]

ÜÇ AYLIK DÖNEMLER İTİBARİYLE
BAŞLICA SANAYİ MADDELERİ ÜRETİMİ =
Production of main industrial products
by quarters / Başbakanlık Devlet
İstatistik Enstitüsü
Ankara, [19--?]-[19--?]
In Turkish and English

DU:DC: 1974:2/1975:2
[25/4/INDUSTRY/MANUFACTURING]

ÜÇ AYLIK DÖNEMLER VE SEKTÖRLER
İTİBARİYLE İMALAT SANAYİİ,
İSTİHDAM VE ÜRETİM = Manufacturing
industry employment and production by
quarters and sectors / Başbakanlık
Devlet İstatistik Enstitüsü
Ankara, [197-?]-[197-?]
In Turkish and English
Nominally quarterly

DU:DC: 1975:3 - 1976:3
[25/4/INDUSTRY/MANUFACTURING]

ÜÇ AYLIK EKONOMİK RAPOR / Ankara Sanayi
Odası
Ankara, [19--?]-

DU:DC: 12.1974 - 6.1977
[25/4/INDUSTRY/GENERAL]

UCHENYE ZAPISKI
See: ELMİ GEYDLĚR

UCHENYE ZAPISKI INSTITUTA
VOSTOKOVEDENIĬĀ
See: ŞĚRGŞÜNASLIG İNSTİTUNUN ELMİ
ĚSĚRLĚRİ

ULAŞTIRMA İSTATİSTİKLERİ
See: ULAŞTIRMA VE TRAFİK KAZALARI
İSTATİSTİKLERİ

ULAŞTIRMA VE TRAFİK KAZALARI
İSTATİSTİKLERİ = Transportation and
road traffic accidents statistics /
Başbakanlık Devlet İstatistik
Enstitüsü
Ankara, [19--?]-
Original title: Ulaştırma
istatistikleri = Transportation
statistics
In Turkish and English
Annual; some issues cumulated

SU:IDS: 1970; 1973/1974; 1981 - 1986;
1989 -   [SERIALS/OFFICIAL/TURKEY]

ÜLKEMİZ: aylık mecmua = Nash kraĭ:
ezhemesĭachynĭ zhurnal: organ
severo-kavkasskoĭ natsional'noĭ
mysli
No. 1 (1-ci Teşrin 1937) - [?] No. 7
(Nisan 1938)
Warsaw
Superseded by: Cagiris.= Prizyv
In Istanbul Turkish and Russian

BL:OIOC: 3 (12.1937) - 6/7 (3-4. 1938)
[ITA.1986.a.390]

ÜLKÜ [1. SERİ]: Halkevleri mecmuası
Cilt 1, sayı 1 (Şubat 1933) - Cild 17,
sayı 102 (Ağustos 1941)
Ankara
Later subtitles: Halkevleri dergisi;
Halkevleri ve Halkodaları dergisi
Monthly

BL:OIOC: 1:1 (2.1933) - 17:102 (8.1941)
[14498.cc.52/1]
LO:SOAS: 1 - 80; 82 - 89
[L.E.Per.96053]
OX:BOD: 1:1 - 17:102   [Turk.d.576]

ÜLKÜ [2. SERİ]: millî kültür dergisi
1. cilt, sayı 1 (1 Ekim 1941) - Cilt 11,
sayı 126 (16 Aralık 1946)
Ankara
Fortnightly

BL:OIOC: 1:1 (1.10.1941) - 11:126
(16.12.1946)   [14498.a.88]
LO:SOAS: 1:1 - 8:89 (1.6.1945); lacking
7:81 (1.2.1945)   [L.E.Per.96053]

ÜLKÜ [3. SERİ]: halkevleri ve
halkodaları mecmuası
Cilt 1, sayı 1 (Ocak 1947) - Cilt 4,
sayı 44 (Ağustos 1950)
Ankara
Monthly

BL:OIOC: 1:1 (1.1947) - 4:44 (8.1950)
[14498.cc.52/3]
OX:BOD: 1:1 - 4:44; lacking no. 27
[Turk.d.727]

ÜLTTAR
No.1 (Favral 1956)-
Beijing: Ülttar baspası
Illustrated magazine for minority
peoples in China
Kazakh; in Arabic characters (roman from
ca. 1974 to 1982). Also published in
Chinese, Korean, Mongolian, Tibetan, and
Uygur
Monthly

BL:OIOC: 1956:1 - ; lacking 1956:7-12;
1958:3 - 1961:4; 1964:4. 8-12; 1967:1;
1974:1; 1976; 7, 9; 1979:11; 1982:1
[15037.a.36/7]

ULUDAĞ / Bursa Halkevi mecmuası
Sayı 1 (2inci Kanun 1935) - Sayı 101/102
(Mayıs/Haziran 1950)
Bursa
Issues 6 and 8 entitled: Türkün
Irregular; generally 4 or 5 per year

OX:BOD: 1 (1.1935) - 62 (11/12.1943);
lacking 3, 7, 9, 11, 15, 28-30, 33
[Per.Turk.d.3536]
OX:MEC: 1 - 59 (5.1943); lacking 12-13,
16, 55   [APT Ulu 1]

ULUG-HEM: Çeçen çogaal al'managı /
Tiva ASSI-nin Çogaalçılar Évileli
1 (1944) - [?]
Kizil
An annual cultural and literary review
In Tuvan; Russian version also
published, 1957-?

BL:OIOC: 18 (1961) - 24 (1966)
[14499.tt.6]

ULUM GAZETESİ: bu mecmuadan maksad,
neşr-i lezzet-i ulum va maarife bezl-i
himmet eylemekdir ... kısm-ı evvel ...
"Kamus ul-ulum ve'l-maarif", kısm-ı
sanide mesail-i müteferrika ve emsal-i
ilmiye mündericdir
Numero 1 [date? 1287 [1868]] - Numero
[?] [187-?]
Paris
Exact dates of publication unknown
Added title in French: Ouloum gazatassy:
journal encyclopédique turc, bi-mensuel
/ par Suavi Effendi
Bi-monthly

BL:OIOC: 21 (1.7.1870) - 24 (15.8.1870)
[14498.cc.92]

ULUM-U İKTİSADİYE VE İCTİMAİYE
MECMUASI
Cild 1, sayı 1 (Nisan 1325 [1909]) -
Cild 3, 2. sene, nu. 27 (1 Mart 1327 [14
Mar. 1911])
Istanbul
Nominally monthly beginning with Cild 2

BL:OIOC: 1:1 (4.1909) - 3:2:24 (3.1911)
[14498.cc.67]
CA:UL: 1:1 - 2:2:[17] (?.1909)
[Q.830.c.6]
DU:UL: 1:1 - 3:12 (12.1909)   [Per./PL8]
OX:BOD: 1:1 - 3:2:26 (?.1911)
[Per.Turk.d.984]
OX:MEC: 1:1 (4.1909) - 1:4 (7.1909)
[APT Ulu 2]

ULUS
Sayı 1 (14 Eylül 1335 [1919]) -
Ankara
Published from 14.9.1919 at Sivas as
İrade-i milliye; from 10.1.1920 at
Ankara as Hâkimiyet-i milliye; and
since 1934 at Ankara as Ulus
Daily newspaper

BL:OIOC: 17.4.1940 - 13.8.1945; 1.3.1946
- 31.5.1946; 1.7.1946 - 31.7.1946
[O.P.638]
LO:SOAS: 16:4904 (25.3.1935) - 16:4944
(4.5.1935); 16:4949 (9.5.1935)
[L.E.Per.33762]

ULUSAL KÜLTÜR: üç ayda bir yayınlanır
kültür dergisi / Kültür Bakanlığı
Yıl 1, sayı 1 (Temmuz 1978) - Yıl 2,
sayı 6 (Ekim 1979)
Ankara

BL:OIOC: 1:1 (7.1978) - 2:6 (10.1979)
[14498.cc.42]
CA:UL: 1:1 - 2:6   [P.617.c.61]
DU:UL: 1:2 (10.1978) - 2:6   [Per./PL 1]
OX:BOD: 1:1 - 2:6   [Per.Turk.d.2676]

UMRAN: onbeş günde bir defa Cumartesi
günleri çıkar ve edebiyat, fünun,
teracim-i ahval, seyahât, roman ve
lataifden bahis Osmanlı risale-i
mevkutesi
1. sene, aded 1 (21 Eylül 1304 [4 Oct.
1888]) - 2. sene, numero 29 (26
Teşrinievvel 1304 [8 Nov. 1888])
Istanbul
Subtitle varies

BL:OIOC: 1:1 (4.10.1888) - 2:29
(8.11.1888)   [14498.a.109]

ÜN / Isparta Halkevi mecmuası
Cilt 1, sayı 1 (Haziran 1934) - Cilt 13,
sayı 171-172 (Temmuz-Aralık 1949)
Isparta
Nominally monthly

BL:OIOC: 1:1 (6.1934) - 4:46 (1.1938)
[14498.cc.37]
OX:BOD: 1:1 - 12:135-136 (6-7.1945)
[Per.Turk.d.3539]

UNESCO HABERLERİ, SERİ 3: aylık dergi /
UNESCO Türkiye Millî Komisyonu
Sayı 1 ([Mayıs?] 1958) - [?]
Ankara
Cultural journal mainly concerned with
UNESCO projects involving Turkey

BL:HSS: 30 (11.1960) - 42 (11.1962)
[S.Q.177/3]

ÜNİVERSİTE YAYINLARI: Türkiye
üniversitelerinde yayımlanan
makale-kitap konusal kaynakçası
1989/1 -
Istanbul: Türk Kütüphaneciler
Derneği İstanbul Şubesi
Four-monthly

BL:OIOC: 1989:1 -   [ZOR.1989.a.92]

URBAN PLACES HOUSEHOLD LABOUR FORCE SURVEY
STATISTICS
See: KENTSEL YERLER HANEHALKI İŞGÜCÜ
ANKET SONUÇLARI

URFA İL YILLIĞI
[1] (1967) - [2] (1973)
Sivas

BL:OIOC: [1] (1967)   [14498.a.36]
OX:BOD: [1]   [Turk.d.3324/63]

UŞAK İL YILLIĞI
[1] (1967) - [2] (1973)
Istanbul; Izmir, 1968-1973

BL:OIOC: [1] (1967)   [14498.a.29]
OX:BOD: [1]   [Turk.d.3324/64]

ÜZBEK TİLİ VA ADABİYOTİ / Üzbekiston
SSR Fanlar Akademiyasi, A.S. Puşkin
nomidagi Til va Adabiyot İnstituti
1958, no.1 -
Tashkent: Fan
Original title, 1958-1962: Üzbek tili
va adabiyoti masalalari
In Uzbek
Bi-monthly

BL:OIOC: 1958:1 -; lacking 1958:5-6,
1959:4-6, 1961:2, 1964:6, 1971:4,
1974:5, 1975:6, 1977:1, 1978:1-6,
1979:1, 1983:1-6, 1984:1-2
[14499.p.52]
LO:SOAS: 1964:6, 1978:5, 1981:1 -
[Per.10.189708]
OX:BOD: 1960:1 -; lacking 1961:2,
1974:5, 1975:6   [Per.Turk.d.375]

ÜZBEK TİLİ VA ADABİYOTİ MASALALARİ
See: ÜZBEK TİLİ VA ADABİYOTİ

UZBEKISTAN
See: NAFOSAT

UZBEKISTAN
See: ÜZBEKİSTON

ÜZBEKİSTON
See: NAFOSAT

ÜZBEKİSTON: oyda bir marta çıkadıgan
ictimoiy-siyosiy, adabiy-badiy suratli
curnal
1942, no. 1 -
Tashkent: Üzbekiston KP Markaziy
Komitetining birlaşgan naşriyoti
Russian title: Uzbekistan
In Uzbek

BL:OIOC: 1961:1 (229) - 1969:12 (336);
lacking 1965:7, 1966:9, 1967:5, 10, 12
[14499.tt.2]

ÜZBEKİSTON ADABİYOTİ VA SAN'ATİ /
Üzbekiston SSR Yozuvçilar Soyuzi va
Üzbekiston SSR Madaniyat
Ministrligining organı
No. 1 (4 Yanvar 1956) -
Tashkent
Previous title: Üzbekiston madaniyati
In Uzbek
Twice weekly

BL:OIOC: 1979:10 (2.2.1979) -; lacking
1979:56, 67, 77; 1980:25-27, 29;
1981:11, n.n.8, 24; 1982:22; 1984:49
[O.P.1028]

ÜZBEKİSTON-CONTACT: suvratli oynoma
1984 yil, san 1 (Yanvar) -
Tashkent
ISSN 0202-6333
General-interest magazine
Title before July 1991: Sovet
Üzbekistoni
In Uzbek

BL:OIOC: 1988:1 -   [ZOR.1988.a.80]

ÜZBEKİSTON MADANİYATİ
See: ÜZBEKİSTON ADABİYOTİ VA
SAN'ATİ

ÜZBEKİSTON MATBUOTİ / Üzbekiston SSR
Ministrlar Soveti matbuot davlat
komiteti va Üzbekiston curnalistlar
soyuzining oylik curnali
1 ([Mart 1960?]) - [?]
Tashkent
Uzbek; also published in Russian

BL:OIOC: 9 [91] (9.1967)   [14499.tt.14]

ÜZBEKİSTON SSR FANLAR AKADEMİYASİNİNG
AHBOROTİ, İCTİMOİY FANLAR =
Izvestiia Akademii Nauk Uzbekskoǐ
SSR, seriia obshchestvennykh nauk
Tashkent, [19--?]-
Title unchanged as of early 1993
Articles in Russian or Uzbek
Bimonthly

BL:HSS: 1957:2, 1957:4; 1958:1 - 1960:6
[Ac.1162.b.5/3]

ÜZBEKİSTONDA İCTİMOİY FANLAR =
Obshchestvennye nauki v Uzbekistane /
Üzbekiston SSR Fanlar Akademiyasi
1957, 1 (May 1957) -
Tashkent: Fan
ISSN 0202-151X
Mainly in Russian; some Uzbek
Monthly

BL:HSS: 1957:1 - 1982:12; lacking
1966:12   [Ac.1162.b/12]
LO:SOAS: 11:1 (1.1967) -
[Per.10.203294]
OX:BOD: 1961:1 (1.1961) -
[Per.24725.d.586]

V SOKROVISHCHNİTŠE RUKOPISEǏ
See: ÉLYAZMALAR HĒZİNĒSİNDĒ

VAKIFLAR DERGİSİ / sahibi, Vakıflar
Genel Müdürlüğü
1 [1938] -
Ankara
Studies on historical monuments and
vakıflar
Occasional

BL:OIOC: 1 [1938] -   [14498.c.4]
LO:SOAS: 1 -   [Per.10.L.36883]
CA:UL: 1 -   [T.830.b.1]
OX:BOD: 1 -   [Per.Turk.d.846]
OX:MEC: 7 (1968) - 8 (1969)   [APT Vak]

VAKİT: siyasi, ilmî ve iktisadî gazete
Sene 1, numero 1 (21 Kanunuevvel 1334
[1917]) - [?] ([date?] 1967)
Istanbul
Other titles used during 1919: Muvakkat,
Mütevakkit. Title from 22.11.1934 to
1.1.1939: Kurun

BL:OIOC: 1:116 (14.2.1918) - 1:296
(16.8.1918); 328 (22.9.1918) - 337
(1.10.1918); lacking 33 issues
[OR.MIC.11703 (O.P.252)]

VAN İL YILLIĞI
[1] (1967) - [2] (1973)
Ankara, 1968-1973

OX:BOD: [1] (1967)   [Turk.d.3324/65]

VARLIK: aylık edebiyat ve sanat dergisi
Sayı 1 (15 Temmuz 1933) -
Istanbul
Subtitle prior to 48:884 (5.1981): her
ayın başında çıkar, sanat ve fikir
dergisi
Monthly; initially fortnightly

BL:OIOC: 41:796 (1.1.1974)-
[14498.a.67]
OX:BOD: 39:748-   [Per.Turk.c.97]
OX:MEC: 1 (15.7.1933) - 39:772 (1.1972);
a few issues lacking   [APT Var]

VĀRLĪK: āylıḵ Türkçĕ vĕ Fārscā
fĕrhĕngi nĕşriyyĕ = Vārlıq:
majallah-i māhanah-i farhangī-'i
Fārsī va Turkī-'i Āzarī
Birinci şāyı (Urdibihişt 1358
[Apr.-May 1979]) -
Tehran
Azeri (Arabic characters) and Persian

LO:SOAS: 1 (4-5.1979) -
[Per.10.591404]

VARLIK YILLIĞI
1 (1960) -
Istanbul
A literary yearbook

BL:OIOC: 1 (1960) - ; lacking 2 (1961),
3 (1962), 5 (1964), 20 (1979)
[14472.a.38]
LO:SOAS: 2 (1961) -   [Per.10.96464]
DU:UL: 14 (1973) - 16 (1975), 21 (1980),
23 (1982), 25 (1984), 26 (1985)
[Per./PL1]

VĀRLĪQ
See: VĀRLĪK

VATAN: Londrada, onbeş günde bir çıkar
bağımsız gazete
Yıl 1, sayı 1 (30 Ağustos 1968) - [?]
Ankara
Newspaper for Turkish Cypriots in
Britain
Title of first issue: Yeni Vatan.
Subtitle varies
Fortnightly until Yıl 2, sayı 39 (13
Feb. 1970); weekly thereafter

BL:OIOC: 1:1 (30.8.1968) - 2:66
(28.8.1970)   [OR.MIC.12824 (O.P.1163)]

VATAN
Yıl 1, sayı 1 (19 Ağustos 1940) -
Istanbul
National daily newspaper

BL:OIOC: 1,12,18,28,31.5.1960; 1-4,
14-30.6.1960; 1-30.7.1960; 15-28,
30-31.10.1960; 1-15,22,24-25.11.1960; 1,
5-8,10,13.12.1960; 21.4.1961;
27-28.7.1961; 8,28.8.1961
[OR.MIC.12602 (O.P.552/2)]

VATAN YILLIĞI
[1] (1960)
Istanbul: Vatan gazetesi

BL:OIOC: [1] (1960)   [14498.cc.8]
OX:BOD: [1]   [Per.Turk.e.7282]

VEHICLES AND VESSELS, COASTWISE AND
INTERNATIONAL SEA TRAFFIC AND SHIPPING
See: KARA VE DENİZ TAŞITLARI, KABOTAJ
VE MİLLETLERARASI DENİZ TRAFİĞİ VE
NAKLİYATI

VERGİ VE ARAZİ MECMUASI: ayda bir defa
neşr olunur
1. sene, nusha 1 (31 Mart 1301 [13 Apr.
1885]) - 2. sene, nusha 23 (31
Kanunusani 1302 [13 Feb. 1887])
Istanbul

BL:OIOC: 1:1 (13.4.1885) - 2:23
(13.2.1887)   [ITA.1987.a.530]

LA VÉRITÉ
See: HAKİKAT

VESTNIK AKADEMII NAUK KAZAKHSKOĬ SSR
See: ҚАЗАҚ SSR ĞILIM AKADEMİYASINIÑ
ḤABARŞISI

VİLAYET MERKEZLERİNDEKİ ÖLÜMLER
See: ÖLÜM İSTATİSTİKLERİ (İL VE
İLÇE MERKEZLERİNDE)

VİLÂYET VE KAZA MERKEZLERİNDEKİ
ÖLÜMLER
See: ÖLÜM İSTATİSTİKLERİ (İL VE
İLÇE MERKEZLERİNDE)

VOICE OF EASTERN TURKISTAN
See: DOĞU TÜRKİSTAN'IN SESİ

VYSOTA
See: PĚRVAZ

WHOLESALE AND CONSUMER PRICE INDEXES
MONTHLY BULLETIN
See: TOPTAN EŞYA VE TÜKETİCİ
FİYATLARI AYLIK İNDEKS BÜLTENİ

WHOLESALE PRICE STATISTICS
See: TOPTAN FİYAT İSTATİSTİKLERİ

YACH TURKESTAN
See: YAŞ TURKİSTAN

YADİGÂR: tarih ve fünun-u riyaziye ve
sanayi ve tehzib-i ahlâk'a medâr olan
hikayeden bahseder risaledir
Sayı 1 (Teşrinievvel 1295 [Oct.-Nov.
1879]) - Sayı 8 (15 Teşrinisani 1296
[28 Nov. 1880])
Istanbul
Irregular

OX:BOD: 1 (10.1879) - 8 (28.11.1880)
[Turk.d.2050]

YAĞLAMA / Madeniyağ Şube Müdürlüğü
tarafından hazırlanmıştır
Cilt 1, sayı 1 (Eylül 1965) - [?]
Ankara: Petrol Ofisi Genel
Müdürlüğü
Monthly

BL:HSS: 2:1 (9.1966) - 4:7 (11.1970)
[S.Q.158/2]

YAHYA KEMAL ENSTİTÜSÜ MECMUASI
1 [1959] -
Istanbul

BL:OIOC: 1 [1959] - 3 [1988]
[14456.f.80]

YAKIN TARİHİMİZ: haftada bir çıkar
tarih dergisi
Sayı 1 (1 Mart 1962) - Cilt 4, sayı 52
(21 Şubat 1963)
Istanbul
Journal on the history of Turkey since
the First Constitution

BL:OIOC: 1 (1.3.1962) - 4:52 (21.2.1963)
[14456.k.30]

YAÑA MİLLİ YUL: İdel-Ural istiklal
fikri taratuçi aylık mecmua
Yıl 1, san 1 (23 Dekabr 1928nçi yıl) -
Yıl 11, san 7 (135) (İyul 1939)
Berlin
Title in years 1-2: Millî yul. Subtitle
varies
Tatar; Arabic characters
Fortnightly before year 4; then monthly

BL:OIOC: 1:1 (23.12.1928) - 11:7 (135)
(6.1939); lacking 1:2   [14498.c.6]
LO:SOAS: 1:1 - 11:7 (135)
[L.E.Per.21840]

YANGİ YUL: ayda bir katla çıkadırgan
hatun-kızlar curnalidir / Özbekistan
K.P.(B) Markaz Kavmî Hatunlar
Bölimining nâşir-i afkâri
1nçi il, san 1 (Yanvar 1926) - [?]
Tashkent
Uzbek; Arabic characters

BL:OIOC: 1:11/12 (11-12.1926) - 2:7
(7.1927); 3:9 (9.1927)   [14499.tt.16]

YAÑİ ÇOLPAN: her ayın on beşinde bir
defa çıkar, şiyasî, iktisadî,
ictimaî, ilmî, edebî curnal /
muharrirler, Edibler, Mürebbiler ve
Muharrirler Hey'eti
Sayı 1 (Mart 1923) - [?]
Simferopol'
Subtitle varies
Tatar; Arabic characters
Irregular: nominally monthly in 1923,
fortnightly in 1924

BL:OIOC: 1 (3.1923) - 3 (8.1923); 7
(15.4.1924) - 8 (1.9.1924)
[14499.tt.24]

YANI YAPON MOFUBIRI
See: YAÑİ YAPON MUHBİRİ

YAÑİ YAPON MUHBİRİ: ilmî, edebî,
ticarî, sanaî, iktisadî, ictimaî, ve
terbiyevî aylık mecuadır
Aded 1 [Yan. 1933?] - [?]
Tokyo
Magazine for Tatar émigrés in Japan
and the Far East
Added titles: al-Mukhbir al-Yabānī
(Arabic) ; Yani Yapon mofubiri
(Japanese)
Tatar; Arabic characters

BL:OIOC: 14499.t.40

YANYA VİLÂYETİ ŞALNAMESİ
See: SALNAMESİ VİLÂYET-İ YANYA

YAPI: onbeş günlük mimari, güzel
sanatlar, fikir ve kültür dergisi
Yıl 1, sayı 1 (15 İkinci Teşrin 1941)
- Yıl 2, sayı 48-49 (1-15 İkinci
Teşrin 1945)
Istanbul

BL:OIOC: 1:1 (15.11.1941) - 2:48/49
(1-15.11.1943) [ITA.1989.a.240]
LO:SOAS: 2:25 (15.11.1942) - 2:28
(1.1.1943) [L.E.Per.45926]

YAPIT: toplumsal araştırmalar dergisi
Sayı 1 (Ekim 1983) -
Ankara
Series 1 published monthly, 10.1976 to
3.1980
Quarterly

OX:BOD: 1 (10.1983) -
[Per.Turk.d.3310]

YARATIŞ: san'at, fikir, edebiyat
Cilt 1, yıl 1, sayı 1 ([date?] 1955) -
[?]
Lefkoşa
Review devoted to contemporary Turkish
literature and culture
Publication history and frequency
unknown

BL:OIOC: 1:1:2 [14469.d.55]

YARIN: haftalık ilmî, edebî, ictimaî
resimli mecmua
Numero 1 (13 Teşrinievvel 1337 [1921])
- 45. sayı (15 Teşrinievvel 1338
[1922])
Istanbul
Most issues lack subtitle

BL:OIOC: 1 (13.10.1921) - 45
(15.10.1922) [14498.a.102]
CA:UL: 1 - 2:25 (?.1922) [T.830.a.11]

YAŞ TÜRKİSTAN: Türkistannıñ millî
kurtuluşi uçun kuraşuvçi aylik
mecmua
San 1 (Dekabr 1929) - San 115 (İyun
1939)
Nogent s. Marne: Mustafa Çokayoğlu
Subtitle varies. French added title:
Yach Turkestan (le jeune Turkestan)
Uzbek; Arabic characters

BL:OIOC: 26 (1.1932) - 115 (6.1939)
[14498.b.2]
LO:SOAS: 1 (12.1929) - 115
[Per.57.28885]
CA:UL: 1 - 25 (?.1931) [Q.830.c.24]

YAŞLIR BİLİMİ: yaşlır uçun ilmî,
fennî, edebî mecmue
1 ([date?], [1948?]) - [?]
Urumchi; Lanzhou; Nankin
General-interest educational magazine
for children
Uygur; in Arabic characters
Frequency unknown; first issue undated

BL:OIOC: 1 (?.?.1948?)
[ITA.1986.a.1624/6]

YAZI: üç aylık kültür dergisi
Sayı 1 (Kış 1975) - 1980/8 (1980)
Ankara, 1975-1980
Second issue, dated 1978, also numbered
1, numeration incoherent
Irregular; nominally quarterly

BL:OIOC: 1975:1; 1978:1-3; 1979:4-5;
1980:6-8 [14498.cc.77]

YAZKO EDEBİYAT
Cilt 1, sayı 1 (Kasım 1980) - 60/61
(Ocak-Şubat 1986)
Istanbul: Yazarlar ve Çevirmenler Yayın
Üretim Kooperatifi
Monthly

OX:BOD: 1:1 (11.1980) - 60/61 (1-2.1986)
[Per.Turk.d.2917]

YEDİGÜN: Çarşamba günleri çıkar,
herşeyden bahseder haftalık halk ve
aile mecmuası
Sene 1, no. 1 (15 Mart 1933) - Sene 6,
Cilt 11, no. 267 (19 Nisan 1938)
Istanbul

LO:SOAS: 1937 special issue (George VI
coronation) [L.E.Per.33241]

YELKEN: aylık sanat ve edebiyat dergisi
Yıl 1, sayı 1 (Şubat 1957) - Sayı 240
(Mayıs 1977)
Istanbul
Later subtitles: aylık düşün ve sanat
dergisi; öncü sanat dergisi

BL:OIOC: 1:1 (1.1957); 2:13 (2.1958) -
185 (7.1972); lacking 171
[14498.cc.22]

YEMEN SALNAMESİ
Defa 1 (1298 [1880-1881]) - Defa 9 (1313
[1895-1896])
San'a: Yemen Vilâyeti
Some issues entitled: Yemen Vilâyeti
için ... salnamedir

LO:SOAS: 3 (1886) [E.Per.280670]
OX:BOD: 3 [Turk.e.1485]

YEMEN VİLÂYETİ İÇİN SALNAME
See: YEMEN SALNAMESİ

YENGİ YOL
See: YANGİ YUL

YENİ AKIS; aylık fikir dergisi
Yıl 1, sayı 1 (Ağustos 1966) - Yıl 1,
sayı 4 (Kasım 1966)
Ankara

BL:OIOC: 1:1 (8.1966) - 1:4 (11.1966)
[ITA.1993.a.341]

YENİ ASIR
Izmir
Dates of publication not known; place of
publication deduced
Daily newspaper

BL:OIOC: 28.4.1960, 29.5.1960, 31.5.1960
[OR.MIC.12612 (O.P.552/12)]

YENİ BAŞTAN
See: BAŞDAN

YENİ BİLGİ
See: BİLGİ

YENİ BOYUT: plastik sanatlar dergisi
Sayı 1 (Nisan 1982) - Sayı 31 (Nisan
1985)
Ankara
Initially monthly

OX:BOD: 1 (4.1982) - 31 (4.1985)
[Per.Turk.c.189]

YENİ DERGİ: aylık sanat dergisi
Yıl 1, sayı 1 (Ekim 1964) - Yıl 11, sayı
128 (Mayıs 1975)
Istanbul: De Yayınevi

DU:UL: 1:1 [Per./PL3]
OX:BOD: 1:1 - 11:128; lacking 11:126 -
11:127 [Per.Turk.d.1724]
CA:OS: 1:3 (12.1964) - 2:15 (12.1965)
[enquire for callmark]

YENİ EDEBİYAT: aylık edebiyat dergisi
Sayı 1 (Kasım 1969) - cilt 2, sayı 12
(Ekim 1971)
Istanbul

OX:BOD: 1 (11.1969) - 2:12 (10.1971)
[Per.Turk.d.1730]

YENİ FİKİR: millî terbiye'ye çalışır
ve mekteblerde çiftçilik gayesi güder
aylık mecmuadır
1. sene, sayı 1 (15 Kanunuevvel 1327 [28
Oct. 1911]) - Cild 3, sayı 22 (15
Haziran 1330 [28 June 1914])
Istanbul
Issues 1-4 were published from Manastır
Subtitle varies considerably

BL:OIOC: 1:1 (28.10.1911) - 3:22
(28.6.1914)   [14480.d.235]

YENİ FORUM: onbeş günlük tarafsız
siyaset-iktisat-kültür dergisi
Cilt 1, sayı 1 (15 Eylül 1979) -
Ankara

OX:BOD: 1:1 (15.9.1979) -
[Per.Turk.b.16]

YENİ GAZETE: günlük siyasî ve
iktisadî müstakil gazete
Istanbul
Daily newspaper

CA:OS: 5:1633 (1.7.1969) - 6:1814
(31.12.1969)   [enquire for location]

YENİ İRŞAD: gündelik çıkan siyasî,
edebî, iktisadî, fennî, Türk
dilinde musalman gazetesidir
1. sene, numero 1 (19 Ramazan 1329 [31
Oct. 1911]) - [?]
Baku
Added title: Eni Irshad'
Azeri; Arabic characters

LO:SOAS: 1:10 (9.9.1911) - 1:20
(23.9.1911)   [L.E.Per.33817]

YENİ İSTANBUL: siyasi, iktisadi,
müstakil gazete
Yıl 1, sayı 1 ([date?] 1949) - [?]
Istanbul
Daily

BL:OIOC: 31.5.1960, 29.12.1960; 12, 15,
31.12.1961; 3, 4.1.1962
[OR.MIC.12613 (O.P.552/13)]

YENİ KALEM: perşembe günleri
neşrolunur edebî, ictimaî mizah
mecmuası
Numero 1 (6 Teşrinievvel 1927) - 1.
sene, numero 25 (5 Nisan [1]928)
Istanbul

BL:OIOC: 1 (6.10.1927) - 1:25 (5.4.1928)
[OR.FICHE 449]

YENİ KÜLTÜR: ailede çocuk, mektepte
çocuk
Sayı 1 ([date?], 1936) - Yıl 10, sayı 92
([date?], 1945)
Istanbul
Journal on education
Monthly; some issues not dated

LO:SOAS: 73 (3.1943); 77 (9.1943) - 81
(1.1944); 10:91 (1945) - 10:92 (1945)
[Per.10.47880]

YENİ MECMUA: ilim, sanat ve ahlâk'a dair
haftalık mecmua
1. sene, 1. cild, sayı 1 (12 Temmuz
1917) - 4. cild, sayı 90 (20 Kanunusani
1923)
Istanbul
Not published between 1919 and 1922; new
series begins with Vol.4, no.67

BL:OIOC: 1:1 (12.7.1917) - 4:90
(20.1.1923) (microfiche and hard copy)
[OR. MICROFICHE 19 (microfiche);
14456.ggg.3 (hard copy)]
LO:SOAS: 1:1 - 4:90   [L.E.Per.136640]
CA:UL: 1:1 - 3:66 (26.10.1918)
[T.830.b.11]
OX:BOD: 1:1 - 3:66   [Per.Turk.c.71]
OX:MEC: 1:1 - 4:90   [APT Yen]

YENİ MEKTEB / Azerbaycan Helk
Mearif Komisarlığı ilmi-metodik
şurasının aylık pedagoji mecmuasıdır
1. yıl, sayı 1 (Nisan 1924) - [?]
Baku
Azeri; Arabic characters

BL:OIOC: 1:1 (4.1924) - 1:2 (5.1924)
[ITA.1986.a.392]

YENİ MUSİKİ MECMUASI
See: MUSİKİ MECMUASI

YENİ SABAH: günlük tarafsız siyasi
gazete
1. yıl, sayı 1 ([Date?] 1938) -
Istanbul

BL:OIOC: 27.5.1960 - 28.5.1960;
30.5.1960 - 31.5.1960; 16.12.1960
[OR.MIC.12607 (O.P.552/7)]

YENİ SANAT: aylık sanat-edebiyat dergisi
Yıl 1, sayı 1 (Aralık 1973) - Yıl 2,
sayı 10 (Mayıs 1975)
Istanbul
Nominally monthly

OX:BOD: 1:1 (12.1973) - 2:10 (5.1975)
[Per.Turk.d.3316]

YENİ ŞİİRLER
[1] (1949) - [10] (1959)
Istanbul: Varlık, 1949-1958
Yearbook of new Turkish poetry.
Continued from 1960 by: Varlık yıllığı

LO:SOAS: [1] (1949) - [10] (1959);
lacking [9] (1958)   [Per.10.96464]

YENİ TARİH DERGİSİ: her ayın başında
çıkar
1 (Ocak 1957) - 45 (Eylül 1960)
Istanbul

BL:OIOC: 1 (1.1957) - 36 (12.1959)
[14498.c.15]
OX:MEC: 1 (1.1957) - 45 (9.1960)
[APT Yen 2]

YENİ TARİH DÜNYASI
Yıl 1, sayı 1 (Eylül 1953) - Yıl 2,
sayı 22 (1 Ağustos 1954)
Istanbul
Continuation of: Tarih dünyası
Generally fortnightly

LO:SOAS: 1:1 - 2:22 + 3 supplements
[Per.10.296640]
OX:MEC: 1:1 (9.1953) - 2:22 (1.8.1954)
[APT Tar 6]

YENİ TASVİR-İ EFKÂR
See: TEVHİD-İ EFKÂR

YENI TURKESTAN
See: YENİ TÜRKİSTAN

YENİ TÜRKİSTAN: Türkistan millî
istiklâl fikrine çalışan aylık mecmua
Sayı 1 (5 Haziran 1927) - Sayı 39
(Eylül 1931)
İstanbul
Subtitle varies

  LO:SOAS: 1:1 (5.6.1927) - 1:10/12
  (5-7.1928); 3:15 (27) (2.1930); 3:17
  (29) (10.1930); 4:30 (12.1930) - 5:34
  (4.1931)   [Per.10.136639]
  DU:UL: 3:17 (11.1930) ; 5:32 (2.1931) -
  5:39 (9.1931)   [Per./PL 2746.6]

YENİ VATAN
  See: VATAN

YENİ YAYINLAR: aylık bibliyografya
dergisi
Cilt 1, sayı 1 (Ocak 1956) - Cilt 23,
sayı 12 (Aralık 1978)
Ankara

  LO:SOAS: 1:1 (1.1956) - 23:12 (12.1978);
  slightly incomplete   [Per.10.249875]
  OX:BOD: 6:12 (12.1961) - 17:7 (7.1972)
    [Per.Turk.d.1675]

YENİLİK: aylık fikir ve sanat mecmuası
Sayı 1 (15 Aralık 1952-15 Ocak 1952
[i.e. 1953]) - Cilt 12, sayı 61-62
(Kasım-Aralık 1957)
İstanbul

  BL:OIOC: 1 (15.12.1952-15.1.1953) -
  12:61/62 (11-12.1957)   [14480.d.182]

YER YÜZİ
  See: YİR YÜZİ

YĚŞ KÖSTĚR
  1 [1952?] -
  Ufa
  Literary annual containing poems,
  stories, playlets and essays
  In Bashkir

  BL:OIOC: 11 (1962), 13 (1964)
  [ITA.1987.a.120]

YEŞİL ADA: ayda bir çıkar terbiyevî,
edebî ve biraz da mıskalcı Tatarca bir
curnaldır
Sayı 1 (15 April 1920) - [?]
Simferopol'
Added title in Cyrillic characters:
Eshil' ada
Tatar; Arabic characters
Irregular; nominally monthly

  BL:OIOC: 1 (15.4.1920) - 4 (10.1920)
    [14499.tt.25]

YILDIS / Altaydıñ biçiktör çıgarar
izdatel'stvozınıñ Tuulu Altaydagı
bölügi
1 [1963?] - [?]
Gorno-Altaisk
Literary journal
In Altai
Annual?

  BL:OIOC: 4 (1966)   [14499.t.19]

YILDIZ: bu gazete umum-u Osmanlıların
hukuk-u magsuba ve zayia'larını taharrî
ve taleb eyler ve delalet ve
irşâdâtta bulunacak namuslu
Osmanlıların tercümanıdır
1. sene, numero 1 (1 Şubat-ı efrencî
1898) - 1. sene, numero 6 (15 Haziran-ı
efrencî 1898)
Cairo
Added title: The Yıldız
Ottoman; with one page per issue in
English
Monthly; semi-monthly for 3 issues only

  BL:OIOC: 1:1 (1.2.1898) - 1:6
  (15.6.1898)   [14498.d.11 (2)]

YILDIZ: ěki aylık' içtimaiy-siyasiy ve
ědebiy-bediy curnal / Oz'bekstan SSR
Yazıdcıları Birliginin' organı
1980, no. 1 ([month?]) -
[Tashkent]: G'afur G'ulam adına
ědebiyat ve san'at neşriyatı
ISSN 0207-642X
In Crimean Tatar

  BL:OIOC: 1985:1 -   [14499.t.38]

YILLIK / A.Ü. Siyasal Bilgiler Fakültesi
Basın ve Yayın Yüksek Okulu
[1] (1977-1978) -
Ankara, 1979-

  BL:OIOC: 1 (1977-1978)   [14479.b.58]

YILLIK / Türk Dil Kurumu
[1] (1943) - [?]
Ankara

  BL:OIOC: (a) [1] (1943) - [3]
  (1945/1946); (b) [2] (1944) - [3]
  [(a) 14498.bb.6; (b) 14498.cc.7]
  CA:UL: [1]   [L.830.c.42]
  DU:UL: [1] - [3]   [Per./PL2]

YILLIK / T[ürkiye] B[üyük] M[illet]
M[eclisi]
1 ([1928?]) - [?]
Ankara

  BL:OIOC: 2 (1929); 4 (1931)
  [14429.e.1]

YILLIK / İslâmî İlimler Araştırma
Vakfı
1 (1978) -
İstanbul
Mainly concerned with Islamic law

  BL:OIOC: 1 (1978)   [14415.d.132]

YILLIK / Türk Edebiyatçılar Birliği
[1] (1962) -
İstanbul

  BL:OIOC: [3] (1964)   [14456.gg.33]
  DU:UL: [1] (1962)   [Per./PL3]

YILLIK / Gazetecilik Enstitüsü dergisi
1 (1961) - 3/4 (1963)
İstanbul: İstanbul Üniversitesi
İktisat Fakültesi Gazetecilik
Fakültesi

  BL:OIOC: 1 (1961) - 3/4 (1963)
  [14498.cc.10]
  OX:BOD: 1 - 3/4   [Turk.d.2040]

YILLIK / Topkapı Sarayı Müzesi
1 (1986) -
İstanbul: Topkapı Sarayı Müzesi
Müdürlüğü: Topkapı Sarayı Müzesini
Sevenler Derneği

  BL:OIOC: 1 (1986) - 2 (1987)
  [ITA.1988.a.860]
  LO:SOAS: 1 -   [Per.107.552551]
  OX:BOD: 1 -   [Per.Turk.d.3953]

YILLIK ARAŞTIRMALAR DERGİSİ / Ankara
Üniversitesi İlâhiyat Fakültesi
Türk ve İslâm San'atları Tarihi
Enstitüsü yayınları
1 (1956) - 3 (1981)
Ankara, 1957-1981
Mainly concerned with Islamic
architecture and epigraphy
Includes English or French translations
or summaries of some articles
Irregular

BL:OIOC: 1 (1956) - 2 (1957)
[14448.e.7]
LO:SOAS: 1 - 2   [Per.10.L.285570]
DU:UL: 1 - 2   [Per./PL14]
OX:BOD: 1 - 3 (1981)   [Per.Turk.d.612]

YILLIK ARAŞTIRMALAR DERGİSİ / Ankara
Üniversitesi Dil ve Tarih-Coğrafya
Fakültesi
1 (1940-1941)
Ankara, 1944

BL:OIOC: 1 (1940/1941)   [14498.c.17]
OX:BOD: 1   [Per.Turk.d.2356]

YILLIK / CUMHURIYET
See: CUMHURİYET YILLIK

YILLIK EKONOMİK RAPOR: malî yıl bütçe
tasarısı ile birlikte T.B.M.M.'ne
sunulmuştur
Ankara: [T.C. Maliye Bakanlığı?],
[19--?]-
Date of first publication unknown

DU:DC: 1977-1978
[25/4/ECONOMY/GENERAL]

YILLIK İMALAT SANAYİ ANKET SONUÇLARI
See: YILLIK İMALAT SANAYİ
İSTATİSTİKLERİ

YILLIK İMALAT SANAYİ İSTATİSTİKLERİ
= Annual manufacturing industry
statistics / Başbakanlık Devlet
İstatistik Enstitüsü
Ankara, [19--?]-
Former title: Yıllık imalat sanayi anket
sonuçları
In Turkish; generally also in English
Some early issues cumulated

BL:HSS: 1976/1979   [SQ.170/55]
DU:DC: 1964/1968; 1971-1972; 1975-1976;
1976/1979 -
[25/4/INDUSTRY/MANUFACTURING]
SU:IDS: 1972 -
[SERIALS/OFFICIAL/TURKEY]

YILLIK METEOROLOJİ BÜLTENİ / Tarım
Bakanlığı Devlet Meteoroloji İşleri
Umum Müdürlüğü
Sene 1 ve 2 (1925-1926) - 34 (1958)
Ankara
Original title of issuing body: Ziraat
Vekâleti Meteoroloji Enstitüsü
Previous titles: Türkiyede meteoroloji
rasatları, Meteoroloji rasatları
First issues printed in Arabic
characters

BL:HSS: 39 (1963) - 48 (1972)
[S.Q.152/3]
DU:DC: 1/2 (1925/1926) - 22 (1946); 26
(1950) - 34 (1958)   [25/2/CLIMATE]

YILLIK RAPOR / Türkiye Cumhuriyeti Merkez
Bankası
1 (1932) -
Ankara: Türkiye Cumhuriyeti Merkez
Bankası, 1932-
Subtitle varies. Some issues entitled:
... yılı raporu
In Turkish. Also published in French
(until 1961 or later), and in English
(from 1964 or earlier)

DU:DC: 1970; 1975; 1982; 1964 - 1974;
1976 -   [25/4/BANKING]
SU:IDS: 1983 -
[SERIALS/NON-OFFICIAL/72]

YILLIK RAPOR / Türk Halk Bankası
Ankara, 1938-

DU:DC: 1969   [25/4/BANKING]

YILLIK TİCARET VE HİZMET
İSTATİSTİKLERİ = Annual statistics
of trade and service / Başbakanlık
Devlet İstatistik Enstitüsü
[1] (1981-1982) -
Ankara, 1986-
In Turkish and English
Nominally annual; published in
cumulations

BL:HSS: [1] (1981-1982) -   [SQ.170/60]
SU:IDS: 1983/1984
[SERIALS/OFFICIAL/TURKEY]

YİR YÜZİ / Kızıl Özbekistan
gazitasining naşri
1. yil, san 1 ([date?], 1925) - [?]
Tashkent
Current news and features on life in
Uzbekistan and elsewhere
Uzbek; Arabic characters
Monthly

BL:OIOC: 2:18 (14.1.1927) - 2:21
(20.4.1927); 2:25 (12.8.1927) - 2:27
(30.9.1927)   [14499.tt.17]

YİRMİNCİ ASIRDA ZEKÂ
See: ZEKÂ

YOL-İŞ: aylık eğitim ve meslekî
bülten / Türkiye Yol-İş Federasyonu
Sayı 1 (Şubat 1966) -
Ankara
Monthly

DU:DC: 4:38 (3.1969); 4:44 - 4:45;
5:49/50 - 6:64; 6:67 (8.1971)
[25/3/TRADE UNIONS]

YÖN: haftalık fikir ve sanat gazetesi
Yıl 1, sayı 1 (20 Aralık 1961) - Yıl 6,
sayı 222 (30 Haziran 1967)
Ankara

BL:OIOC: 1:10 (21.2.1962) - 1:24
(30.5.1962); lacking 1:13, 1:22
[OR.MIC.11804 (O.P.736)]

YÖNELİŞLER: aylık sanat ve kültür
dergisi
Yıl 1, sayı 1 (Nisan 1981) -
Istanbul

OX:BOD: 1:1 (6.1981) -
[Per.Turk.d.3317]

YÖNETİM / İstanbul Üniversitesi
İşletme Fakültesi İktisadı
Enstitüsü dergisi
Yıl 1, sayı 1 ([1978]) - [?]
Istanbul
Issues not dated. Nominally quarterly

SU:IDS: 2:7 [?.1978] - 3:11 [4.1979]
[SERIALS/NON-OFFICIAL/72]

YOZGAT İL YILLIĞI
[1] (1967) - [2] (1973)
Sivas, [ca. 1968]-[ca. 1973]

  OX:BOD: [1] (1967)   [Turk.d.3324/66]

YÜCEL: aylık sanat ve fikir mecmuası
Sayı 1 (Şubat 1935) - [3. seri], sayı
163 (Ağustos 1956)
Istanbul; later Ankara
Series 1 and 2 published at Istanbul,
1935-1950; series 3 at Ankara,
1955-1956.
Subtitle varies slightly

  BL:OIOC: 2. [yeni] seri, 1:1 [=146]
  (1.1950) - [3. seri], 10 [=163] (8.1956)
  [14498.cc.81]
  OX:BOD: [3. seri], 1 (11.1955) - 10
  (8.1956)   [Turk.d.2387]

YÜKSEK TİCARETLİLER / İstanbul Yüksek
İktisat ve Ticaret Mektebi Mezunları
Cemiyeti neşir organıdır
Yıl 1, sayı 1 (Ağustos 1958) - Cilt 4,
sayı 16-17 (Nisan-Temmuz 1961)
Ankara
Mainly bimonthly

  BL:HSS: 1:1 (8.1970) - 4:16/17
  (4-7.1961)   [S.Q.60/21]

YURT VE DÜNYA: aylık mecmua
Cilt 1, sayı 1 (Sonkânun 1941) - Cilt
5, sayı 42 (15 Mart 1944)
Ankara
Cultural and literary review
Monthly; fortnightly in 1944

  BL:OIOC: 1:1 (1.1941) - 5:42 (15.3.1944)
  [OR. MICROFICHE 94]
  LO:SOAS: 3:24; 3:29 - 3:32; 3:36
  [Per.10.45930]

ZAFER: siyasî sabah gazetesi
Yıl 1, sayı 1 (30 Nisan 1948) -
Ankara
National daily newspaper

  BL:OIOC: 1.1.1955 - 31.3.1956; 1.10.1956
  - 30.9.1957; 1.1.1958 - 21.3.1958;
  lacking very few issues from those dates
  [OR.MIC.12590 (O.P.552/10)]

ZAMAN: günlük siyasî gazete
Izmir, 1957-[19--?]
Publication dates not known

  BL:OIOC: 4:1177 (28.5.1960) - 4:1178
  (29.5.1960)   [OR.MIC.12610
  (O.P.552/10)]

ZEITSCHRIFT FÜR SOZIOLOGIE
See SOSYOLOJİ DERGİSİ

ZEKÂ: felsefî, edebî her türlü
terakki ve teceddüdlerden bahis ...
onbeş günlük gazetedir
1. sene, numero 1 (5 Mart 1328 [18 Mar.
1912]) - Numero 34 (2. cild) (19 Haziran
1330 [2 July 1914])
İstanbul
Title on masthead of nos.1-16 : Yirminci
asırda Zekâ

  BL:OIOC: 1:1 (18.3.1912) - 2:34
  (2.7.1914)   [14498.a.103]

ZERDE / Kazakstan LKSM Ortalık
Komitetinin ayına bir ret şiğatın
ğılımi-köpşilik curnalı
No. 1 (346) (Yanvar' 1989) -
Alma-Ata
ISSN 0134-353X
Continuation of: Bilim cêne eñbek
In Kazakh

  BL:OIOC: 1989:1 -   [ZOR.1990.a.32]   95

ZERKALO
See: AYNA

ZEYTİNCİLİK İSTATİSTİĞİ / T. C.
Başbakanlık Devlet İstatistik Genel
Müdürlüğü
[1] (1944-1949)
Ankara
Apparently only one issue published

  BL:HSS: [1] (1944-1949)   [S.Q.170/28]

ZİRAİ BÜNYE VE İSTİHSAL
See: TARIMSAL YAPI VE ÜRETİM

ZİRAİ İSTATİSTİK ÖZETLERİ
See: TARIM İSTATİSTİKLERİ ÖZETİ

ZİYA GÖKALP / Ziya Gökalp Derneği'nce
yayımlanır kültür dergisi
Cilt 1, sayı 1 (Kasım 1974) -
Ankara
Cultural and literary journal concerned
principally with the ideas of Z. Gökalp
Frequency varies: 1974-1977,
approximately semi-annual; 1978 onwards,
quarterly

  BL:OIOC: 1:1 (11.1974) - 5:30 (5-6.1983)
  [14456.cc.373]

ZONGULDAK İL YILLIĞI
[1] (1967) - [2] (1973)
Ankara

  OX:BOD: [1] (1967)   [Turk.d.3324/67]